Allied Armour 1939–1945

Allied Armour
1939–1945

British and American Tanks at War

Anthony Tucker-Jones

Pen & Sword
MILITARY

This volume is for Rupert Harding, my commissioning editor at Pen & Sword Books. I have had the pleasure of working with him for well over a decade. He nurtured my second career from the start and has overseen some 50 of my titles – not bad going and clearly a very fruitful partnership. Rupert, my heartfelt thanks for all your help and guidance over the years.

First published in Great Britain in 2020 by
PEN & SWORD MILITARY

An imprint of
Pen & Sword Books Ltd
Yorkshire – Philadelphia

ISBN 978-1-52677-797-3

Typeset in 11.5/15 by Ehrhardt

Printed and bound by TJ Books Limited

Pen & Sword Books Ltd incorporates the imprints of Pen & Sword Archaeology, Atlas, Aviation, Battleground, Discovery, Family History, History, Maritime, Military, Naval, Politics, Social History, Transport, True Crime, Claymore Press, Frontline Books, Praetorian Press, Seaforth Publishing and White Owl

For a complete list of Pen & Sword titles please contact

PEN & SWORD BOOKS LTD
47 Church Street, Barnsley, South Yorkshire, S70 2AS, England
E-mail: enquiries@pen-and-sword.co.uk
Website: www.pen-and-sword.co.uk

Or

PEN AND SWORD BOOKS
1950 Lawrence Rd, Havertown, PA 19083, USA
E-mail: Uspen-and-sword@casematepublishers.com
Website: www.penandswordbooks.com

Contents

List of Illustrations

1. Early production Matilda II identifiable by the Vickers machine gun mounted in the right-hand side of the turret. The smaller Besa 7.92mm was fitted in the Mk IIA. (All images sourced by author)

2. The British Mk VI series of light tanks were numerically the most significant armoured fighting vehicles with the British Army in 1939–40.

3. The Matilda I, or Infantry Tank Mk I, was much bettered armoured than the light Mk VI, but was very slow and armed with just a machine gun.

4. These Mk IVA (A13) cruiser tanks belong to the 2nd Royal Tank Regiment, 1st Armoured Division, deployed to France in 1940.

5. A Matilda II lost during the fighting at Arras. In 1940 it was the heaviest tank in British service, but was not available in sufficient numbers.

6. German troops pose on their prize – a captured Matilda, numbers of which were lost during both Operations Brevity and Battleaxe in North Africa in May and June 1941.

7. The Crusader proved mechanically unreliable, but went into battle during Operation Crusader and continued in service until the end of the fighting in North Africa.

8. The Valentine joined the 8th Army's tank brigades in the summer of 1941 and played a key role in Operation Crusader.

9. A welcome addition to the British tank inventory was the American-supplied M3 Stuart light tank. It first arrived in Egypt in July 1941.

10. The American M3 medium tank, while far from perfect, was an ideal stopgap remedy to the firepower of Rommel's panzers. This version is the Lee with the machine-gun cupola.

11. A British Sherman, which appears to be the cast hull M4A1, takes on ammunition. The British 8th Army had received about 270 Shermans by October 1942.

12. Grant tanks plough their way through the mud and rain in Tunisia. After the campaign ended those remaining were sent to the Far East to fight the Japanese.

13. M3 Lee with the 2nd Battalion, 12th Armored Regiment, US 1st Armored Division at Souk el Arba in Tunisia.

14. A troop of welded-hull M4A2 Shermans poised for action. Armed with a 75mm gun the Sherman first saw action at El Alamein and was a reasonable match for the panzers in Egypt and Libya.

15. A British Crusader II Close Support Tank, armed with a 3in howitzer, leads two Crusader IIIs (armed with the 6-pounder gun) through the town of El Hamma.

16. American Sherman M4A2s gathered at La Pêcherie, a French naval base in Tunisia, in July 1943 ready for the invasion of Sicily.

17. A veteran of the North African battles comes ashore in Sicily.

18. Following the German surrender in Tunisia in May 1943, British Shermans were next deployed in the invasion of Sicily – this one is north of Rammacca.

19. *LST-77* offloading M4A2 Sherman tanks at Anzio, Italy, May 1944.

20. The remains of a New Zealand welded-hull Sherman. During the battles for Cassino in Italy tanks proved to be of limited value.

21. British Honey light tank on its way to the Sangro River from Baglieta, 9 December 1943.

22. Churchill tanks in Italy. After fighting against the Gustav Line, the British 8th Army captured Rimini and established a bridgehead over the Marno in mid-September 1944.

23. Upgunned Churchill IV (NA 75) shelling the Gothic Line in Italy. These were converted in Tunisia, North Africa (hence NA) when 120 Churchill IVs were fitted with M3 75mm guns and mantlets salvaged from damaged Shermans.

24. M4A4 Shermans in the town of Portomaggiore, north of Argenta, which was captured by the 8th Army on 19 April 1945.

25. M24 Chaffee, US 1st Armored Division, on the streets of Milan in late April 1945. Although work to develop a new light tank started in early 1943, the Chaffee was not standardized until mid-1944.

26. M3 Lee medium tanks supporting the Gurkhas during the Battle of Imphal in 1944.

27. Chinese M3A3 or M5A1 light tanks involved in the fighting at Bhamo, Burma in 1944.

28. Chinese-crewed Shermans on the Burma Road in 1945.

29. Stuart light tanks supporting Australian troops at Buna, during the New Guinea campaign fought from January 1942 to August 1945.

30. Disabled Sherman on the shoreline of Betio, Tarawa Atoll, Gilbert Islands, which the US Marines assaulted on 20 November 1943.

31. Flooded Sherman in the Tarawa Lagoon.

32. 'Lucky Legs II' supporting US troops on Bougainville in March 1944. The island was assaulted on 1 November 1943, but the Japanese garrison held out until the end of the war.

33. 'Cover Girl' of the US 775th Tank Battalion engaging Japanese troops on Luzon in the Philippines in early 1945.

34. The most common Allied tanks in Normandy were the Sherman M4 and M4A1 – they equipped the bulk of the American, British, Canadian, French and Polish armoured forces.

35. At the time of D-Day upgunned Shermans were in short supply. Only 800 M4s armed with a 105mm howitzer were produced during 1943. The follow-on M4A3 105mm only went into production in April 1944.

36. The M4A1 and M4A3 equipped with a 76mm gun only became available in early 1944.

37. To compensate for the Sherman's lack of punch, in June 1942 the Americans began to produce the M10, armed with a 3in gun, using the Sherman chassis.

38. The British Sherman IIC, IVC and VC Firefly were the only Allied tanks capable of taking on the Panther or Tiger on equal terms (using the M4A1, M4A3 and M4A4 respectively).

39. Specialized armour supporting D-Day included the Sherman Crab. Designed to clear minefields and barbed wire, it consisted of the M4A4 fitted with a rotating flail.

40. This mobile Normandy hedgerow is concealing an American M10. To the right is a burnt-out Sherman.

41. Sherman with the Canadian 2nd Armoured Brigade, which consisted of the 6th, 10th and 27th Armoured Regiments.

42. Cromwell tanks of the 4th County of London Yeomanry (Sharpshooters), 7th Armoured Division, who were mauled at Villers-Bocage.

43. US Military Policeman directs an M5 light tank bearing the name 'Concrete' in Normandy.

44. M5 light tank engages enemy targets as a GI dashes for cover.

45. Another US Army M5. Note the prong on the front of the hull designed to dig up the Normandy hedgerows.

46. French half-tracks and a M8 Howitzer Motor Carriage, Free French 2nd Armored Division, on parade through the Arc de Triomphe, Paris.

47. Churchill Mk VI, armed with a 75mm gun, in the Netherlands.

48. Sherman with the call sign 'Bramble 5', serving with the 79th Armoured Division in the Netherlands.

49. US Sherman and supporting infantry crossing the Siegfried Line in September 1944.

50. M10 tank destroyer with the Régiment Blindé de Fusiliers Marins, Free French 2nd Armored Division, outside Halloville, France on 13 November 1944.

51. Camouflaged Sherman tank, belonging to the French 5th Armored Division, engaging enemy targets during the liberation of Belfort on 20 November 1944.

Introduction

Although the British military were keen enthusiasts of the tank after their experiences during the First World War, cost and the country's love affair with mounted cavalry greatly slowed progress during the 1930s. While tank proponents, such as Captain Liddell Hart and Generals Fuller and Hobart, helped develop and train tank units that were unique in concept, very few officers were experienced in mechanized warfare. Like the French, the British developed two kinds of armoured force: the fast moving, all-arms groups that were the basis for future armoured divisions, and tank battalions assigned an infantry support role. In 1937 it was decided to equip a number of British cavalry regiments with tanks, instead of expanding the existing Tank Corps. Two years later, with the outbreak of war Britain's tank forces remained very weak in comparison to France and Germany's.

Both the Germans and the French fielded large numbers of tanks in 1940. However, while the Germans concentrated theirs in powerful panzer divisions, French tanks were dispersed to support their infantry divisions. This decision cost France dearly and it was a mistake the Allies did not repeat. Subsequently both Britain and America expanded their dedicated armoured forces considerably, to the point where they created the spearhead of their armies. The deployment of armoured divisions was shaped foremost by geography, firstly in Europe and then North Africa. Certainly environmental conditions impacted greatly on constantly-developing tactics. For the Allies the lessons learned in North Africa were not entirely applicable to northern Europe, the Far East and the Pacific. While there was some similarity between the mountains of North Africa and Italy, these other diverse regions presented tankers with vastly different challenges and priorities. The initial fighting in France though paved the way.

Hitler wanted to attack France as soon as possible, to secure his western borders in the wake of defeating Poland in September 1939, before then turning east again to tackle the Soviet Union. However, he was informed that it would take time to refit his panzers. After six months Hitler invaded Norway and Denmark on 9 April 1940. The outnumbered Danes offered virtually no resistance, but the Norwegians (with belated British and French military assistance) lasted until early June. France and the Low Countries (The Netherlands and Belgium) now braced themselves for the inevitable German attack.

Ironically from the very start on 10 May 1940 both the Germans and the Allies played out Hitler's envisaged campaign to perfection. The moment the German Blitzkrieg commenced the Allies drove north to confront Army Group B, which in the event overran the Netherlands in the space of just five days. In Belgium other units of Army Group B shoved the Allies back after securing Belgium's much-vaunted strongpoint Fort Eben Emael. As all this played out Hitler and his generals rubbed their hands together. Now that the Allies were committed in the Low Countries and with the garrisons of the French Maginot line pinned down, Army Group A smashed through the Ardennes to reach the French coast in a mere 10 days.

Once it had turned north Army Group A was able to assist Army Group B drive the cornered Allies into a pocket around Lille on 24 May 1940. Three days later the left flank of the salient dissolved when the Belgian defenders surrendered and by 30 May the remaining Allied forces were hemmed in behind a 7-mile wide, last-ditch perimeter around the port of Dunkirk. The British Army had little option but escape back over the English Channel.

During late May and early June the British, French and Belgian defenders at Dunkirk held on while almost a quarter of a million British and over 141,000 French and Belgian troops were evacuated to Britain during Operation Dynamo. The success of the latter in part has to be attributed to the tanks of 'Frankforce' at Arras. In the debacle that was the 1940 French Campaign this shines out as one of the few bright moments. Shortly afterwards the Germans entered Paris without a fight and French morale collapsed completely. An armistice was signed on 22 June 1940 leaving a divided and humiliated France.

The battles fought in North Africa during the Second World War are largely remembered for the exploits of Erwin Rommel, which gained him the title of the 'Desert Fox', and the British 7th Armoured Division, better known as the 'Desert Rats'. The future Field Marshal Bernard Montgomery also made his reputation there with his decisive victory at El Alamein that sealed Rommel's fate. The highly mobile armoured warfare in North Africa was essentially a clean war, a soldier's war. The open desert wastes in Egypt and Libya were ideal for tanks, with few towns and civilians to distract from the business of fighting or indeed result in atrocities. Once the fighting moved into Tunisia the landscape changed yet again with the Axis forces taking to the mountains. North Africa's geography and climate meant that the style of mechanized warfare fought there was far removed from that fought in France, Italy and Russia.

The vast Western Desert stretches almost 400 miles from El Alamein in Egypt to Gazala in Libya, 150 miles to the south lie the Jarabub and Siwa oases, while north of the coastal road are the shores of the Mediterranean Sea. Running west along the coast of Libya's Cyrenaica province lays Bardia, Tobruk, then the bulge at Djebel Akhdar with the towns of Derna and Benghazi, and westward to Mersa Brega and El Agheila. Key choke points are at the Fuka, Halfaya and Sidi Rezegh passes. It was from Agheila to Alamein and back again that the critical battles between the tanks of 8th Army and the panzers of the Deutsches Afrika Korps (DAK), or more precisely Panzerarmee Afrika, took place. The key British armoured units that fought in North Africa were the 1st, 7th and 10th Armoured Divisions.

While the vast, open desert sands of North Africa seemed an ideal place to fight decisive tank battles, things are rarely that simple. Both sides suffered from the problem of terribly long and exposed lines of communication; victory inevitably meant a supply problem for the victor, that then in turn tilted the battle in favour of the vanquished. Moving, re-supplying and reconnaissance soaked up the lion's share of the time. Typically fighting was restricted to daylight and then combat only accounted for about three or four hours a day. British armoured and infantry units at nightfall often withdrew up to five miles from the scene of the action to form protective laagers. At rest, like old-fashioned wagon trains, both sides formed protective boxes with all-round covering fire providing mutual defence.

Mussolini's invasion of Egypt in 1940 had turned out to be half-hearted to say the least. Unfortunately, Churchill missed his chance to finish the Italian army after the remarkable victory at Beda Fomm, as he was distracted by Mussolini's ill-conceived invasion of Greece and British momentum in North Africa was lost. At this point Hitler propped up his Axis ally by despatching Rommel's Afrika Korps. Within two weeks he had reached the Egyptian frontier, with just Tobruk holding out. The Australian defenders refused to give up and it was the first time that the panzers drove through infantry who did not automatically surrender. All Generals Wavell and O'Connor's successes were swept away in a month.

For the next two years Rommel was to fight a succession of British commanders and he was to perfect his defensive-offensive method of mechanized warfare – in Rommel's parlance, first the shield then the sword. Initially repeated British efforts to drive Rommel away from the frontier were continually unsuccessful. Despite his skills as an armoured tactician, thanks to Hitler's indifference to the North African campaign until it was too late, Rommel found himself fighting a war of attrition that he could not win. The turning point finally came in October–November 1942 by which time the Axis forces were completely outnumbered in terms of manpower and equipment. Denied the resources he needed to deliver a knockout blow, Rommel was forced to fight a two-front war following the Allied landings in French North Africa that was ultimately unwinnable.

While the campaigns fought in North Africa, the Eastern Front and North-west Europe were very much dominated by armoured warfare, the battles in Italy were not. The mountainous topography running the length of the Italian peninsula ensured that it was foremost an infantry war, with tanks playing a secondary supporting role. At the beginning of the campaign the mountainous terrain of southern and central Italy greatly impeded the Allied advance. When they were able to use the roads, after German demolition damage had been repaired and mines cleared, they still had to drive huge distances up zigzagging routes just to cover a few miles as the crow flies.

As well as Italy's mountains and numerous rivers, the Allies also had to overcome half a dozen key German defensive positions known as the Bernhardt, Gustav, Senger, Caesar, Albert, Heinrich and Gothic Lines respectively. This was a job for infantry and artillery, not tanks. On top of this the Italian weather was an additional curse on Allied operations. For over half the year there was rain and snow, both of which resulted in mud.

Only six Allied armoured divisions fought in Italy and not at the same time. In fact, only one US armoured division served with the multinational US 5th Army fighting in western Italy (though there were independent tank battalions assigned to support the infantry units). This was 'Old Ironsides' as the US 1st Armored Division was affectionately known. This unit was the founding father of America's tank force during the Second World War, supplying cadres for all the other fifteen US armoured divisions.

However, the US 5th Army at various times was strengthened by the British 6th and 7th Armoured Divisions, the South African 6th Armoured Division and the Canadian 1st Armoured Brigade. In contrast the key armoured units with the British 8th Army, fighting its way up eastern Italy, were the British 1st Armoured and Canadian 5th Armoured Divisions. The Canadians were not very happy at being equipped with the 7th Armoured Division's worn out Sherman tanks when the latter was shipped back to Britain to take part in the Normandy landings.

In the Far East conditions were completely different to those in Europe and the Mediterranean. Initially British and American forces lacked tanks and suffered the consequences. Geography also played its part in the evolution of armoured warfare in this part of the world. Perhaps understandably, at the time the jungles of Burma, Malaya and Thailand and the coral islands of the Pacific were considered wholly unsuitable tank country. Events were to prove otherwise, but this initial mindset stifled the use of armour.

The fighting in China, South-east Asia and the Pacific is not generally known for its armoured or mechanized warfare. Nevertheless, a wide range of units with the American, Australian, British, Chinese and Indian armies employed armoured fighting vehicles to varying degrees during the various campaigns fought in the Far East and the Pacific. On 7 December 1941, Japanese carrier aircraft struck at Pearl Harbor; the next day Japanese forces occupied Shanghai and Siam (Thailand) and landed in British Malaya. Trundling down the roads through Malaya's rubber plantations came Japanese light and medium tanks. These caused chaos and panic and swiftly overran British defences to reach Singapore.

Just after Pearl Harbor the Japanese captured the American island of Guam. Then in the New Year they attacked the Philippines, with tanks spearheading the assault on Luzon. British Hong Kong fell to the Japanese in late December 1941. Shortly after having been driven from Malaya, British forces at Singapore surrendered in February 1942. The following month the Japanese occupied most of Java, Sumatra and other islands of the Dutch East Indies. In Burma British and Chinese troops were swiftly driven back toward the Indian border. An Imperial Tokyo communiqué announced on 9 March 1942 that Rangoon, the capital of Burma, had been seized. This threatened

India and China's western frontier. Japanese tanks then helped humiliate American and Filipino troops trapped at Bataan.

In the Pacific in the opening stages of the war, America light tanks did nothing to stave off America's defeat in the Philippines. American light tank crews arrived on Luzon ill-prepared to fight armoured warfare against the Japanese. The Stuart tank found itself bested by the Japanese Type 97 and the small American tank force was soon lost during the retreat to Bataan. Once the American-built Lee and Sherman medium tanks entered the fray Japanese tanks became obsolete overnight. Stuart, Grant and Sherman tanks were called on to perform a wide variety of combat missions in both the Far East and Pacific ranging from mobile pillboxes to bunker busting. In Burma they were employed to knock out enemy positions, scale steep defended hills and clear trees for advancing troops. Japanese anti-tank guns, anti-tank mines and artillery ensured that the advance of enemy tanks was severely contested. On the whole British tanks were utilized in their more traditional role of infantry support – it was only during the Imphal–Kohima and Meiktila–Mandalay battles that anything like true mechanized warfare was waged against the Japanese.

American tanks provided an advantage, but certainly not a decisive one, once operations commenced to drive the Japanese back across the Pacific. In many places the medium tanks were simply too heavy and troops relied on light tanks to provide support. Despite the massive resources of the US Navy and Marine Corps, once a tank crew were ashore they were pretty much on their own. Often on the confines of the small atolls tanks provided tempting and vulnerable targets for Japanese gunners. In the Pacific US tank crews sweltered inside their tanks enduring heat exhaustion, dehydration and malaria.

The Japanese were expert at burrowing into the volcanic hills and mountains that covered the larger islands. These they these turned into natural fortresses with hidden gun positions and connecting subterranean passageways. Such defensive positions created deadly interconnecting fields of fire that dominated the exits off the beaches and inland. Nearer the beaches they built log bunkers using felled palm trees packed with coral and sand. These were protected by mines, anti-tank ditches and heavy artillery and proved highly resilient. Where naval gunfire and dive-bombers failed to silence Japanese strongpoints, tanks and flamethrowers were called on to smash them open at point-blank range.

Shermans supporting US infantry and marines found before they ever reached the beaches they had to negotiate reefs and treacherous shallows that could suddenly swallow a wading tank. Even when the crew managed to escape they found themselves running the deadly gauntlet of enemy fire raking the water and the shoreline. Like the beaches themselves these shallows were obstructed by obstacles and covered by large-calibre guns and mines. Quite often for the opening attack the Americans had to rely on their amphibious tractors or amtracs which were progressively up-armoured and upgunned as the war progressed.

In Europe the D-Day landings, on 6 June 1944, presented Allied military planners with a unique set of problems when it came to liberating Nazi-occupied France. Not only did they have to successfully ferry their armoured forces across the English Channel and overcome German coastal defences, but also fend off and then defeat the inevitable counter-attack by Hitler's panzers. The Dieppe Raid in 1942 had shown how not to do it: attempting to seize and hold a French port had resulted in Allied tanks becoming trapped in the town. Instead it was decided to assault the open beaches of Normandy. These were potentially deadly killing grounds.

A major concern was the beach obstacles in the selected landing zones, which posed a threat to the smaller assault craft. These consisted of steel and wooden posts, many of which had mines attached, capable of tearing a craft's hull open. The Navy conducted various experiments to determine their effect on the different types of landing craft; General Hobart's 79th Armoured Division, which operated the specialized assault vehicles known as the 'Funnies', was given the task of clearing the way and breaking though the crust of Hitler's 'Fortress Europe'.

After the Second Front was opened, the Americans, British, French, Canadians and Poles committed over a dozen armoured divisions and numerous independent armoured brigades to the Battle for Normandy. This battlefield was very different to the wide-open spaces of the deserts of North Africa and the sweeping steppe of the Eastern Front. Both sides found themselves engaged in bitter battles amidst Normandy's fields, orchards and cities. Initially the anticipated mobile armoured warfare did not materialize as the Allies were hemmed in at their bridgehead. Instead there was a brutal slogging match in which the Allies were forced to trade their superior resources with the battle-hardened panzers in an effort to secure first Cherbourg and turn the German flank either side of Caen. The latter, in the British and Canadian sector, become the lynchpin of the whole battle, because beyond it lay open tank country.

Hitler only had eight divisions engaged during the first six weeks of the campaign; the Allies were expecting at least twice as many. More and more German units were eventually drawn into the battle and by the end of June facing the British were approximately 725 panzers, while on the American front there were less than 200. The desperately-needed German infantry divisions that could free up their armour for a massed counter-attack remained north of the Seine. This was thanks to the Allies' elaborate deception plans, which convinced Hitler that the Normandy landings were just a feint and that a second assault would take place across the Pas de Calais.

Following the American breakout, even as part of Army Group B was being overwhelmed in the Falaise Pocket, far to the south the Americans were in a headlong rush toward the Seine to trap even more German forces. It seemed as if Hitler's generals were on the verge of a second much bigger disaster. Unfortunately determined resistance held up the Americans as the retreating troops fought desperate rearguard actions along the Seine.

The armoured battles fought from the Riviera to the Rhine were characterized by a rapid advance by American and French armoured divisions, until they reached the mountains on the Franco-German border. This was part of General Eisenhower's broad front strategy following the Allies' defeat at Arnhem. Remarkably although General Johannes Blaskowitz's German Army Group G lost most of its panzers to the fighting in Normandy, it was still able to keep the American and French armour at bay in southern France.

Unlike Normandy, where there was a three-month deadlock following D-Day, the Operation Dragoon landings in the Riviera saw the Allies swiftly overcome the German defences. However, Blaskowitz conducted an exemplary fighting withdrawal thanks to the actions of the 11th Panzer Division. It was not until the Battle of Arracourt and the creation of the Montélimar and Colmar Pockets that the Germans suffered their first major defeats in South-west Europe and opened the way into Germany across the Rhine.

The plan had been to capitalize on the Allies' success in Normandy with an invasion of the Riviera in mid-1944, with the intention of trapping the Germans as they had done in the north. Churchill, the wily old politician, avoided an inconvenient truth that most of the German army in southern of France had escaped the clutches of the Allies and where now offering a determined rearguard defence west of the Rhine.

By the summer of 1944 in the wake of the Allied landings on the French Riviera, Hitler's forces were in full flight from southern France. He watched in dismay as his defences in the region unravelled. To make matters worse German resistance in Normandy was almost at an end. In the south the swift advance of General Jean de Lattre de Tassigny's French 1st Army and General Alexander Patch's US 7th Army caught Hitler by surprise. Leaving Toulon and Marseilles to de Lattre's forces, Patch's advance guard raced to reach the city of Grenoble on 22 August with the objective of linking up with elements of General George Patton's US 3rd Army near Dijon.

The sole remaining escape route for Hitler's troops lay in the network of roads and rail lines in the 15-mile-wide Belfort Gap, between the Vosges Mountains to the north and the Jura Mountains to the south-east. Hitler despatched the 11th Panzer Division to Besançon on the evening of 5 September to cover the retreating German 19th Army moving into Belfort. Hitler's high command also ordered the 30th Waffen-SS Division to France. This arrived in Strasbourg on 18 August with instructions to hold the Belfort Gap and counter any Free French units operating in the area.

Fighting in the freezing snows covering Alsace, the French Army avenged its humiliating defeat of 1940. Supported by American forces, French troops first surrounded and then overwhelmed some eight divisions inflicting almost 40,000 casualties on the German 19th Army. This though was no daring Blitzkrieg; it was warfare at its worst with General Charles de Gaulle's vengeful French literally bludgeoning the Germans to death. General Joseph de Goislard de Monsabert's troops launched their attack in the winter of 1944–5 determined to destroy the last Nazi foothold on French soil.

For those German troops abandoned by Adolf Hitler west of the Rhine a miserable fate that awaited them. They had prepared their trenches, bunkers and minefields in full knowledge that they would be far safer on the eastern bank of this mighty barrier. As ever, though, Hitler even in this late stage of the war would hear no talk of tactical or strategic withdrawals; his men must fight and die where they stood. Shivering in the bitter cold, wrapped in tatty greatcoats, their breath a misty vapour, they knew they were standing in the way of the Allies southern thrust into the Nazi heartland. Now an army of frightened schoolboys and pensioners, with most of the veterans long gone, they lacked everything from bullets to food. This was no way to fight a war, but they had no choice, their families were depending on them.

The vast Nazi bridgehead on the west bank of the Rhine 40 miles long and 30 miles deep was created when Hitler's defences in the Vosges Mountains collapsed following attack from the US 6th Army Group in late 1944. By this stage the reinvigorated French Army consisted of highly experienced colonial troops who had fought their way up from the south of France and green recruits who had recently come from the Free French forces of the FFI (the French Army of the Interior, better known as the Resistance). This reorganization plus a lack of supporting arms, such as artillery, meant that the French forces were weaker than the other Allied field armies. It was this situation that permitted Hitler to hold the Colmar Pocket against an unsuccessful French offensive from 15–22 December 1944.

In January 1945, despite Hitler's Ardennes offensive running out of steam, he launched Operation North Wind hoping to recapture Strasbourg. Joining in were the 198th Infantry Division and the 106th Panzer Brigade attacking north from the Colmar Pocket from 7–13 January. Although the defending French 2nd Corps suffered some minor losses during this attack, they held south of Strasbourg and frustrated Hitler's attempts to grab the city. Following the failure of Nordwind, the 6th Army Group was ordered to crush the Colmar Pocket as part of General Dwight D. Eisenhower's plan for all Allied forces to reach the Rhine prior to invading Nazi Germany. Since the bulk of Allied troops surrounding the pocket were French, the honour of destroying the German 19th Army was granted to the French 1st Army. In the meantime to the north all eyes were turned on Montgomery and Patton as they vied for position to be the first to cross the Rhine.

The armoured warfare conducted in North-west Europe was characterized principally by a series of battles to overcome the continent's major rivers. Initially following the D-Day landings in June 1944 the Allies struggled to get over the Orne north and south of Caen. It was only when the Americans broke out to the west that the German defences were finally compromised and they fought a desperate rearguard action on the River Dives in late August. The Allies then raced to the Seine where they had to overcome another German rearguard at Rouen. Allied plans to hasten the end of the war came unstuck when the attempt to reach the Rhine in the Netherlands was defeated at Arnhem. This delayed securing the vital port of Antwerp and resulted in the brutal battle for the Scheldt. The Germans then launched a panzer counteroffensive to try and reach the bridges over the Meuse in an attempt to recapture Antwerp. In the closing months of the war the Allies launched their last major offensive with their armoured assault over the mighty Rhine.

The Allies substituted the Germans' daring Blitzkrieg with a strategy of rollback, based largely on superior firepower and numbers. Since the failure of Operation Market-Garden, Eisenhower remained averse to risking his flanks. The Germans could not understand why the Allies' advance was so laborious and on such a broad front. Despite the collapse at Falaise Hitler was able to organize a massive counter-stroke against the Allies to grab back the initiative. He intended to punch his armour through the lightly defended Ardennes region in Belgium and seize Antwerp. This was not to be some feeble counter-attack but a full-blown counteroffensive using two whole reconstituted panzer armies. It was a race against time and the weather; once the snow-laden skies cleared Allied fighter-bombers inevitably wrested back the initiative. Hitler's panzers were stopped in their tracks and then sent reeling.

The Rhineland was the scene of two costly campaigns in the closing months of the war. The US 1st Army fought from September 1944 through to February 1945 clearing German forces from the Hürtgen Forest, losing 24,000 men in the process. The Allies then geared themselves up to reach and subsequently cross the Rhine itself. Although the Allies assessed that the Wehrmacht was in disarray, they had been very shaken by Hitler's surprise Ardennes offensive and subsequent tough fighting in the Hürtgen and Reichswald. In addition, with Montgomery in charge, assaulting the Rhine was another set piece battle. The preparations for the crossing took two weeks which many felt unnecessary. The Americans were particularly unhappy with Montgomery's cautious preparations and meticulous planning. For the push across the Rhine, Montgomery wanted the 1st Canadian Army's 2nd Corps and the US 9th Army's 16th Corps to be allocated to the British 2nd Army. The Americans objected and this led to the parallel Operation Flashpoint.

In late March 1945 the Allies crossed Germany's last major defensive barrier – the Rhine. After Operation Overlord this was the second largest operation undertaken by the British Army during the entire war. Fortunately for the Allies, Montgomery decided to attack upstream of Emmerich where the British 2nd Army faced the weakened German 1st Parachute Army that had no panzers. Once the Allies were over the Rhine Hitler's panzers were a completely spent force with the survivors surrendering in the Ruhr Pocket. By early May the war was over.

Chapter 1

Matildas at Arras

Britain only had a single armoured division in May 1940 and this was still undergoing training in England. In the meantime, the 1st Army Tank Brigade was deployed to France consisting of two battalions of 'I' or Infantry tanks. Also supporting the British Expeditionary Force (BEF) were seven light armoured regiments equipped with light tanks. Their task was reconnaissance, similar to the traditional cavalry role. On 9 May 1940 the BEF had a total of 210 light tanks with the light armoured regiments and 100 'I' tanks with the 1st Army Tank Brigade. An additional 174 light tanks and 156 new cruiser tanks with the 1st Armoured Division were ready to cross the Channel as battle commenced. Nonetheless, the greatest thing that hampered both the British and the French armoured forces was lack of training and experience. In contrast the German panzer crews had cut their teeth in Poland and knew exactly what they were doing.

The French Chief of Staff was General Gamelin, while General Georges was his theatre commander for the north-east front. Georges organized his forces with General Huntziger's French 2nd Army on the coast, then General Gort's BEF, followed by Corap's 9th Army, with Blanchard's 1st Army on the Meuse and Sambre and finally Giraud's 7th Army covering Sedan. On paper these forces looked impressive, but their lack of flexibility and mobility was to be their undoing.

Britain's paucity of tanks at the outbreak of war was a significant deficiency for the British Army. Those tanks available were too lightly armoured and their guns lacked a punch capable of tackling Hitler's panzers on anything like equal terms. Most of the BEF's tank strength was made up of the small Mk VIB light tank, armed with two Vickers machine guns, which went into production in 1936. Although designed as a reconnaissance tank, it was often used in a cruiser role. Its inadequate armour and armament invariably lead to heavy losses when facing anything bigger than a Panzer I. They served in the 1st Army Tank Brigade's headquarters.

The much heavier Matilda Mk I (A11) Infantry Tank was also first delivered to the British Army in 1936. Like the Mk VI it was only armed with a machine gun and was not capable of withstanding the Panzers' firepower. In contrast the Matilda Mk II (A12) Infantry Tank was the best in the British inventory. When war broke out in 1939 there were just two in service. Although heavily armoured, some 78mm on the front, cross country it was slow and its' 2-pounder (40mm) main armament was inadequate.

Within the 1st Army Tank Brigade, three battalions of the Royal Tank Regiment (RTR) were to be equipped with the Matilda II, consisting of the 4th at Farnborough, 7th at Catterick and the 8th at Perham Down on Salisbury Plain. The only unit ready to be shipped to France was the 4th Battalion equipped with fifty Mk I Infantry Tanks and seven Mk VI light tanks. Production of the Matilda II remained grindingly slow and it was not until the eve of the German Blitzkrieg that the 1st Tank Brigade HQ and the 7RTR shipped to France. Frustratingly 8RTR was not up to strength and was left behind; the 7RTR arrived on the continent with twenty-three Mk IIs, twenty-seven Mk Is and seven light tanks. The unit commander, Brigadier Douglas H. Pratt, found himself under the direct control of the CinC BEF, General the Viscount Gort, who had a total of nine divisions under his command.

Two days after Hitler launched his offensive in the West, Brigadier Pratt and his men moved toward Brussels. In the meantime, over ninety German divisions swarmed into Belgium, France, the Netherlands and Luxembourg. Lacking tank transporters, Pratt's armour was shipped by train while the rest of the brigade struggled up the line by road. Little did Brigadier Pratt realize what a key role his brigade was to play in the unfolding disaster that was about to engulf the Allies in northern Europe.

The 1st Tank Brigade was directed to Tournai, but arriving at Enghein Pratt's' tanks found that the railway station had been bombed by the Luftwaffe and all the engines dispersed. There was no choice but to take to the road. The brigade gathered at Ath on 17 May, only to be sent on a fool's errand in response to reports of a German breakthrough. Eventually reaching Orchies, 16 miles south-east of Lille, Brigadier Pratt joined a scratch force under Major General Frank Mason Macfarlane, Director of Military Intelligence at GHQ, dubbed 'Macforce.' British tanks were designed to cover just 10 miles a day before maintenance; by the time they arrived back in Arras on 18 May they had travelled 120 miles.

Alarmingly, by the 17th the French had exhausted all their reserves trying to stem the German tide and were not in a position to defend Paris. In a desperate all or nothing attempt to slice through the German spearhead, General de Gaulle launched his unsuccessful counter-attack at Montcornet. Assuming the Germans would now turn on the French capital, General Alphonse Georges wanted to throw six divisions against the Germans' southern and north-western flanks. In reality his scattered and harassed forces were unable to concentrate for such a counter-attack. On 19 May Gamelin was sacked by French Premier Reynaud and replaced by the 72-year-old General Maxime Weygand. That day General Erwin Rommel's 7th Panzer Division reached Cambrai, just 24 miles south of Orchies.

Within a week of getting over the Meuse seven German panzer divisions had pierced the French defences and on 20 May General Heinz Guderian's 19th Panzer Corps reached the Channel west of Abbeville. It should be pointed out that the panzers did not have it all their own way. The bulk of the panzer divisions comprised Panzer Is and Panzer IIs and by the time the forward units were gazing out over the English Channel at Abbeville many vehicles had suffered mechanical failure. At this stage the panzers had lost 40 per cent of their strength and could have suffered a defeat if the Allies had any strategic reserves available. Nonetheless, they had still conducted one of the greatest flanking movements in history – the encirclement of the Allies in Belgium. Now the French generals were in a state of despair and the British were alarmed at the prospect of being cut off from Cherbourg and Le Havre and home.

In an effort to cut off those British and French forces north of the River Somme, Guderian swept northward toward the ports of Boulogne, Calais and Dunkirk. Meanwhile early on 20 May the British 1st Tank Brigade and the 5th Division were ordered to the Vimy area north of Arras to reinforce the 50th Northumbrian Division. Placed under Major General Harold E. Franklyn, General Officer Commanding 5th Division, this force was dubbed 'Frankforce'.

After reaching Cambrai, Rommel halted to allow his troops to catch their breath. He planned to resume his advance on 19 May, his destination the high ground south-east of Arras, where the British Rear GHQ was located. General Hoth arrived and ordered Rommel to stay his hand. 'The troops have been twenty hours in the same place,' argued an exasperated Rommel, 'and a night attack during moonlight will result in fewer losses.' Hoth acquiesced. On 20 May Rommel's panzer spearhead reached Beaurains just two and a half miles south of Arras at 0600 hours. Unfortunately, the motorized infantry was lagging behind so Rommel sped off to hurry them up. French troops caused him a few headaches for the next few hours until his infantry and artillery arrived.

Although Lord Gort had dismissed the Allied High Command's call for a joint Anglo-French counter-attack, he could not ignore the wishes of Prime Minister Winston Churchill. Aware of the deteriorating situation in France, General Sir Edmund Ironside, Chief of the Imperial General Staff, the most senior British Army officer was sent to France to see Gort in person. Ironside wanted Gort to commit the whole of the BEF to an attack, but Gort could not withdraw those troops fighting on the Scheldt without opening up a gap in the defence between the BEF and the Belgian Army. To make matters worse the Germans were moving around the British right flank between Arras and the Somme.

The situation for the British was very desperate; the BEF had just four days' worth of supplies remaining and barely sufficient ammunition for another grapple with the Germans. Although Gort's options were limited and diminishing by the day, he still had the 5th and 50th Divisions that could strike toward the Somme. It was hoped that the new French CinC General Weygand might gather his forces and attack the gap from the south.

Seeking out General Billotte, Ironside found him at Lens with the commander of the French 1st Army, General Georges Blanchard. Ironside was appalled by the apathy exhibited by the French generals and shaking Billotte in a fit of rage declared, 'You must make a plan. Attack at once to the south with all your forces on Amiens.' The French 1st Army informed General Franklyn that it could not mount an attack towards Cambrai for two whole days.

General Franklyn tried to coordinate his efforts with two senior French officers, Generals Prioux of the Cavalry Corps and Altmayer of the French 5th Corps, on 20 May. Also present was General Billotte, in theory Lord Gort's superior, but Franklyn had no idea who he was. Altmayer encouragingly announced he planned to launch the 250 tanks of the French 3rd Light Mechanized Division south the following day. However, the French were unable to get into position until the 22nd due to fuel shortages and the exhaustion of the crews. In reality all the 3rd Light Mechanized could muster were about sixty Somua S-35 tanks, having already lost its H-35 tanks.

Altmayer, though, was a broken man. Liaison officer, Major Vautrin, was sent to the general's HQ to get him to commit to the venture. Vautrin reported back to the High Command, 'General Altmayer, who seemed tired out and thoroughly disheartened, wept silently on his bed. He told me his troops had buggered off. He was ready to accept all the consequences of his refusal (to go to Arras) ... but he could no longer continue to sacrifice the Army Corps of which he had already lost half.' In contrast GHQ were considering 'Frankforce' as a major element of the forthcoming British and French counter-attack.

Franklyn, intent on supporting the Arras garrison, deployed 5th Division's 13th Brigade to the east on the Scarpe facing Pelves, while its 17th Brigade was held in reserved north of Arras. The 150th Brigade from 50th Division took up position east of the town on the 13th's right flank. To the west the 151st Brigade joined the armour of 4RTR and 7RTR from 1st Tank Brigade.

British tanks struggled along choked roads through Carvin and Lens to cover the 30 miles between Orchies and Vimy. The last of the 1st Tank Brigade reached Vimy at 0500 hours on 21 May, thereby delaying Franklyn's plans. The lack of the trains meant the tanks had covered 120 miles in five days and this took its toll in wear and tear; of the seventy-seven Matilda Mk Is nineteen were lost and of the twenty-three Mk IIs seven of these were unserviceable. While the more numerous Matilda Is' armour was almost impervious to the Germans' standard 37mm anti-tank gun, its Vickers machine gun lacked real bite. Lacking an anti-tank gun, it was not able to take on the panzers on equal terms.

The 50th Division's commander, Major General Martel, was instructed to clear the south of Arras as far as the Cojeul River a distance of just 10 miles. Following this the 5th Division's 13th Brigade was to advance south to link up with the 151st Brigade from 50th Division. These combined forces were to then push on to a line on the River Sensee to the south-east. In total Martel's attack force numbered just 3,500 troops supported by 74 tanks. He organized them into two mobile battle groups, each consisting of a tank and infantry battalion, supported by field artillery and anti-tank batteries. For the opening of the Arras attack the French 3rd Light Mechanized Division's Somua S-35 tanks were supposedly to screen the British right flank.

The two British columns were to sweep south-east of Arras. The right-hand column spearheaded by the 7RTR, with twenty-three Matilda Is and nine Matilda IIs, was to push through Duisans, Walrus and Berneville to the Beaumetz-Arras highway. From there it was to attack toward Wailly, Ficheux and onto the Cojeul River. The left-hand column lead by the 4RTR, with thirty-five Matilda Is and seven Matilda IIs, was to drive through Dainville, Achicourt, then split clearing Agny to the south to Mercatel and the Cojeul; while just to the north the rest would attack through Beaurains, Neuville and then onto Wancourt on the Cojeul.

The infantry units supporting the tanks were from 6th and 8th Battalions of the Durham Light Infantry (DLI) assigned to the 4RTR and 7RTR respectively. These were Territorial Army units from north-east England and had only half their number of Bren light machine guns, no radios and little artillery. Each column was supported by a battery of just twelve field guns and twelve 2-pounder anti-tank guns. The lack of radios severely hampered communication with the tanks. The DLIs, also lacking adequate transport, were suffering with their feet. They spent the night in the shadow of a much earlier battlefield near the Canadian memorial at Vimy Ridge.

Facing them was Rommel's tough 7th Panzer Division, consisting of the 25th Panzer Regiment with about 180 tanks and the 7th Rifle Brigade numbering about 4,000 men. They were well supported with thirty-six 105mm field guns and howitzers and thirty-six 37mm anti-tank guns. Crucially the 23rd Flak Regiment included a battery of 88mm anti-aircraft guns, which could be used in an anti-tank role. Even without the assistance of the nearby 5th Panzer Division, Rommel easily out-gunned and outnumbered Martel's attacking force from the start.

Rommel, aware of the concentrating British and French forces north of Arras, intended to strike west of Arras with the SS Totenkopf Division screening his left flank toward Beaumetz, while the 5th Panzer Division would punch east on his right. To guard his right flank, south-east of Arras, Rommel established a defensive line extending from Wailly to the west to Neuville in the east.

At 1315 hours on 21 May 1941 the British tanks began moving the eight miles to their Arras-Doullens road start line, without the DLI who had been delayed. They did not catch up with the tanks until 1600 hours. Martel found that Maroeuil was already under shellfire at 1430 hours and that German troops were in Duisans to the south. The day did not start off well when British tanks accidentally engaged some French ones near the village. Luckily there were no losses before the error was realized.

Rommel takes up the story, 'At about 1500 hours I gave the Panzer Regiment orders to attack. Although the armour had by this time been seriously reduced in numbers due to breakdowns and casualties.' He must have been wrong about the timing, because the French reported seeing panzers on the right flank as the British attack got underway. Discovering the panzers also had no infantry support Rommel sped off toward Ficheux, finding part of the 6th Rifle Regiment he headed toward Wailly. 'One of our howitzer batteries was already in position at the northern exit from the village,' recalled Rommel, 'firing rapid on enemy tanks attacking south-ward from Arras.'

After capturing Duisans, two companies of the 8th DLI and two troops of the 260th Anti-Tank Battery were left to defend the village. The 8th DLI's anti-tank guns and support platoon soon went into action against some French tanks! The latter then supported the DLI's attack on the cemetery near Duisans. The number of German prisoners reported taken there varies, the implication being that some were shot out of hand. The SS were later to cite the DLI's behaviour at Arras as the excuse for murdering British PoWs at Le Cornet and Wormhoudt.

Certainly heavy casualties amongst the DLI's officers meant that PoWs received little sympathy from their captors. An officer of 7RTR escorting a German non-commissioned officer was appalled at the treatment the man received. 'I continued into Dainville and handed over the prisoner to a Captain of the DLI for conveyance to Provost Personnel. The troops displayed great animosity towards the prisoner, and I was compelled to draw my revolver and order them off before I could reach their officer.'

By mid-afternoon with Warlus and Berneville in British possession the 8th DLI finally found themselves on the Arras-Doullens road/railway start line. German defences around Berneville inflicted heavy casualties on the DLI and a Stuka dive-bomber attack showed the glaring lack of air support available to the British. However, the 7RTR's tanks pressed on, reaching Wailly. There Rommel discovered, 'The enemy tank fire had created chaos and confusion among our troops in the village and they were jamming up the roads and yards with their vehicles, instead of going into action with every available weapon to fight off the oncoming enemy.' Moving west of Wailly with his staff officer Lieutenant Most at his side, Rommel saw that the advancing British tanks, spearheaded by a Matilda II, had already crossed the Arras-Beaumetz railway and set about a Panzer III. British tanks were also pressing in from the north from Bac du Nord, which lay north-west of Wailly. Some of his infantry took flight taking the crew of a howitzer battery with them.

At this point the British were suddenly taken by surprise by Rommel's well-concealed anti-tank guns and anti-aircraft troop, who were hiding in the hollows and a small wood. Rommel and Most crept amongst the guns and personally assigned each its targets. Some of his officers pointed out that the range was too great, but Rommel knew they could not wait or they would be overrun. He then ordered a furious and rapid fire in an attempt to halt the oncoming tanks. Despite being under fire themselves Rommel's gunners kept their nerve and opened up.

'It did not look as though the battery would have much difficulty in dealing with the enemy tanks,' recalls Rommel, 'for the gunners were calmly hurling round after round into them in complete disregard of the return fire.' The leading vehicles soon lurched to a halt. Just 150 yards west of the small wood a Matilda II was stopped after its driver was killed: in a daze a British captain emerged from the tank and staggered hands in the air toward the Germans' lines. At a range of up to 1,500 yards beyond the abandoned howitzer battery the reception was so hot that the British veered away. 'One tank [Mk II] showed as many as 14 direct hits,' a British tank officer recalled, 'and the only indication the crew had of being hit was a red glow for a few seconds on the inside of the armour plate.'

One of Rommel's field guns claimed Lieutenant Colonel Fitzmaurice, commanding 4 RTR, when his Mk IV light tank was hit. The 7RTR commander Lieutenant Colonel Heyland was also killed by machine-gun fire after dismounting from his vehicle. Rommel now turned his attention on those tanks approaching from Bac du Nord. Some caught fire; others were halted while the rest turned tail.

But then, in Rommel's moment of triumph, personal tragedy struck. 'The worst seemed to be over and the attack beaten off, when suddenly Most sank to the ground behind a 20mm anti-aircraft gun close beside me,' recalled Rommel.

> He was mortally wounded and blood gushed from his mouth. I had no idea that there was any firing in our vicinity at that moment apart from that of the 20mm gun. Now, however, the enemy suddenly started dropping heavy gunfire into our position in the wood. Poor Most was beyond help and died before he could be carried into cover beside the gun position. The death of this brave man, a magnificent soldier, touched me deeply.

The British left-hand column got as far as Neuville and Wancourt, but ran into Rommel's screening defences consisting of 20mm and 88mm anti-aircraft guns and 105mm howitzers. In the area of Tilloy-Beaurains-Agny the British overran the German's light anti-tank guns and the SS were put to flight. The British success was short lived, as Rommel recalled: 'Finally, the divisional artillery and 88mm anti-aircraft batteries succeeded in bringing the enemy armour to a halt south of the line Beaurains-Agny.' The carnage amongst the British armour was considerable, according to Rommel, 'Twenty-eight enemy tanks were destroyed by the artillery alone, while the anti-aircraft guns accounted for one heavy and seven light [tanks].'

At 1900 hours Rommel ordered the 25th Panzer Regiment to strike southeastwards in order to take the British in the rear. South of Agnez, which lay west of Arras and Duisans respectively, the panzers ran into a superior force of British tanks. In the following tank battle the Germans lost ten panzers, but knocked out seven Matilda IIs and six anti-tank guns. The panzers broke through and the defeated British headed back toward Arras.

By 2215 hours the British left-hand column was withdrawing on Achicourt south of Arras, where the 6th DLI conducted a hotly-contested rearguard action. On the right, six French tanks and two armoured personnel carriers got through to Warlus past midnight and covered the retreat. Ten Bren gun carriers from the 9th DLI screened the withdrawal of those men still at Duisans. Although Rommel had received a bloody nose he had kept his nerve and thrown back the brave but futile British tank counter-attack.

Belatedly the French 3rd Light Mechanized Division went into action on 23 May, only to be pounded to a halt by German dive-bombers and artillery fire. The French crews abandoned their stricken vehicles and fled. That evening the British left Arras, withdrawing 18 miles north to the canal line running through La Bassée and Bethune, to Gravelines on the coast south-west of Dunkirk. Despite this retreat the fighting at Arras enabled four British divisions and most of the French 1st Army to withdraw toward the coast in reasonably good order.

Remarkably, during the fighting around Arras against the British, the Germans lost four times the number of casualties they had suffered during the actual break through into France, consisting of 89 dead, 116 wounded and 173 missing. On 27 May Rommel gained the distinction of becoming the first German divisional commander in France to receive the Knight's Cross. In some quarters the British attack at Arras was seen as a waste of dwindling resources, ill conceived and executed, achieving little result. This was not the case, as the Germans were now alarmed at the prospect of their panzer divisions being cut off before their infantry could reach them. While the Germans dismissed all the French counter-attacks, the British effort at Arras caused Generals Kluge and Kleist to pause. Guderian's drive on Boulogne, Calais and Dunkirk was slowed. This ripple of unease passed up the chain of command to Hitler, who halted his forces for two crucial days, allowing the British time to prepare their desperate rearguard defences at Dunkirk.

Afterwards von Rundstedt paid British achievements at Arras the highest compliment saying,

> A critical moment in the drive came just as my forces had reached the Channel. It was caused by a British counter-strike southwards from Arras on May 21st. For a short time, it was feared that our armoured divisions would be cut off before the infantry divisions could come up and support them. None of the French counter-attacks carried any threat such as this one did.

This was praise indeed for the brave British efforts. Although by 24 May the 6th Panzer Division was poised to attack Cassel, HQ of the BEF, Hitler stopped thereby saving the BEF from total destruction. When the attack did come the British 145th Infantry Brigade were as prepared as they could be, only when they attempted to retreat was the garrison lost.

First Lieutenant Bake and his Czech-built light tanks were involved in stopping the British armour breaking out from Cassel in the direction of Waten. Circling south Bake caught them in the flank and his sixteen tanks opened fire at once. The first two British tanks were blown to pieces followed by six others. The Germans then pressed home their attack and soon Bake had accounted for another three British tanks. When the fighting came to a stop fifty tanks had been destroyed, several hundred British soldiers killed and 2,000 captured. In total his division took sixty tanks, five armoured cars, ten artillery pieces and eleven anti-tank guns, thirty motor cars and 233 trucks. The 6th Panzer Division then pursued the retreating French. Under attack by the 10th Panzer Division and the Luftwaffe's Stukas, the port of Calais surrendered on 26 May and the Germans took 20,000 prisoners, 3,500 of them British.

It was Hitler's 'Halt Order' at Dunkirk that marred his incredibly successful Blitzkrieg against France and prevented the BEF from being annihilated. Operation Dynamo between 27 May and 4 June 1940 scooped 224,685 British soldiers and another 141,445 Allied troops from the German net. There were though sound strategic reasons for Hitler's actions. He was worried about protecting his southern flank and seizing Paris, as after all his main purpose was the defeat of France. With her armies scattered France signed an armistice on 22 June and Hitler told General von Kleist that, 'They [Britain] will not come back in this war.'

In terms of saving manpower, the evacuation of the BEF from Dunkirk was a miracle; in terms of equipment losses it was disaster of the first magnitude. Hitler captured almost every tank the British Army possessed and most of its motor transport; his haul included 600 tanks. By the summer of 1940, Britain's armoured units possessed just 240 medium tanks, 108 cruiser tanks and 514 largely useless light tanks. Britain was completely exposed to the threat of German invasion by Hitler's panzers.

Chapter 2

Cruisers Against Mussolini

Whilst Britain braced itself for invasion, British-held Egypt also faced attack from Libya following Italy's declaration of war on 10 June 1940. Churchill was not blind to the very real danger that Italian dictator Benito Mussolini would drive the under-strength British forces from western Egypt and back across the strategically vital Suez Canal. In reality Mussolini's armour was to prove a pale shadow of their German cousins wreaking havoc throughout Europe, but at the time Churchill had no way of knowing this. Ironically it was the inadequacies of Mussolini's tanks that was to embroil Hitler in this secondary theatre of operations. What Churchill did know was that Hitler was threatening Britain from across the English Channel, while Mussolini was greedily eyeing British interests in North Africa.

Following the 1938 'Munich Crisis' a British mobile force had been put together in Egypt, but such were its capabilities that it had been derisively dubbed the 'immobile farce'. The following year it was supposed to be expanded to a full armoured division, but equipped with various Vickers light tanks, 1920 pattern Rolls-Royce armoured cars and few old Vickers medium tanks it clearly lacked punch. One armoured regiment even had to make do with 3.7in mountain guns and machine guns mounted on lorries.

By the time war broke out the Western Desert Force (predecessor of the 8th Army), under Lieutenant General Richard O'Connor, who answered to General Archibald Wavell, Commander-in-Chief Middle East, included the 7th Armoured Division, soon to be known as the 'Desert Rats'. They were equipped with inadequate A9 and A10 cruiser tanks as well as Mk VI light tanks. Only the 7th Royal Tank Regiment (RTR) was equipped with the much heavier Matilda II infantry support tanks. Prior to the Italian offensive the cruisers were withdrawn from the frontier. Amidst sporadic skirmishing a lone squadron of tanks was left behind to watch the border along with some armoured cars.

At the outbreak of hostilities Wavell had less than 10,000 men available to protect Egypt, so a series of aggressive operations were conducted to keep the Italians off balance. Maddalena and Capuzzo were temporarily seized on 14 June 1940. Three days later the Western Desert Force was officially created out of the headquarters of 6th Division under O'Connor. He only had a single armoured unit, two tank and two artillery regiments, and two infantry battalions in the immediate vicinity of Mersa Matruh. When Italy declared war the RAF or Desert Air Force (DAF) could muster a few Gladiator fighters, some Blenheim medium bombers, and a few Wellington and Bombay medium bombers in Egypt, but from the start they aggressively attacked enemy airfields, the Italian air base at El Adem outside Tobruk being raided on the first day of the war.

By the summer of 1940, despite the low priority placed on tank production, Britain's armoured units possessed about 830 tanks. As the fighting with the Italians in North Africa escalated many were despatched to Egypt. In October 1940 Churchill's reinforcements began to arrive in Egypt, most significant of which were fifty Matilda tanks. These represented the most powerful weapon in the British tank inventory and their frontal armour could withstand every Italian gun in service.

After Mussolini's declaration of war it seemed certain that he would strike eastward from the port of Bardia and Fort Capuzzo in Libya, with the intent of seizing the strategically vital railhead 50 miles away at Mersa Matruh in Egypt. His 5th Army, equivalent to nine divisions, stationed in Tripolitania (western Libya), initially guarded the French Tunisian border, but with the defeat of France and the formation of the pro-German Vichy government, Tunisia was no longer a threat, although Mussolini rapidly began to fear the Free French in Equatorial Africa. His 10th Army in Cyrenaica (eastern Libya) consisting of five divisions was bolstered with four from the 5th Army in June 1940, bringing Mussolini's forces facing Egypt up to about 250,000 men.

General d'Armata Berti's 10th Army was scheduled to move against Sollum, Halfaya pass and Sidi Barrani in August. Under him was 21st Corps consisting of three divisions supported by the Libyan divisions and the Motorized Maletti Group. The attack though never took place and Marshal Maresciallo Graziani, Italian CinC North Africa, in Tripoli came under increasing pressure from an exasperated Mussolini seeking to emulate Hitler's Blitzkrieg across France.

Graziani was finally forced to launch his attack the following month. Ironically those divisions with desert experience were in Albania ready for Mussolini's foolhardy invasion of Greece. Graziani massed six divisions with Libyan troops spearheading General Annabale Bergonzoli's 23rd Corps, supported by the Maletti Group which was to act as flank guard. The offensive commenced on 13 September 1940 with Graziani commanding the operation from way back at Tobruk using inadequate radio communication.

Bergonzoli's 'Blitzkrieg' advanced 65 miles into Egypt before his men dug in at Sidi Barrani and refused to go any further for lack of armour and artillery. Back in London Churchill and his generals were able to heave a sigh of relief; clearly Mussolini was living up to his reputation for bluff and bluster. The British Western Desert Force was given valuable breathing space and clear indication of poor Italian leadership.

Some 36,000 men under General Wavell launched a counter-raid that soon developed into a full offensive. Outmatched and poorly motivated, the Italians did slowly improve their performance but by learning the hard way, and then it was largely too late. Initially they did not know how to conduct armoured warfare against the British. At Alam Nibeiwa on 9 November 1940 General Pietro Maletti's artillery continued to fire ineffectually until overrun by British tanks, while at Sidi Barrani and Bardia the British armour caused widespread panic. All the M11/39 tanks were taken by surprise and destroyed without a fight by the advancing Matildas at Nibeiwa. O'Connor slipped behind the Italians and their defences simply collapsed.

The 4th Indian Division recorded that at Nibeiwa,

> Frightened, dazed or desperate Italians erupted from tents and slit trenches, some to surrender supinely, others to leap gallantly into battle, hurling grenades or blazing machine guns in futile belabour of the impregnable intruders ... General Maletti, the Italian commander, sprang from his dug-out, machine gun in hand. He fell from an answering burst; his son beside him was struck down and captured.

The Italians valiantly resisted for another two and a half hours and one British tank crewman was struck by their bravery, 'The Italians may have been a push-over afterwards, but they fought like hell at Nibeiwa.'

O'Connor and Wavell launched their major counterstroke on 9 December 1940; employing the impregnable Matilda tank, Operation Compass rolled the Italians completely out of Egypt. Trooper 'Topper' Brown with the 2nd Royal Tank Regiment was in the thick of it. 'Practically all morning we never stopped firing, at wagon loads of infantry or tanks. I haven't a clue how many enemy I killed, but it must have run into hundreds. We definitely had a score of 20 M13s at the end of the day …' He took out the last M13 with his final two rounds, 'We had started out with 112 rounds of 2-pounder, 97 in the racks and 15 extra. Hughes had let us get down to the last two. … so you can understand the amount of firing I had done.'

The King's Royal Rifles passing through the destruction reported, 'After we had gone a few miles south … we came upon the scene … an imposing mess of shattered Italian tanks, abandoned guns and derelict lorries. There was the familiar sight of hordes of prisoners being rounded up; processions of staff cars, containing General Bergonzoli and his entourage, passed up the road towards Benghazi.' In just three days they captured 38,000 Italian and Libyan troops, 73 tanks, 1,000 vehicles and 237 guns.

Bardia fell on 3 January 1941 with the loss of another 40,000 Italian troops followed on the 22nd by Tobruk, which gave up 27,000 prisoners, 90 tanks, 200 vehicles and 200 guns of various calibres. Mussolini's remaining forces were dramatically cut off at Beda Fomm on 5–7 February 1941. General Valentino Babini's armoured brigade only had a few days to become familiar with the newly arrived replacement M13/40 tanks. Again these were too lightly armoured and lacked radios. Over 100 were found around Beda Fomm. Some were burnt out, but many were simply abandoned by inexperienced crews. 'You were too soon, that is all,' said General Bergonzoli when questioned about his army's performance. 'But we gave battle at once … And always, here as everywhere else, we were grossly outnumbered. So when our second attack was unable to prevail we had no choice but to make an honourable surrender.'

O'Connor sent Wavell a message that summed up the end of Mussolini's aspirations in North Africa, it simply read 'Fox killed in the open'. Following his defeat General Graziani, full of doom and gloom, wrote to his wife,

'One cannot break steel armour with finger nails alone.' He considered withdrawing on Tripoli but Mussolini would have none of it, raging, 'This man has lost his mind or at least his senses. Here is another man with whom I cannot get angry, because I despise him.'

Wavell was understandably full of praise for his troops' efforts, 'The Army of the Nile, as our Prime Minister has called us, has in two months advanced over 400 miles, has destroyed the large army that had gathered to invade Egypt, taking some 125,000 prisoners and well over 1,000 guns besides innumerable quantities of weapons and material of all kinds. These achievements will always be remembered.' In Britain the headlines triumphantly ran 'Wavell's Wave Sweeps over Libya.'

Mussolini's forces were in complete disarray, Hitler's Blitzkrieg in North Africa by proxy had ended as a complete and utter shambles, leaving Churchill occupying half of Libya. In total Mussolini's 10th Army lost 130,000 prisoners, almost 500 tanks, and thousands of wheeled vehicles. The Italian Army was left reeling and Mussolini was furious that his military might had been squandered. His defeat in Africa also ensued that Spain's dictator General Franco did not side with Hitler.

O'Connor was understandably disappointed that he was not allowed to have a go at Tripoli. When asked could he have taken it, he responded,

> I think we could have done so at once, or fairly shortly after, before the Luftwaffe came into the picture. Of course, the question of supplies would have been difficult. But this would have been greatly eased by the Italian rations, which we could have picked up at Sirte and Tripoli. Like the rest of the campaign it would have been a risk, but I think personally not a dangerous one.

O'Connor's dramatic victory at Beda Fomm was the defining moment of the first round of the war in North Africa. 'Thus ended,' said Churchill 'Mussolini's dream of an African Empire to be built by conquest and colonised in the spirit of ancient Rome.'

Churchill's ill-fated attempts to help Greece, as well as distract Mussolini and Hitler from North Africa, threw away the victory at Beda Fomm. The 1st Armoured Brigade, New Zealand Division and 6th Australian Division, fully equipped at the expense of those forces in the Middle East, were despatched in early March 1941. The armoured brigade consisted of the light tanks of the 4th Hussars and the Matildas of the 3RTR plus infantry, anti-tank gun and artillery support. Mussolini's armour was no threat to Churchill's tanks, but Greek geography and Hitler's panzers proved fatal.

Following their victory over the Italians in North Africa in early 1941, the British 7th Armoured Division was withdrawn to Egypt for a refit just as Rommel's Afrika Korps was arriving in Libya. The replacement 2nd Armoured Division comprised a divisional Support Group and the 3rd Armoured Brigade; the latter had just 86 of the 156 tanks it was supposed to have. There was no hiding the fact that 3rd Armoured was an improvised formation equipped with a regiment of inadequate cruiser tanks, a regiment of equally useless light tanks and a regiment with captured Italian tanks. Notably the 6th Royal Tank Regiment (6RTR) was issued with Italian M13 tanks which, although they had been repaired, lacked radios. All of this equipment was to swiftly end up in Rommel's hands.

In mid-May 1941 Wavell's tank force was increased by 135 Matildas and 82 cruisers, 50 of which were the brand new Cruiser Mk VI (A15) Crusader I, enough to re-equip a whole tank regiment, and twenty-one light tanks. All the tanks except the Crusader were slow. While the Germans and Italians respected the Matilda, the Crusader I, which came with Churchill's 'Tiger' convoy, carried the same inadequate 2-pounder gun and its superior cross-country handling was nullified by its niggling engine problems. The Crusader had been rushed into service before its teething problems could be ironed out. It showed the same defects of its predecessors, principally thin armour and mechanical unreliability. While it was fast and could manage up to 40mph in the desert (with the right modifications) the engine was elderly and suffered cooling problems, especially with the fan's drive shafts and clogged air filters.

Churchill was keen to strike back at Rommel immediately, but to his irritation once in Egypt his 'Cubs' had to be worked up in the workshops, sand filters had to be fitted and cooling systems modified. The mechanics had to wade through the voluminous manuals to appreciate the manufacturers' do's and don'ts. Despite the Crusaders' and Mk IV's (A13) shortcomings, these tanks were issued to Major General Michael O'Moore Creagh's 7th Armoured Division. The unit had been without tanks for four months, so needed time to familiarize itself with them, particularly the Crusader.

By September 1941 13th Corps had been reinforced by 30th Corps to form the 8th Army under General Cunningham. The 7th Armoured Division was now mainly composed of Crusaders, but still had A13s and some even older Cruiser tanks, while 4th Armoured Brigade comprised entirely of American supplied Stuart light tanks, known by the British as 'Honeys'. The two army tank brigades (one with 13th Corps and the other with the Tobruk garrison) had a combination of Matilda and Valentine tanks. The South African Marmon-Herrington Mk II was the main armoured car, while American and Canadian vehicles were phasing out the older British models. By November 1941 a second generation of British infantry and cruiser tanks along with the American light tanks had reached North Africa.

The 1st Armoured Division learned the hard way not to overestimate Rommel's capabilities. In January 1942 he first enveloped and then put to flight its divisional combat group, which lost three-quarters of its 150 tanks along with 85 guns. While most armoured units were despatched to the Middle East as whole divisions or tanks brigades, part of the ill-fated 2nd Armoured Division ended up in Greece and a brigade from 1st Armoured was incorporated into 7th Armoured for the Crusader operation. Likewise, losses sometime meant the end of units, such as the 7th Armoured Brigade in early 1942 and the 8th Armoured Division just before Alamein (where its HQ was used to fool Rommel). By the time of Alamein, the 8th Army included the 1st, 7th and 10th Armoured Divisions.

Commonwealth support for the war in the Western Desert was considerable with the 6th and 9th Australian Divisions, the New Zealand Division, 1st and 2nd South African Divisions and various aviation and naval units all seeing action. Likewise, the Indian Army supplied the 4th and 5th Indian Divisions under British officers. They all included armoured support units, but no dedicated armoured divisions.

Chapter 3

Rommel Turns the Tide

The first elements of the DAK arrived in Tripoli on 14 February 1941 with the disembarkation of the 3rd Reconnaissance Battalion, 5th Light Division; other units, most notably two battalions of the 5th Panzer Regiment, followed. Shortly after the 5th Light was renamed the 21st Panzer Division and along with the 15th Panzer Division formed the core of the DAK. The ad hoc 90th Light 'Afrika' Division controlled those units not assigned to either of the panzer divisions. The key units of the latter were the tank regiments, the 5th with 21st Panzer and the 8th with the 15th Panzer.

Strictly speaking the term Afrika Korps only applies to the 15th and 21st Panzer Divisions. Rather confusingly, all other formations including the 90th Light Division, Ramcke Brigade and Italian armoured and motorized divisions were part of Panzerarmee Afrika. Rommel commanded the latter, while Generals Cruewell, Nehring and von Thoma commanded the DAK. What is remarkable is that although this force only existed for two years, thanks to its operations in the desert it has acquired a certain mystique.

When the 5th Panzer Regiment landed in North Africa it brought with it 150 tanks, comprising 70 light Panzer IIs, while the rest were Panzer IIIs with the L/42 50mm gun and Panzer IVs with the L/24 75mm gun. In the face of inevitable battle losses, the Panzer IIs were replaced with the two newer models and for much of the campaign there were two Panzer IIIs for every Panzer II and IV. The 5th and 8th Panzer Regiments took 40 Panzer IV Ausf D and Es to North Africa.

The 605th Panzerjäger Battalion, part of the 5th Light Division, also arrived with the DAK's first self-propelled gun, the 47mm PaK(t) (Sf) auf PzKpfw I Ausf B (which was a Panzer I chassis fitted with a captured Czech 47mm gun). These vehicles were later supplemented by the Marder, utilizing a Czech tank chassis. The tanks were also supported by the assault gun and armoured car units. By March 1941 Rommel massed almost 160 panzers supported by 60 Italian tanks in Libya. Rommel, after his experiences in

France, was only too familiar with British armour. Following Dunkirk two captured Matilda Mk Is and two Mk IIs had been despatched to Germany.

There were two main anti-tank guns deployed by the DAK; the 50mm L/42 and later L/60 PaK 38 and the famous dual-role 88mm flak gun. The excellent 75mm PaK 40 was a later development and did not see service until the closing stages of the campaign. The reputation of the '88' in North Africa almost reached mythical proportions and was both feared and respected by the Allies in the Western Desert, as no tank could stand up to its killing power. Rommel to hold Libya dug-in his 88s at Sollum and Halfaya. These guns reaped a rich harvest from Churchill's 'Tiger Cubs' which had been rushed straight from Britain's training grounds to the desert battlefield.

Having co-opted Mussolini's armour, Rommel quickly recycled abandoned Italian vehicles and artillery. Italian guns appeared in German positions and reconditioned Italian lorries, cars and motorcycles were soon on the roads sporting the palm tree and swastika insignia of the Afrika Korps. When General Gariboldi, Italian CinC North Africa, complained that the equipment was Italian property and should be promptly returned, Rommel was of a different opinion. His ally would have no real further say in the prosecution of the war in North Africa.

British armour could cope with the Panzer I and II but not the subsequent two models. War correspondent Alexander Clifford, who covered the 1941 North African campaign, soon became aware of this:

> The [Panzer] Mk IIIs and Mk IVs both had more firepower than anything we had got. We found ourselves up against the Mk III's 50mm guns firing four-and-a-half-pound shells … It meant that the British had to start every battle with a sprint of half a mile under fire before they could fire back. He calculated that to combat the Germans technological advantage the British would need to start with a thirty per cent superiority in numbers, adding gloomily: 'Of course our military authorities had known and expected it. It was one of the risks they were prepared to take.'

When Rommel struck at Agheila on 24 March 1941 the British 2nd Armoured Division conducted a fighting withdrawal. Losses were not serious but the mechanical reliability of its tanks was a concern and there were many breakdowns. Then on 2 April Rommel's panzers bounced the Support Group from Agedabia and a large part of the division was overrun. The 3rd Armoured Brigade was sent to Mechili to cover the withdrawal. By the time Rommel reached Mechili the 3rd Armoured Brigade had little or no fighting capability. The remains of the brigade short of petrol and with just a dozen tanks sped north to Derna only to be ambushed and destroyed on 6 April.

Churchill was furious at the loss of the 3rd Armoured Brigade and in early April 1941 cabled General Wavell demanding to know what had happened. Wavell explained the units involved were not ready for action and that his cruiser tanks were appallingly unreliable stating, '3rd Armoured Brigade practically melted away from mechanical and administrative breakdowns during the retreat, without much fighting, while the unpractised headquarters of the 2nd Armoured Division seems to have lost control.'

Quickly recovering from the shock of Wavell's unwelcome expulsion from Libya, Churchill rallied to secure the defence of Egypt. He ordered Britain be stripped of every tank and aircraft that could be spared. This was at a time when the country's factories were taking a hammering from the Luftwaffe. Excitedly Churchill wrote to Wavell on 22 April 1941:

> I have been working hard for you in the last few days, and you will, I am sure, be glad to know that we are sending you 307 of our best tanks through the Mediterranean, hoping they will reach you around 10 May. Of these 99 are cruisers, Mark IV and Mark VI [Crusader I], with necessary spare parts for the latter, and 180 'I' tanks [Matilda].

The five ships of Churchill's 'Tiger' convoy escorted by the Royal Navy passed Gibraltar on 6 May. One ship, the *Empire Song*, with 57 tanks and 10 Hurricane fighters aboard, was sunk after striking mines in the waters south of Malta, though luckily no one was killed. The rest reached Malta and pressed on to Alexandria unscathed on the 12th delivering 238 much-needed tanks and 43 Hurricanes. While the 'Tiger Cubs' were prepared for action the British attempted to drive Rommel away from the frontier before 15th Panzer was ready for battle.

Launched on 15 May 1941, Operation Brevity saw Wavell lose yet more tanks to Rommel. The 22nd Guards Brigade, with twenty-six Matildas, was to capture Fort Capuzzo via Halfaya, while to the south 2nd Armoured's Support Group, with twenty-nine old cruiser tanks, was to screen the attack with a push on Sidi Azeiz. The Guards made little headway, losing five Matildas and thirteen damaged. Many of the cruiser tanks broke down on the way to Sidi Azeiz and more broke down on the way back. At Halfaya Pass the 15th Panzer captured seven Matilda tanks, three of which were still operational.

By 9 June 1941 all the British tank squadrons had received their new vehicles, but at General Creagh's request were given another five days training before the launch of Operation Battleaxe. Later Creagh admitted he was not confident about their chances of victory. 'An answer was difficult since it depended on which side could reinforce the quicker – though we could concentrate on undoubted initial superiority, the Germans could reinforce with their second armoured division from Tobruk, only 80 miles distant, while as far as I knew we had no means of reinforcement at all.'

Lieutenant General Sir Noel Beresford-Peirse was placed in command, with the 7th Armoured and 4th Indian Divisions acting as his strike force, though both lacked a brigade each. The latter was to push along the coast through Halfaya toward Sollum and Capuzzo. The 7th Armoured comprised the 4th and 7th Armoured Brigades – the former had two regiments, 4RTR and 7RTR, equipped with Matildas, while the latter's 2RTR had to make do with inadequate A9, A10 and A13 cruiser tanks, which although old designs were recently delivered new builds, and the 6RTR was issued with the Crusaders. Ninety-eight Hurricanes and Tomahawks as well as over 100 bombers supported the ground forces.

In Battleaxe Churchill's ill-prepared 'Tiger Cubs' were thrown perhaps recklessly into action on 15 June with the intention of overwhelming Rommel. Lieutenant Colonel Walter O'Carroll, commander 4RTR watched the attack on Halfaya Pass go in, 'The sun was rising behind and light forward was excellent. No guns sounded. The tanks crept on. At Halfaya the month before, Major Miles had found the enemy still in bed or shaving when he arrived, but they were Italians. Now it seemed almost too good to be true that the [German] garrison should be so caught again . . .'

He was right. At 0600 hours Rommel's 88mm guns opened and all but one of thirteen Matildas went up in flames and the attack along the top of the escarpment collapsed. At the bottom of the pass six tanks of A Squadron 4RTR ran into a minefield and four blew up, blocking in the survivors. The attack on the pass ended in a confused shambles. 7RTR reached Capuzzo only to lose five Matildas to German counter-attacks, with another four damaged.

The 2RTR attacked, with 6RTR's Crusaders held back for a surprise blow, but both were bested to the west at Hafid Ridge. Two A9s were lost to German 88mms: equipped only with solid shot there was nothing they could do against the dug-in anti-tank guns. To the south a flanking attack failed and five tanks were lost after they could not be recalled for the lack of radios. The Crusaders were then thrown in and ran straight into a German gun line, losing eleven tanks immediately and another six damaged. Others simply broke down. In the face of over thirty panzers and failing light the rest withdrew.

By the end of the day of the 100 Matildas committed to the battle only 37 remained operational, although the mechanics had another 11 battleworthy by the following day. It was discovered that 7th Armoured Brigade had lost half its tanks, while 2RTR had twenty-eight tanks and 6RTR some fifty remaining. Disastrously for Beresford-Peirse, he had lost half his tanks without even bringing Rommel's main panzer force to battle.

Rommel though was feeling the pressure. Having lost Capuzzo, he had men isolated at Halfaya, suffered casualties along Hafid Ridge and lost Point 206. He must have been very reassured by the reports filtering in that the surrounding landscape was littered with knocked-out and broken down British tanks. Also a panzer battalion from the 5th Light Division had just arrived at Hafid Ridge and the rest of the division was en route. Similarly, the 15th Panzer Division had yet to fully commit itself to the fight, its artillery and anti-tank units having borne the brunt of most of the British attack. Those panzers involved around Capuzzo had been used solely to lure the 'Tiger Cubs' onto the waiting anti-tank guns.

Lieutenant Heinz Werner Schmidt accompanied Rommel to view the battle recalling,

> It was bonny fighting that we saw. Wavell's tanks broke into a number of infantry positions, despite the intensive fire from our 88mm

guns, which they had scarcely expected to meet. The crews manning the 88's sat high up and unprotected at their sights. When one man fell, another of the crew took his place. ... despite the heavy losses caused by the artillery, the British infantry with rare gallantry pressed forward across the Halfaya wadis.

By the afternoon of 16 June the 6RTR had withdrawn to the frontier with just ten operational Crusaders. The panzers launched another attack at 1900 and rolled over 6RTR and 2RTR, only the onset of darkness saved them from compete annihilation. The following day, massing his panzers, Rommel struck west of Sidi Suleiman reaching the town at 0600 hours. The Matildas withdrew from their exposed position at Capuzzo and a six-hour battle followed. Battleaxe had been stopped in its tracks and the Germans were left in possession of the battlefield. Rommel witnessed, 'Great numbers of destroyed British tanks littered the country through which the two divisions had passed.'

'Thus the three-day battle of Sollum was over,' observed Rommel, 'It had finished with a complete victory for the defence, although we might have dealt the enemy far greater damage than we actually had done. The British had lost in all, over 200 tanks and their casualties in men had been tremendous. We, on the other hand, had lost about twenty-five tanks totally destroyed.' In fact, according to British figures, sixty-four Matildas were lost along with twenty-seven cruiser tanks, though more Crusader tanks fell into German hands due to mechanical troubles than through battle damage. Although the Crusader was under-gunned, Rommel was quite impressed by it, noting, 'Had this tank been equipped with a heavier gun, it could have made things extremely unpleasant for us.'

Generals Wavell and O'Connor's previous successes had been swept away. Churchill by his own admission was disconsolate at the failure of Battleaxe, 'Although this action may seem small compared with the scale of the Mediterranean in all its various campaigns, its failure was to me a most bitter blow. Success in the Desert would have meant the destruction of Rommel's audacious force.' On the 21st Wavell fell on his sword and signalled Churchill, 'Am very sorry for the failure of Battleaxe and the loss of so many Tiger Cubs, ... I was over optimistic and should have advised you that

7th Armoured Division required more training before going into battle. . . . but ... I was impressed by the apparent need for immediate action.'

Churchill, still smarting about the very public failure of his 'Tiger Cubs', wrote to his Minister of Supply and the Chief of the Imperial General Staff in a state of irritation in late August, bemoaning:

> We ought to try sometimes to look ahead. The Germans turned up in Libya with 6-pounder guns in their tanks, yet I suppose it would have been reasonable for us to have imagined they would do something to break up the ordinary 'I' tank. This had baffled the Italians at Bardia, etc. The Germans had specimens of it in their possession taken at Dunkirk, also some cruiser tanks, so it was not difficult for them to prepare weapons which would defeat our tanks.

The 'Tiger' convoy had stretched Britain's resources to the limit and by early July 1941 for the defence of the British Isles Churchill could muster 1,141 infantry and cruiser tanks, of which just 391 were considered fit for action. British repair facilities at this stage remained lamentable and a month later 25 per cent of the infantry tanks were still out of action, as were 157 of the 400 cruiser tanks. After the success of the 'Tiger' convoy the Royal Navy, feeling its luck could not hold in the Mediterranean, escorted another fifty cruiser and fifty infantry tanks round the Cape, but they did not reach Suez until mid-July.

When Panzergruppe Afrika was established consisting of the 15th and 21st Panzer, they were equipped with about 170 Panzer II, III and IVs, as well as a dozen British Matildas and 17 Valentines. Rommel's 'Tiger Cubs' went into action with 21st Panzer on 14 September 1941, when three columns pushed into Egypt. By November the 8th Army had come into being, and a second generation of British infantry and cruiser tanks along with the American Stuart light tank had reached North Africa. The production runs for Britain's early cruiser tanks was fairly limited (125 A9s, 175 A10s and 335 A13s) and all were withdrawn from service in late 1941 having been replaced by the Crusader and Stuart. The British massed 756 tanks, mostly Matildas and Valentines, for Operation Crusader. They enjoyed mixed success when this was launched on 20 November 1941 employing two whole corps.

The intention for Crusader was that 13th Corps (1st Army Tank Brigade plus the 2nd New Zealand and 4th Indian Divisions) bypass Axis frontier defences to the south and attack along the Via Balbia towards Tobruk. To the south 30th Corps (7th Armoured and 1st South African Divisions plus 22nd Guards Brigade) was to advance north-westward across the desert and smash the enemy's panzers in the area of Sidi Rezegh airfield and link up with the Tobruk garrison, which was to break out in the Belhamed–Ed Duda area. The powerful 7th Armoured consisted of three armoured brigades: the 4th armed with the newly arrived American M3 Stuarts, and the 7th and 22nd both equipped with the British cruiser tanks. The Tobruk garrison included the 32nd Army Tank Brigade, which comprised four Matilda squadrons and a regiment of cruiser and light tanks.

Major General F.W. von Mellenthin recalled:

> To meet this attack the Panzergruppe had 249 German and 146 Italian tanks. ... Of the German tanks, 70 were Mark IIs, which only mounted a heavy machine gun, and could therefore play no part in the tank battle, except as reconnaissance vehicles. The bulk of our strength consisted of 35 Mk IVs and 139 Mk IIIs, we also had five British Matildas, of which we thought highly.

Once more the British tanks were lured into a trap sprung by concealed armour and anti-tank guns and the attack quickly came unstuck. Nonetheless, the British held on and Rommel, his two panzer and single Italian armoured division over extended, was forced to retreat. During these engagements the 'Tiger Cubs' caused confusion on both sides.

Lieutenant Schmidt, posted to 15th Panzer, was involved in the capture of a British tank recovery vehicle in November 1941 near Sidi Azeiz. Afterward heading southward toward Maddalena he was alarmed to be informed that he had British tanks behind him. Three anti-tank guns were set up to block twelve advancing Matildas, two were destroyed and the rest fanned out. Schmidt and his gunners were in danger of being surrounded and were considering retreating when two more Matildas came up behind them. Schmidt takes up the story, 'I glanced back with a vague idea of withdrawal if that were possible amid this fire. To my horror I saw two more British Mark IIs moving towards us. Then to my gasping relief I recognized swastika markings on them: they were two of the British tanks that had been captured at Halfaya during "Battleaxe" months before.'

When the German commander surrendered at Bardia, Rommel lost 9,000 German and Italian troops who went into captivity. A total of 4,000 Germans and 10,000 Italians were taken at Bardia, Sollum and Halfaya. The campaign also cost them about 300 tanks, while the British lost 278. Since Bardia was one of Rommel's major supply bases, perhaps far worse was the loss of the vast quantities of supplies, guns and ammunition. This was irreplaceable and despite his subsequent victories in 1942, he never really recovered. Rommel attempted not to repeat the same mistake at the end of the year when he sought to evacuate at least part of the 10,000 tons of Axis material at Tobruk. British air raids destroyed 2,000 tons of precious fuel at Benghazi. Likewise, when he was forced from Tripoli in early 1943 he managed to spirit away almost all of his supplies and quite remarkably most of it by road.

By late 1941 Rommel had 249 panzers, of which 174 were the more powerful Mk III and IVs, supported by 146 obsolescent Italian M13s of the Ariete Division. Against these the British could field 765 cruiser, Matilda and Valentine tanks. Getting reinforcements to Libya meant running the gauntlet of the Royal Navy and the RAF so replacement panzers were always something of a problem. For example, after the Battle of Sidi Rezegh in November 1941 the two panzer divisions deployed no more than 100 tanks between them and on a number of occasions their strength fell even lower.

Despite Rommel's setbacks, the god of war smiled on him in early January 1942 when a convoy berthed in Tripoli carrying seventy-five much-needed panzers and armoured cars. By 20 January his Afrika Korps had 111 combat-ready tanks with another 28 undergoing maintenance; the Italian Motorized Corps had 89 tanks. Crucially, ammunition and petrol also arrived and over 300 Axis aircraft could be put into the air. The Panzergruppe Afrika was restructured as Panzerarmee Afrika, which included the Ariete Armoured and the Trieste Motorized Divisions. This enabled him to bounce back and go over to the offensive again.

In response to the Matilda the Germans despatched the Marder self-propelled anti-gun to 15th Panzer – though the units did not arrive until May 1942; it was really the 88mm flak gun that ended the Matilda's reign as the 'Queen of the Battlefield'. The Matilda was withdrawn from service in North Africa by the end of July 1942. The British also seemed unable to learn from their mistakes. The Ariete and part of 21st Panzer Division overran the isolated 3rd Motorized Brigade in the spring of 1942 and shortly after 15th Panzer caught the 4th Armoured Brigade on its own which lost nearly half its strength.

During June 1942 following Rommel's successful attack on the Gazala Line, he withdrew his armour into the 'Cauldron', in which the three German mobile divisions plus two Italian ones were cut off for a while. Rommel though triumphed thanks to his tactics, especially his anti-tank screen, and forced the British (including the 1st and 32nd Tank Brigades) to retreat with the disastrous loss of Tobruk.

Rommel employed superior tactics, training and communications; he appreciated the necessity of local superiority and the value of artillery and anti-tank guns. Both were used offensively in support of his panzers rather than as purely defensive weapons. Ironically in June 1942 Rommel was far more appreciative of General Wavell's efforts than Churchill, remarking:

> Wavell's strategic planning of the offensive had been excellent. ... He knew very well the necessity of avoiding any operation which would enable his opponent to fight on interior lines and destroy his formations one by one with locally superior concentrations. But he was put at great disadvantage by the slow speed of his infantry tanks, which prevented him from reacting quickly enough to the moves of our faster vehicles.

Chapter 4

Enter the Sherman

America supplied the 8th Army with three main types of tank, the M3 light tank or Stuart, and the M3 Lee/Grant and M4 Sherman medium tanks. While the Sherman became the single most important tank in the British inventory by virtue of its vast numbers, it was the Grant that arrived in the nick of time to save the 8th Army. The Germans first came up against American-built armour fighting with the British Army in Egypt and Libya and subsequently with the US Army in Tunisia. The very first Stuarts were delivered in July 1941 and used to replace British-built light tanks, these were followed by the General Grant. The introduction of the American Lend-Lease Act in March 1941 also enabled Britain to receive numbers of the slightly differently armed General Lee.

After the British Army's escape from Dunkirk and the loss of all its equipment, a British Tank Commission was despatched to Washington in June 1940 with a view to getting British tanks built in America and procuring American tanks. In the event they ordered 500 M3 medium tanks, dubbed the Grant by the British after General Ulysses S. Grant. The first 200 were shipped to the 8th Army starting in early 1942. For the coming Gazala battle the 4th Armoured Brigade were equipped with 167 Grants, at last giving them a tank with superior firepower to any German armoured fighting vehicle. By June 1942 a further 250 M3s had been successfully shipped to Egypt along with American instructors.

Following Rommel's capture of Tobruk that month, President Roosevelt proposed sending the US 2nd Armored Division to help, but as it would take up to five months to get them there it was decided to despatch their Sherman tanks instead. Around 300 M4 Shermans, mainly the cast-hull M4A1 variant, were shipped to the 8th Army by October 1942, along with 100 new M7 self-propelled howitzers. Washington generously made good convoy losses by withdrawing further tanks issued to American units. Elements of the British 2nd Armoured Brigade, 1st Armoured Division, 8th and 24th Armoured

Brigades, 10th Armoured Division and 9th Armoured Brigade, 2nd New Zealand Division were issued with the M4A1s. While the Sherman was easily superior to the obsolescent British cruisers, the British crews soon nicknamed them 'The Ronson Lighter' and the Germans the 'Tommy Cooker', as they caught fire very easily.

The American-built Grant met with general approval, importantly it was reasonably fast, reliable (unlike the Matilda and Crusader) and its 75mm gun could take on German armour and anti-tank crews on a more equal footing. The only problem was that the gun was mounted in the right side of the hull, thereby greatly restricting its arch of fire. The Grants first went into action in North Africa in May 1942 at Gazala and its 75mm gave the Germans a nasty shock. 'Up to May of 1942 our tanks had in general been superior in quality to corresponding British types,' noted Rommel in his diary. 'This was now no longer true, at least not to the same extent.' He adds, 'The advent of the new American tank had torn great holes in our ranks. Our entire force now stood in heavy and destructive combat with a superior enemy.' Rommel had seized Tobruk on 21 June 1941, where he captured about fifty tanks from the dispirited garrison. By that time his forces had taken or destroyed over 1,000 armoured fighting vehicles and almost 400 guns, as well as seizing 45,000 prisoners. Rommel's reward was elevation to Field Marshal. However, by October 1942 600 Grants had arrived in Egypt.

While the concept of the M3 was good, it was only really an interim fix and both the Grant/Lee tank types were replaced as the Sherman became available. Montgomery's 8th Army had 294 Crusaders, 170 Grants, 252 Shermans, 119 Stuarts and 194 Valentines ready for its knockout blow. Four British Churchill tanks were also present at El Alamein. Initial Sherman casualties lost to German mines and anti-tank guns occurred with the British 9th Armoured Brigade, during the opening stages of the Battle of El Alamein on 23 October 1942. The first tank-to-tank engagement took place the following day between Shermans of the 2nd Armoured Brigade and tanks of Rommel's 15th Panzer Division. Both sides suffered casualties, but it was the Germans who withdrew to the north.

Rommel was impressed by the Sherman, 'Their new tank, the General Sherman, which came into action for the first time during this battle, showed itself to be far superior to ours.' Understandably he was not happy about this development. Indeed, the turning point for Rommel had come. By this stage his forces were completely outnumbered in terms of manpower and equipment. After fierce fighting he was thrown back with the loss of over 400 panzers. Montgomery lost half his tank force, but 350 were repairable.

American-built armour first went into action with the US Army against the Vichy French in North Africa. When American units were deployed overseas they normally exchanged their medium M3s for M4s, the only unit not to do this was the US 1st Armored Division. This unit formed part of the Centre Task Force of Operation Torch during the landings in Algeria on 7–8 November 1942. Although Shermans replaced 1st Armored's battle casualties, M3s remained on its strength throughout the campaign. The Sherman first went into action with the Americans in Tunisia in January 1943.

Armour enhancements were not all one-sided. During early 1942 Rommel was supplied with the Panzer III Ausf J armed with the long-barrelled KwK 39 L/60 gun, that proved very useful against the Grant and the Valentine. Adolf Hitler initially wanted the L/60 installed in the Panzer III in the summer of 1940 so was not pleased to see the initial Ausf J armed with the shorter L/42 when it went into production in 1941. While this variant ended up armed with either the L/42 or L/60, all subsequent Panzer III Ausf L and M were fitted with the longer gun. From April 1942 spaced armour 20mm thick was also fitted to the gun mantlet and hull front, including to those tanks deployed to North Africa.

The most common Panzer IVs were the Ausf D, E and F1 which made up around 25 per cent of Rommel's armoured formations. They were armed with the short 75mm KwK37 L/24 anti-tank gun, which was inferior to the later 50mm gun of the Panzer IIIs. In the summer of 1942 Rommel began to receive the upgunned F2 armed with the long-barrelled 75mm KwK40 L/43, which could penetrate 85mm of armour at 1,000 yards and was superior to the British 6-pounder and the Grant's 75mm gun (the latter could only pierce 45mm of armour at 1,000 yards).

At the same time Rommel also received the Panzerjäger 38(t) which married captured Russian 76.2mm anti-tank guns with the Czech-manufactured 38(t) tank chassis and the Geschützwagon Lorraine Schlepper (f), which comprised a tracked French artillery tractor mounting a German 150mm howitzer. None of these vehicles were supplied in any significant numbers. Similarly, Rommel received just three Sturmgeschütz Ausf D assault guns (armed with the short 75mm gun) and just twelve sIG 33 (which mounted a 150mm infantry gun on a stretched Panzer II chassis) during 1942. The Tiger I with the powerful 88mm KwK36 L/56 anti-tank gun did not arrive until the following year, by which time the Allies were already well aware of its capabilities following its performance on the Eastern Front. By mid-1942 Rommel increasingly lacked adequate armoured fighting vehicles, supplies and reinforcements in the face of ever-growing numbers of America- supplied tanks.

Once General Claude Auchinleck had relieved General Ritchie in the summer of 1942, he realized that holding western Egypt was not possible and prepared a mobile defence in depth between Mersa Matruh and El Alamein. The latter was the only defensive line in North Africa that could not outflanked and was fortified by the 8th Army. While Rommel was aiming to push his panzers all the way through to Alexandria, Cairo and the Suez Canal, Auchinleck in turn planned to stop him and breakthrough to the west. Rommel was handicapped by a long supply line that tailed back as far as Tripoli.

After Rommel had taken Mersa Matruh this led to the first Battle of Alamein, though by this point his armoured forces were reduced to about a dozen tanks. Rommel spent two weeks trying to dislodge the British, who then in turn spent two weeks trying to drive back the Germans. This series of engagements lasted 27 days and commenced in 1 July 1942. The Ruweisat Ridge was the scene of especially heavy fighting. While the New Zealanders and Indians drove the Italians from their positions on 14 July they bypassed the 8th Panzer Regiment.

The following day there was no sign of the 22nd Armoured Brigade, which was supposed to support the New Zealanders. Predictably the panzers counter-attacked, catching the New Zealanders on three sides and were only checked by the belated appearance of the British tanks. Having fought each other to a standstill, the battle tailed off by 27 July; Axis losses amounted to 22,000 men and 100 tanks, while the British lost 13,000 men and 193 tanks.

Unfortunately, Auchinleck's decision to give ground and his failure to decisively defeat Rommel cost him his job. The Afrika Korps' situation was such that lacking panzers, exhausted and under strength a British victory was largely assured. Montgomery arrived to take command of the 8th Army's gathering strength on 13 August 1942. In light of his enemy's numerical superiority, with typical flare Rommel sought to catch Monty off balance by attacking first.

Due to the slowness of the Italian Ariete and Trieste divisions getting through the British defences and refuelling problems, Rommel was unable to strike Alam Halfa until 31 August. Nonetheless, when his new Panzer IVs with their high-velocity 75mm guns supported by Stuka dive-bombers did attack they caused heavy losses to the dug-in British Grant tanks. Times had changed though and things did not go to plan, his attack becoming bogged down. For the first time the British also had substantial numbers of the 6-pounder anti-tank guns. Rommel's forces, under constant attack by the RAF, had little choice but withdraw to their original start line.

Montgomery, never a man to rush headlong into anything, did not give chase, but instead chose to bide his time while gathering even greater strength ready for a decisive knockout blow. Before Alamein a divisional headquarters staff (from 8th Armoured) was used to create the impression that Montgomery had an extra armoured division simply through radio traffic. In reality it had no tanks at all. Montgomery though went into battle with a superiority of about 2:1 in troops and 1,100 tanks to Rommel's 500 (of which 300 were of an inferior type). On top of this Montgomery had almost 1,000 field guns, and 800 6-pounder and 500 2-pounder anti-tank guns. On 23 October 1942 a massive British artillery bombardment heralded the second battle of El Alamein.

Montgomery had finally learned it was not wise to throw his tanks against Rommel's gun line, so directed his infantry to first breach the enemy minefields. Once two corridors had been secured he planned to push through the 1st and 10th Armoured Divisions to Tel el Aqqaqir, to prepare for an enemy counter-attack. Near the Qattara Depression in the far south the 7th Armoured launched a diversionary attack with the view of pinning down Rommel's reserves, most notably 21st Panzer. While Monty's infantry engaged the Axis defences his armour, despite its overwhelming numbers, at first was unable to break through. The battle turned into a slugging match that Rommel could not win. He could clearly see the writing was on the wall for the Axis cause in North Africa. This battle is 'turning the tide of war in Africa against us,' Rommel wrote, 'and, in fact, probably representing the turning point of the whole vast struggle. The conditions under which my gallant troops entered the battle were so disheartening that there was practically no hope of our coming out of it victorious.'

By 26 October Major General Raymond Briggs' 1st Armoured Division had reached Kidney Ridge and was threatening to cut the Axis main north-south line of communication along the Rahman Track. The 2nd Rifle Brigade was sent forward to set up Outpost Snipe and came into contact with 15th Panzer and the Italian Littorio Armoured Division. Although only of battalion strength, the 2nd Rifle Brigade fortunately had almost twenty 6-pounder anti-tank guns and drove off the enemy attacks. The 21st Panzer then found itself caught between the anti-tank guns and the rest of 1st Armoured. Afterwards the battlefield around the Snipe position was found littered with twenty-one panzers, eleven Italian tanks and five tank destroyers; it was also assessed that another twenty tanks had been knocked out but recovered by the Axis.

On 27 October Montgomery reorganized his forces and despite mounting losses maintained the pressure in the northern sector of the battle. Rommel was in an unenviable position – despite all his skills by the end of October he knew the British had still not committed the bulk of their 800 tanks, against which he could field 90 panzers and 140 Italian tanks. Then on 1 November Operation Supercharge finally overwhelmed the exhausted Axis troops.

Rommel received the brunt of Montgomery's expected major attack that night. South-west of Hill 28 the British broke through 15th Panzer's front. Captured documents showed they were facing up to 500 tanks, which drove west and overran a unit from the Trieste Armoured Division. To Rommel's dismay his observers reported another 400 British tanks waiting east of the minefields. By the evening of 2 November Rommel had just thirty-five serviceable panzers, and by the 4th this had fallen to just twenty.

Despite the British armour's breakthrough, on 4 November Rommel was already retiring back toward Libya. Thanks to Montgomery's caution, bad weather and fuel shortages the British pursuit was delayed. Rommel with his remaining troops, the equivalent of two divisions from his original dozen, rumbled back along the coast road, harried by the RAF as he went. This was no rout and Rommel turned to fight at every defensive position. Instead of throwing everything he had at Rommel, Montgomery kept trying to outflank him. As a result, the retreating Axis kept slipping the net.

Fuel became an increasing problem for Rommel, not only getting it shipped to Tripoli, but also getting it up to the front. After his defeat at Alamein 21st Panzer was almost completely immobilized south-west of Quasaba for the want of fuel; only the timely arrival of the Voss Group prevented the division being overrun. Nonetheless, 21st Panzer was forced to destroy all but four of its remaining thirty tanks and withdraw westward in its surviving wheeled transport.

On 8 November 1942, just four days after Montgomery's breakthrough at El Alamein, the US Army landed in Vichy-controlled French Algeria and Morocco west of Rommel in Libya. Due to a lack of tank landing craft, the Moroccan ports of Casablanca and Safi on the Atlantic coast and the Algerian ports of Oran and Algiers on the Mediterranean had to be secured as quickly as possible in order for the Americans to land their tanks over the quayside.

There were around 120,000 French and colonial troops in Algeria, Morocco and Tunisia, supported by up to 500 aircraft. French and French colonial forces were largely infantry formations, equipped with 25mm and 37mm anti-tank guns. However, according to American intelligence they were supported by around 250 armoured cars and tanks, which constituted a direct threat to the American landing forces. Armour in French North Africa included the tiny Renault FT-17, Renault R-35 and the Hotchkiss H-35/39 light tanks.

General Ernest H. Harmon, commanding the American landings, found he was without armour, despite intended support from the US 1st and 2nd Armored Divisions. Those light tanks that had been landed were inoperable due to faulty batteries or drowned engines. To make matters worse the two ships carrying additional tanks suffered critical delays unloading their cargo due to crane problems. When the Shermans of Task Force Blackstone finally landed near Safi they arrived too late to see any combat. Task Force Goalpost, assigned to capture the airport at Lyautey and Sale, included M5 light tanks of the 66th Armoured Regiment, 2nd Armoured.

The 1st Armored Division comprised the 1st and 13th Armored Regiments, each equipped with one battalion of light and two battalions of medium tanks. Whilst the medium tanks were dry-landed at the portside, the light tanks were brought ashore via shallow-draft oil tankers and pontoon bridging. M3 light tanks of the 13th Armored Reconnaissance Company spearheading Red Task Force seized Tafaraoui airfield. Green Task Force including M3s of the 1st Battalion plus elements of the 701st Tank Destroyer Battalion secured La Senia airfield. Luckily the American light tanks were more than a match for the elderly Renault tanks. It was only when Sherman tanks were finally put ashore at Safi and Oran that the Allies were able to field any substantial quantity of medium armour and by then the French had called for a ceasefire.

While elements of the US 2nd Armored Division took part in Operation Torch, only the US 1st Armored fought in Tunisia. Its sister division remained in French Morocco as a deterrent to General Franco's Spain joining the Axis. Also during the winter of 1942–3 the 2nd Armored was cannibalized to provide equipment for the newly-raised French 2nd Armoured Division and to flesh out 1st Armored after its mauling at Kasserine.

If the French had co-operated, the Allies could have pushed into Tunisia within two days of the landings in Algeria. Instead, the Germans struck eastward from Tunis, successfully safeguarding the panzers' escape from Libya into Tunisia. Under the French-Italian armistice, Mussolini had imposed a 50-mile demilitarized zone between Libya and Tunisia, but this now counted for nothing, as German and Italian tanks were soon crossing to secure their exposed western flank. The French garrison in Tunisia chose to observe the ceasefire and join the Allies as elements of the British 1st Army, after landing in eastern Algeria, moved into western Tunisia. Unfortunately, in Tunis a quarter of the French garrison remained loyal to Vichy and did nothing to impede the arriving Germans. At Bizerte, some Vichy French units even joined the Germans who were moving to reinforce Tunisia.

The Allies' inability to extend the landings eastward into Tunisia was to prove a major failing of Operation Torch. Within days of the Allied landings German aircraft were flying troops and equipment into Tunis and by the end of the month 15,000 German and 9,000 Italian troops were in position to prevent the British 1st Army from cutting through Tunisia to link up with the 8th Army advancing through Libya.

In the wake of the Torch landings the French had to support the Allies' forces in Tunisia, maintain their garrison forces and equip a new army to take part in the forthcoming liberation of Europe. This meant that ill-equipped existing units were rushed into battle before they were really combat ready. Initially the French 19th Corps, some 13,000 men, moved to the front between the British 1st Army and the US 2nd Corps. Crucially they lacked tanks. A similar number of Free French Forces were also committed and they were issued with Stuarts and Shermans.

Shortly after the German build-up in Tunisia, the 8th Army rolled up to the Libyan border and during the second week of December Rommel decided to pull back from El Agheila, the Axis stop line during the two previous British advances. Instead he chose to make a stand on the Mareth Line in Tunisia. Ironically this had been built by the French to keep the Italians out and was superior to the Alamein positions.

From Oran the US 1st Armored Division was rushed to Tunisia and came under the command of the British 1st Army for the drive on Tunis. The division's 2nd Battalion, 13th Armored Regiment, lost forty-two tanks to the panzers in fighting around Djedeiba and Tebourba. Despite receiving Sherman replacements, by the time of the Axis surrender the 1st Armored still had fifty-one M3s on its strength. These were handed over to the Free French Forces for driver training. The M3 was then withdrawn from service in the Mediterranean and European theatres of operation.

Montgomery was always able to trade hardware that Rommel could ill-afford. The Second Battle of Alamein was hard won, but Monty's heavy tank losses were not fatal, whereas Rommel's were. By mid-January 1943 Montgomery deployed 450 tanks against Rommel's 36 panzers and 57 Italian tanks. The 7th Armoured Division's attack on 15th Panzer on 15 January 1943 cost thirty-three tanks for just two panzers, and the following day the British lost another twenty tanks. The attack toward Tarhuna resulted in further severe losses for the British, but Rommel had nothing with which to hold on to Tripoli that was captured on the 23rd. Britain's armoured formations also enjoyed increasingly effective air support. By the time of the Second Battle of Alamein the DAF was able to fly 2,500 fighter and fighter-bomber sorties and 800 bomber sorties on a daily basis. The Luftwaffe could only manage 100 fighter sorties and 60 dive-bomber sorties in support of Rommel's beleaguered panzers.

By the end of January 1943 the Afrika Korps had been forced back into Tunisia, having abandoned Mussolini's Libyan colony with the evacuation of Tripoli. With his front secured on the Mareth Line, Rommel knew that he would be granted breathing space by Montgomery that would enable him to turn and face the US Army advancing on Tunisia. Rommel kept hoping that Hitler would spare him reinforcements, but when they arrived it was too little, too late.

When Rommel's forces arrived in Tunisia they numbered about 30,000 Germans and 48,000 Italians. His 21st Panzer had been sent back to the Gabes-Sfax area, while the Italian Centauro Armoured Division had moved to guard the El Guettar defile facing the Americans at Gafsa. The German units though only had about one third of their complement of tanks, a quarter of their anti-tank guns and a sixth of their artillery; of 130 panzers less than half were combat-worthy.

Hitler, having starved Rommel of resources throughout 1941–2, was now determined to hold on in Tunisia at all costs and by the beginning of February Axis forces had risen to a total of up to 100,000 Germans and 26,000 Italians. Armoured forces were now almost entirely German and numbered 280 tanks, 110 with 10th Panzer, 91 with 21st Panzer, a dozen Tiger tanks and 26 tanks in a unit reinforcing the 23 surviving Italian tanks with the battered Centauro Division.

While Rommel was keen to strike before Montgomery gained the full benefit of the port of Tripoli, his chain of command was now complicated. His 21st Panzer was under General von Arnim's Tunisian command. At the end of January 21st Panzer gained a foothold at the Faid Pass from where it could launch an attack on the Americans. Rommel and von Arnim must have secretly despaired of fighting a two-front war in Tunisia. At last having received fresh armoured units (which included the 501st Heavy Tank Battalion equipped with the Tiger tank and the Herman Göring Division), Rommel chose to set about the Americans at Kasserine.

Only at Kasserine Pass did the exhausted Germans enjoy any real success against the inexperienced American tank crews pressing on their western flank. On 14 February 1943 Rommel's veteran 21st Panzer Division and von Arnim's 10th Panzer Division swept through the Americans positions. The raw American troops were no match for the battle-hardened panzers. The 21st Panzer first set about the US 1st Armored Division at Sidi Bou Zid, destroying large numbers of Grant, Lee and Sherman tanks with ease. The Germans then rolled through Kasserine and Sbeitla. To the embarrassment of the US Army they lost over 150 tanks as well as 300 killed, 3,000 wounded and 1,600 captured in the heavy fighting. A week later the Germans captured another twenty tanks, thirty armoured personnel carriers and a similar number of anti-tank guns. However, American losses were swiftly and easily replaced. This gave Rommel his last victory in Africa, but his lack of resources and interference from the high command meant his tactical victory never developed into a strategic success. Shortly after Rommel flew to Berlin to request an evacuation. Not only did Hitler refuse, he also denied Rommel permission to return to his men who were facing final defeat.

Axis forces numbering 120,000 men with around 200 effective tanks were facing over half a million Allied soldiers equipped with 1,800 tanks. Trying to capitalize on their success at Kasserine, on 6 March 1943 a second Axis attack was mounted, this time against the 8th Army opposite the Mareth Line toward Medenine. Up until late February Montgomery only had a single division at Medenine, but by the time of Rommel's attack he had quadrupled his strength, with 400 tanks supported by 500 anti-tank guns and 350 field guns. Montgomery also had air superiority.

Rommel's three panzer divisions mustered only 160 tanks supported by no more than 10,000 infantry and 200 guns. It was an ill-executed operation and was repulsed with heavy losses, including fifty tanks, in the face of British firepower. Although 15th Panzer closed with the enemy, they were driven off. The 21st Panzer, which should have known better, exposed themselves crossing a ridge, received a beating and never closed on the British gun lines. Neither the 10th Panzer or 90th Light Divisions achieved any better results and all suffered losses to mines. The British did not lose a single tank and only suffered minimal casualties – times had changed.

As the Afrika Korps withdrew it could only muster eighty-five German and twenty-four Italian tanks, a dangerously low number with which to hold onto Tunisia. On 9 March Rommel took his long-deferred sick leave and handed over the command of the army group to von Arnim. Rommel's Panzerarmee Afrika was now known as the 1st Italian Army under General Giovanni Messe, against which Montgomery had a 4:1 superiority in tanks.

On 20–22 March Montgomery threw 610 tanks at the Mareth Line, which was defended by just 150 tanks. However, his assault was driven off thanks to the weather, which kept the RAF from the skies, and the panzers. The main defences of the Mareth Line ran along the formidable natural barrier of the Wadi Zigzaou, which after bitter fighting was forced by elements of the British 50th Division. A well-timed counter-attack by 15th Panzer, with less than thirty tanks and two infantry battalions, contained and then almost destroyed the bridgehead.

This forced Montgomery to redeploy Briggs' 1st Armoured Division to the west to support the New Zealand Corps' left hook towards El Hamma. The New Zealanders barged through the Wilder's Gap in the Matmata Hills and across the waterless Dahar to the Tebaga Gap behind the Afrika Korps' flank, forcing them to withdraw from the Mareth Line. Nonetheless, the blocking forces of 21st Panzer at El Hamma ensured that the Axis were not trapped, though the panzer divisions lost most of their tanks during the battle.

Montgomery launched a frontal assault on the Axis' new position at Wadi Akarit, that spanned the Gabes Gap, forcing a breach. Axis commander General Messe with the Americans bearing down on his right flank withdrew north toward Enfidaville. Slowly but surely the Axis forces were trapped in northern Tunisia around the ports of Bizerta and Tunis by the American and British armies.

With 8th Army pushing from the south, 1st Army began an offensive from the west. The key armoured formations were the US 1st Armored and the British 1st, 6th and 7th Armoured Divisions. Still the Axis forces clung to their mountain defences, especially on Longstop Hill where the British 78th Division struggled for four days to retake it from the Germans. In late April the panzers of the Afrika Korps made one last attack in an attempt to staff off the inevitable. General von Arnim gathered all the remaining armoured detachments into the 8th Panzer Regiment, which had first fought during Operation Battleaxe, and counter-attacked at Djebel Bou Aoukaz west of Longstop. The Afrika Korps had sixty-nine panzers still fit for battle, save for one very important detail – petrol.

During early May Allied forces began to encroach onto the Tunisian coastal plain. On the 5th the British 1st Infantry Division took Djebel Bou Aoukaz and the next day the 4th Indian Division secured the Medjez el Bab position. The way was now open for the 'Desert Rats' of 7th Armoured and on 7 May their tanks rolled triumphantly into Tunis. At the same time the Americans took Bizerta leaving the surviving Axis forces trapped in the Cape Bon peninsula. On 12 May 1943 von Arnim was captured and a day later Messe formally surrendered 125,000 German and 115,000 Italian troops. The Axis' remaining 250 immobile tanks fell into the Allies' hands.

Chapter 5

Sicilian Tank Battles

Following the Axis defeat in Tunisia the Allies turned their attention to the Italian island of Sicily. An invasion of Sicily was not a forgone conclusion. Ideally the Allies wanted to open a new front in Western Europe, but at this stage simply did not have the resources in place to conduct a landing in northern France. Other options on the table for Allied planners to consider included invasions of the Italian island of Sardinia or the French island of Corsica, with advances into northern Italy and southern France respectively. On balance it was decided that an attack on Sicily and an advance into southern Italy was the preferred option, as it offered shorter and safer lines of communication with Allied forces in North Africa. Fighter cover could also be provided from Malta. Crucially this Sicilian 'right hook' alternative was intended to serve much grander strategic goals.

Overall command and planning for Operation Husky fell to the 15th Army Group, under General Harold Alexander, which had responsibility for getting Montgomery and Patton's two armies onto the shores of southern Sicily. Committed to the invasion, supporting the infantry divisions of Montgomery's 8th Army, were the British 4th and 23rd Armoured Brigades and the Canadian 1st Tank Brigade. The latter, along with the Canadian 1st Infantry Division, was included on the insistence of the Canadian Prime Minister William Lyon Mackenzie King. Lieutenant General George S. Patton's US 7th Army's principal supporting armoured units were the US 70th and 753rd Tank Battalions and the 601st Tank Destroyer Battalion, plus elements of the 813th Tank Destroyer Battalion. Under the US Provisional Corps was the US 2nd Armored Division. The US 45th Infantry Division was also supported by a tank destroyer battalion

Strategically it was hoped that by attacking southern Italy the Germans would be drawn away from Normandy and the Eastern Front. This was to lead to strong differences of opinion amongst the Allies. The Americans saw the Italian campaign purely as a way to sap Germany's strength from more important fronts, rather than as a major effort to defeat the Axis powers. The British on the other hand saw pushing north through Italy and into Austria and southern Germany as a way of defeating Hitler. This was an important difference, because it meant at a crucial moment in the Italian campaign in mid-1944 the Allied armies were drained of resources to support the fighting in France.

The Germans had two armoured formations deployed on Sicily, the Luftwaffe's Hermann Göring Panzer Division, commanded by General Paul Conrath, and the 15th Panzergrenadier Division, under General Eberhard Rodt. They could field a total of 159 tanks between them. These units were reinforced by General Walter Fries's 29th Panzergrenadier Division, that began to arrive in mid-July and came under General Hans-Valentin Hube's 14th Panzer Corps.

In contrast Italian tank units were negligible, comprising a number of battalions of Renault R-35 tanks, as the bulk of their armour had been lost in the fighting in North Africa. Very limited numbers of armoured fighting vehicles remained scattered in Albania and Greece, while the few remaining medium tanks and assault guns were gathered for the defence of mainland Italy. They were so short of tanks that when Italian officers inspected the Italian divisions on Sicily in June, they confirmed German armour would be needed to help defend the island.

The defence of Sicily was the responsibility of the Italian 6th Army, consisting of two corps, commanded by General Alfredo Guzzoni. However, to confuse matters the specially designated Fortress Areas around the ports came under the Italian Navy. Axis forces on Sicily by early July numbered some 200,000 Italians and 62,000 German Army and Luftwaffe personnel. The Italians were organized into four front-line infantry divisions while the rest consisted of immobile coastal divisions. General Guzzoni's headquarters was based at Enna in the centre of the island, while its subordinate commands consisted of General Matio Arisio's 12th Corps to the west and General Carlo Rossi's 16th Corps to the east. Reserves consisted of a single Italian division and the Hermann Göring and 15th Panzergrenadiers. The Italians were not anticipating any amphibious operations due to the poor weather, so were not on alert along the southern coast.

Husky commenced on the night of 9/10 July 1943. The assault forces comprised three British, three American and one Canadian division. By the evening of 10 July the port of Syracuse had been secured and they were well established. Two days later Field Marshal Kesselring arrived to assess the situation and rapidly came to the view that his troops were on their own. They needed reinforcing as quickly as possible and in order to shorten the front line it was decided to abandon western Sicily. As a result, a defensive line was established from San Stefano on the north coast, via Nicosia, Agira and Cantenanuova down to Catania on the eastern coast.

As the only armoured division supporting the invasion, the US 2nd Armored was divided between two of the US 7th Army's task forces. To the left Combat Command A (66th Armored Regiment) was with the 3rd Infantry Division coming ashore at Licata. The bulk of the division was to act as a floating reserve to support the central invasion around Gela. In the face of counter-attacks by the panzers of Hermann Göring and the Italian Livorno Division and Mobile Force E, reinforcements from the US 2nd Armored were put ashore in the shape of Combat Command B (3rd Battalion, 67th Armored Regiment). While forty panzers were overrunning the positions of the US 1st Infantry Division, the Shermans of 2nd Armored struggled to get off the beaches. Four Shermans under Lieutenant James White finally reached the coastal highway and began to shell the Germans' flank and they eventually withdrew with the loss of sixteen panzers.

At Licata, the westernmost US beachhead, Combat Command A suffered at the hands of the Luftwaffe when a landing ship carrying a company of Shermans, an infantry company's vehicles and half the command's HQ equipment was hit. However, on 11 July the division took Naro only to be bombed by their own air force. On 16 July 2nd Armored was placed in reserve, it then took part in Patton's attack on Palermo on the northern coast. The division rolled into the city on 22 July. Once the island had been occupied the 2nd Armored was sent to England to prepare for the Allied invasion of Normandy.

Despite the very determined German counter-attacks, the Allies drove north with little difficulty until the British 8th Army ground to a halt before Catania. This was just over half way to the army's final objective the port of Messina. Although the key strategic task had been allocated to Montgomery's 8th Army, it was the US 7th Army under the dynamic leadership of General Patton that made the real progress. By 23 July Patton's forces had cleared western Sicily and were heading eastward along the north coast toward the prize of Messina. His advance was assisted by a series of amphibious landings on 8, 11 and 15 August to outflank the resistance now being conducted largely as the Germans as they withdrew.

General Hube was appointed corps commander on 13 July, less than two weeks before Mussolini's downfall on 25 July. German reinforcements sent to Sicily included the 1st Parachute Division and the 29th Panzergrenadier Division, to add to the 15th Panzergrenadiers and the Hermann Göring Division. The 29th Panzergrenadiers were in the northern sector, the 15th in the centre and the Hermann Göring in the east. They were supported by the remnants of three Italian divisions.

The arrival of these reinforcements bolstered the German garrison to some 72,000, with about 160 tanks, including a company of Tigers. Until the 14th Panzer Corps arrived the new units were nominally under the command of the Italians, though in reality they took their orders from General Frido von Senger und Etterlin, who was the German liaison officer with the 6th Italian Army. He answered to Kesselring and Hube eventually took full command of the Sicilian front in early August.

Private H.I. Tait of the 51st Highland Division witnessed the tough time that Allied tanks had in Sicily, 'One point I had particularly noted during the battle was the vulnerability of the Sherman tank, which had a much higher outline than the German tanks, and seemed to be picked off very easily. Our CO [Commanding Officer] was killed whilst in a tank conferring with the tank commander.' Tait also recalled the bitter fighting against the Luftwaffe's panzers for the Gerbini airfield, 'There were several counter-attacks by German troops which were identified as units from the Herman Göring Division and Paratroops. At about 09.00am, 21 July, there was a counter-attack by German tanks supported by about a battalion strength of infantry.' During the fighting Tait was captured, but managed to escape. He noted, 'It was probably early August before out battalion went back into action. I recollect that one of our infantry companies captured a self-propelled 75mm gun by dropping into it from a tree as the gun proceeded along the road. The gun was retained.'

By late July Allied air strikes were concentrating their efforts on the panzers, especially the 15th Panzergrenadiers. They withdrew to a strongly defensive north-south line that ran through Regalbuto conforming with 29th Panzergrenadiers to the north and the Hermann Göring to the south.

All three were prepared to tough it out to the end. The Axis forces moved to a second defensive line, anchored on Mount Etna, starting at San Fratello on the north coast and through Troina and Aderno. The 15th Panzergrenadiers, along with the remains of an Italian infantry division, held the former. For six long days they clung on, launching twenty-four counter-attacks. Once the Americans were on Mount Pellegrino the Troina defences became untenable. The Hermann Göring Division was pushed back by 30th Corps and the 29th Panzergrenadiers' positions were turned at Santa Agata and San Fratello after the Americans landed behind them.

Catania fell on 5 August and two days later Aderno south-west of Mount Etna fell to the British after heavy fighting and an abrupt withdrawal by the Germans. With Aderno and Troina taken the main defence line across north-eastern Sicily was broken. The Americans took Randazzo to the north-west of Mount Etna and some 50 miles from Messina on 13 August. Efforts to trap the enemy were continually thwarted by the speed of the well-organized German withdrawal

It was clear to Kesselring that his forces on Sicily could not hold out much longer. Hube was told to save the three German armoured units, the Hermann Göring and the 15th and 29th Panzergrenadiers. From Calabria the 14th Panzer Corps was instructed to oversee evacuated units. German guns kept enemy fighter-bombers and warships away from the Strait of Messina so the Allies were unable to impede the German escape. Likewise, the Allies' failure to invade Calabria, the toe of Italy, thereby cutting off the Strait sealed mainland Italy's fate in becoming the next battleground.

Between 1 and 10 August 12,000 German troops, 4,500 vehicles and 5,000 tons of equipment were successfully withdrawn to the Italian mainland. A second larger-scale evacuation was conducted from 11 to 17 August. In total General Hube saved 40,000 German troops, 10,000 vehicles, 47 tanks, 94 guns and 17,000 tons of supplies, all of which were redeployed to supplement the defence of the Italian mainland. Despite this achievement Hube did lose vital equipment, including 78 tanks and armoured cars, 287 guns and 3,500 vehicles.

Although the tanks of the 8th Army were pressing on the Germans' heels, the honour of taking Messina fell to the US 3rd Infantry Division. The bloody fighting and resulting stalemate at Gerbina on the plains of Catania had held Montgomery long enough for Patton's tanks to take the laurels for winning the race to Messina. It is ironic that Patton was supposed to safeguard Montgomery's rear while Monty rushed forward as he had done from Alamein to Tunis.

Around 62,000 Italian soldiers, 227 vehicles and 41 artillery pieces were shipped across to the mainland for the loss of 15 landing barges, six minesweepers and many smaller craft before the American and British armies reached Messina on 17 August. Sicily had fallen and a tremor ran through the Italian political elite in Rome. The Sicilian campaign cost the Allies almost 25,000 men, the Germans 10,000–20,000 and the Italians 147,000. Crucially though, an entire panzer corps and its panzer and panzergrenadier divisions got away to fight another day.

Having secured Sicily, the Allies then invaded Italy. The main assault, under the code name Operation Avalanche, took place on the western coast at Salerno, with two subsidiary operations taking place in Calabria and Taranto. The Salerno invasion force consisted of 100,000 British troops and 69,000 Americans with some 20,000 vehicles borne by an armada of 450 vessels. The key armoured unit was once again the British 7th Armoured Division, while supporting forces also included the Royal Scots Greys and the 40th Royal Tank Regiment. The US 5th Amy's reserves included the US 1st Armored Division. Under Operation Baytown the Canadian 1st Armoured came ashore at Reggio di Calabria supporting the British 8th Corps.

Following the Axis surrender in Tunisia, the British 7th Armoured Division had been withdrawn to Tripolitania to refit. It missed out participating in Operation Husky and instead trained for a role in the amphibious assault on mainland Italy. The battle-hardened veterans of 22nd Armoured Brigade were brought back up to strength and issued with new vehicles and equipment. It cast off most of its British tanks and was equipped almost exclusively with the M4 Sherman. Its divisional armoured car regiment had its Daimler and Dingo armoured cars supplemented with White scout cars.

To beef up the division's anti-tank capabilities the Jeep troop was replaced by a self-propelled gun troop, equipped with two 75mm guns mounted in White half-tracks to give immediate fire support. At the same time the 5th Royal Horse Artillery was issued with the Priest 105mm self-propelled gun to work in conjunction with the armoured brigade's tanks. In light of the terrain in Italy the engineers were trained to deploy new Bailey bridges and tank-mounted scissor bridges in order to keep the division moving.

Rommel had taken charge of Army Group B in mid-August with responsibility for all German forces in Italy as far as Pisa. Field Marshal Kesselring and Army Command South remained in charge in southern Italy. The newly formed German 10th Army under General Heinrich von Vietinghoff was activated on 22 August with the task of fending off an Allied invasion. This controlled 14th Panzer Corps (Hermann Göring Panzer, 15th Panzergrenadier and 16th Panzer Divisions) and the 76th Panzer Corps (26th Panzer and 29th Panzergrenadier Divisions). Most notably the 16th Panzer Division was deployed above the Salerno plain.

Following Operation Baytown on 3 September 1943, Kesselring rightly deduced that the Calabria landings were not the main Allied effort and concluded that Salerno or Rome would be their main point of attack. He withdrew General Traugott Herr's 76th Panzer Corps, leaving just a regiment of panzergrenadiers to hold the toe of Italy in the face of the British 8th Army.

On 9 September Operation Slapstick seized Taranto unopposed, followed by Bari and Brindisi. The assault at Salerno also commenced that day, but the Allies soon found elements of 16th Panzer, Hermann Göring Panzer and the 15th and 29th Panzergrenadier Divisions bearing down on them. Private J.C. Jones, from the US 36th Infantry Division, remembered:

> Beyond the beaches in front of the 141st [Regiment], the relatively flat terrain was now invaded by five Mark IV (medium) tanks. The German armour rolled over the American troops who had taken cover in the irrigation ditches, firing continual machine gun bursts into the prone men as they rumbled by. A platoon of B Company, led by Staff Sgt James A. Whitaker of Brownwood, Texas, was caught by these tanks.

By 13 September all German reinforcements were in position, including units from 3rd Panzergrenadier Division, which had been north of Rome. That day they launched a counteroffensive that was halted by naval gunfire and artillery. Two days later 16th Panzer and 29th Panzergrenadier went over to the defensive, but the Hermann Göring Division achieved some success east of Salerno. On 15 September carrying infantry on their backs Shermans of the 40th Royal Tank Regiment departed Salerno town en route for Naples.

When 7th Armoured Division arrived in Italy on 15 September, in support of the US 5th Army, they were soon confronted with bad roads, mountains and impassable rivers. They acted as the follow-up division supporting the British 46th and 56th Infantry Divisions at Salerno. By 16 September the British and American bridgeheads had linked up with the US 5th Army pushing up the west coast and the British 8th Army advancing along the east coast. The 7th Armoured's first real success was taking Scafati on the Sarno River. Having secured the town's road bridge intact, divisional engineers then erected a Bailey bridge next to it. Forward elements of 7th Armoured entered Naples on 1 October 1943.

Once beyond Naples the armour was able to fan out and within four days 7th Armoured reached the Volturno River near Capua. The Germans though had blown all the bridges and were firmly dug in on the far bank. On 12 October 7th Armoured acting in support of an infantry assault, launched a diversionary crossing to keep the Germans preoccupied. The tanks managed to ford the river and help turn the enemy's defences. However, the Germans simply withdrew to their next defence line along the Garigliano River.

In light of the Allies' superior firepower, both 76th and 14th Panzer Corps had little option but break off the battle. Nonetheless, the armoured formations of 10th Army had come very close to overrunning the Salerno beachhead. The initial conduct of 16th Panzer and the Germans' ability to re-deploy their forces quicker than the Allies could reinforce almost tipped the battle.

The whole of southern Italy was in Allied hands with them now poised before a whole series of German defensive lines. These would buy them time, while they constructed the Winter Line south of Rome. In November the 7th Armoured Division was pulled back behind Monte Massico as it had been earmarked to take part in the coming Allied invasion of Normandy. The division handed over all their Sherman tanks and equipment to the Canadian 5th Armoured Division and made their way to Naples ready to be shipped back to England. There it was re-equipped with British-built Cromwell tanks, with dire consequences. By early November Hitler had despatched Rommel to oversee the defence of northern France and Kesselring was left in charge in Italy with instructions to deny Rome to the Allies for as long as possible.

Chapter 6

Heartbreak at Monte Cassino

In Italy it took the Allies until mid-January 1944 to force their way through the Volturno, Barbara and Bernhardt Lines to reach the Gustav Line – the centrepiece of the Winter Line. The Allies launched their next offensive on 12 January 1944, with General Juin's French Expeditionary Corps assaulting Cassino and the British 10th Corps attempting to exploit previous gains on the Garigliano River. Both failed in breaking through Gustav, although limited progress was made.

A week later the US 2nd Corps attacked from the centre of General Mark Clark's US 5th Army, attempting to cross the Rapido River. After just two days the Americans were forced to call a halt. The breakthrough of the Gustav Line, the lynch-pin of the Allied plan of which Operation Shingle, the Anzio landing, was a part, had bogged down. This lack of success at Cassino indicated there would be no progress toward Rome during March. Although the US 5th Army failed to break through it drew German reinforcements in the form of the 29th and 90th Panzergrenadier Divisions away from Rome.

Launched on 22 January 1944. Operation Shingle was an amphibious attack in the area of Anzio and Nettuno, designed to turn the German flank and compromise their defences. Some 36,000 troops and 3,200 vehicles poured ashore. British forces hitting Peter Beach were backed by the 46th Royal Tank Regiment and the American troops coming ashore on X-Ray Beach had armoured support from the US 751st Tank Battalion and 601st Tank Destroyer Battalion. At Anzio the Allies soon found their way blocked by the Hermann Göring Panzer Division and a battle group from the 4th Parachute Division, who were holding the roads from Anzio to the Alban Hills via Campoleone and Cisterna.

Within just two days of the landings the Germans had over 40,000 troops in the area, with the 4th Parachute Division to the west, while the 3rd Panzergrenadiers were in front of the Alban Hills and the Hermann

Göring Division to the east. The invasion forces were rapidly hemmed in by elements of 26th Panzer and Hermann Göring, as well as the 3rd and 16th SS Panzergrenadier Divisions with about 220 panzers. In two weeks of bitter fighting the Anglo-American forces suffered almost 7,000 casualties.

By early February some 76,000 troops were facing 100,000 Germans under the control of 14th Army and the 76th Panzer Corps and 1st Parachute Corps. The Germans launched a counter-attack on 3 February and again on 16 February with both sides fighting each other to a standstill. All the time that the forces at Anzio remained bottled up they were tying up valuable shipping which was keeping them re-supplied. Due to the lack of progress Lieutenant General Lucian Truscott replaced General Lucas as commander at Anzio. Once again the panzers had triumphed.

In an effort to break the disastrous stalemate the Allies launched Operation Diadem on 11 May 1944. The key Allied armoured formations involved in this battle were the US 1st, Canadian 5th and British 6th Armoured Divisions as well as the Polish 2nd Armoured Brigade. This was an all-out armoured thrust designed to pierce the German defences, which also served to distract Hitler from the impending invasions of Normandy and the Riviera and the massive Soviet offensive on the Eastern Front. After months of deadlock the honour of taking Monte Cassino would eventfully fall to Polish Shermans.

Diadem called for a rapid penetration of the Gustav Line at Cassino and a joint thrust northward. Lieutenant General Oliver Leese's British 8th Army was to push up the Liri Valley, as far as Sora, and up the Sacco valley, as far as Valmontone south-east of Rome. Clark's US 5th Army was to drive along the coast to link up with the US 6th Corps that would break out from the Anzio beachhead and strengthen the final push on Rome.

On the left two British divisions were to push up the coast to pin down the 3rd Panzergrenadiers, while in the meantime the US 1st Armoured and 3rd and 45th Infantry Divisions were to conducted the main attack toward Campolene. The fighting was heavy, with the Americans losing 100 tanks, and little progress was made until 1st Armored finally pieced the Caesar Line.

During the fierce battles for Cassino tanks proved to be of limited value; in the town itself Allied armour was hampered by the rubble and craters, that prevented them from moving freely. During the First Battle, when the houses and streets of Cassino were still recognizable, tanks losses were high because they made suicidal frontal assaults and blundered into anti-tank ambushes and well-laid mines. In just twelve days of fighting the US 756th Tank Battalion had twenty-three of its sixty-one tanks knocked out, with another twenty-one damaged. An armoured sortie into the Cassino massif early in the Third Battle was hopelessly mismanaged, resulting in considerable losses.

The defenders had no intention of surrendering any ground. During March and April, the German paratroopers worked on Cassino's defences, hauling up their anti-tank guns to protect the most vulnerable sectors, as well as manning the fortified dugouts and bunkers that overlooked the approaches to the top of the Cassino massif. In addition, between Cassino and Rome the Germans had constructed a whole series of defensive lines upon which they could fall back. One of the strongest was the Hitler Line; this was studded with Panther tank turrets embedded in concrete, ready to exact an appalling toll on Allied tanks and infantry.

The Battle of Monte Cassino required four major engagements involving American, British, Canadian, French, New Zealand and Polish forces. The centrepiece of the battle was the struggle for the monastery overlooking the town of Cassino. By early 1944 the western section of the German Winter Line was held by their forces in the Rapido, Liri and Garigliano valleys and the surrounding mountains and ridges forming the Gustav Line. The Germans did not occupy the monastery and incorporate it into their defences until after American bombers flattened it in mid-February.

After struggling for six weeks through seven miles of the Bernhardt Line at the cost of 16,000 casualties, the US 5th Army finally reached the Gustav Line on 15 January. The first assault was launched two days later. Although US troops got across the Rapido, tanks were unable to reach them leaving then at the mercy of the panzers and self-propelled guns of General Eberhard Rodt's 15th Panzergrenadiers. When the Third Battle commenced on 15 March it was hoped to launch a decisive blow on the German defences in the monastery and town. This included a surprise attack by the British 20th Armoured Brigade moving up a track from Cairo to Albaneta farm toward the Abbey. The conditions were completely unsuitable for tanks. A German counter-attack from the monastery left the tanks stranded round Castle Hill and lacking infantry support by mid-afternoon they were all knocked out.

The final battle commenced with Operation Diadem on 11 May and witnessed the British 8th Corps make two opposed crossings over the Rapido.

Once this was bridged tanks of the Canadian 1st Armoured Brigade moved to support the infantry – something that had been lacking during the first two battles. In the meantime the Polish Corps fought against the German paratroops in and around Cassino in what was clearly a grudge match.

While the Polish Corps consisted of two infantry divisions, the 3rd Carpathian and 5th Kresowa, they had the normal allotment of divisional tanks and were supported by the Polish 2nd Armoured Brigade. The latter consisted of the 1st and 2nd Polish and 6th Kresowa Armoured Regiments, who were equipped with American-supplied Shermans. In total the Poles mustered 50,000 men who had arrived in Italy between December 1943 and January 1844 and first went into the line in March. Around 80 per cent of these troops were former Russian prisoners of war, but they were strengthened with Poles from the Carpathian Brigade that fought with the British 8th Army at Tobruk. A Polish armoured division was formed, but this was committed to the Normandy campaign.

After the failure of the assaults by the Americans, New Zealanders and Indians the same formidable defences confronted the Poles. In particular, the monastery, the south and west of the massif as well as part of the town were held by the paratroops, whose key strongpoints were situated between Colle Sant' Angelo-Point 706-Monte Castellone, in the monastery and the upper reaches of the town, on Points 593 and 569, and around Massa Albaneta.

The German 1st Parachute Division holding Cassino had considerable firepower. It was supported by the 242th Assault Battalion, the 525th Anti-tank Battalion (which was equipped with self-propelled 88mm guns), four artillery battalions from 10th Army and one from the 90th Panzergrenadier Division. In addition, the 71st Werfer Regiment had forty 150mm and 300mm mortars near Pignataro and thirty 150mm and 200mm mortars at Villa Santa Lucia. The Nebelwerfer or 'Moaning Minnie' six-barrelled rocket launcher was a particularly devastating weapon.

The Poles had great difficulties in concentrating their men at the forward jump-off points and were supported by five Cypriot mule companies and two British jeep platoons in moving up their stockpiles for the attack. The 3rd Carpathians had the job of storming the monastery ruins after securing Point 593 and Albaneta Farm to the north-west. The 5th Kresowas were to assault Phantom Ridge and Sant' Angelo to the south. The going was tough for all the Allied forces committed to the offensive. Within 20 minutes of the opening Allied barrage the Carpathians were on Point 593 and the Kresowas had gained Phantom Ridge. They suffered fearful casualties in the process.

Polish tanks with names like 'Claw', 'Pigmy' and 'Pirate' advanced on Albaneta on 15 May firing on burnt-out Allied tanks, the remains of the March attack, which were being used as enemy machine-gun posts. They were soon halted by mines and sappers had to crawl under the tanks for protection from snipers as they worked to clear them. 'We were in utter despair,' said a Polish tank commander, 'being unable to reach our comrades dying in front of Albaneta. With real fury we blasted away at the ruins, and at every suspicious bush or pile of stones.' The tankers took no chances nor showed any mercy. Anything that moved was deluged in machine-gun and gun fire by the Polish tanks. On the night of 17 May the determined Poles finally gained all their main objectives, including Point 593, but not Albaneta where the Germans clung on to the last.

Polish troops moved into the monastery on 18 May to find it abandoned. The 1st Parachute Division had called it a day. Lieutenant Casimir Gurbiel and a platoon of uhlans from the Podolski Lancers were the first Poles to enter the monastery. The only remaining Germans were badly wounded and when asked why they had held out so fanatically they said they had been told the Poles did not take prisoners. Nearly a thousand Poles died in the two attacks. Six days later the Canadian 5th Armoured Division breached the line opening the route to Rome. The Allies hoped that this would break the deadlock that had blighted the Italian campaign to date. It was not to be.

The French took credit for Diadem as it was they who turned the panzers. The French Expeditionary Corps started to arrive in Italy in November 1943 and by May 1944 was fully up to strength. Colonial Moroccan troops first made their presence felt in Italy, when General André Dody's division tipped the balance during Operation Raincoat in mid-December 1943. His men helped push the Germans back to the Gustav Line, but overall the offensive failed to put the Allies in a strong position to support the forthcoming Anzio landings.

While the US 5th Army suggested advancing along the Ausente valley, it was French General Juin who proposed attacking through the mountains while making no attempt to outflank Aurunci. To do this it was necessary to break out of the Garigliano bridgehead so the French could take Monte Majo and the Ausonia defile. General Clark impressed by Juin's boldness agreed.

The 2nd Moroccan Infantry Division under General Dody was given the task of taking Majo and its three spurs. On the right was Brosset's 1st Free French Division and on the left de Monsabert's 3rd Algerian Infantry Division, which was tasked with securing Castleforte to open up the Ausente. Afterwards the Mountain Corps comprising General Savez's 4th Moroccan Mountain Division and General Guillame's Group of Moroccan Tabors could then push to the Aurunci massif.

In the face of stiff German resistance, on 13 May 1944 the Moroccans succeed in breaching the Gustav Line at one of its deepest points (though the weakest defended) at Monte Majo. Ausonia was captured two days later. In particular, the fall of Majo unhinged the 14th Panzer Corps left wing greatly contributing to the Allies success. By 1730 hours on 23 May General B.M. Hoffmeister, commanding the Canadian 5th Armoured Division, felt a large-enough breach had been achieved to commit his tanks. Unfortunately, having to shift its axis of attack the division got tangled up with the tanks of the 25th Armoured Brigade moving to rearm and refuel. By the time the mess was sorted out, frustratingly Hoffmeister was unable to attack until early the next morning. This was to become an all-too-familiar problem.

It was decided to throw everything up the Liri Valley as soon as possible. The net result was that five divisions, the Canadian 5th Armoured, British 6th Armoured, Canadian 1st Infantry, Indian 8th Infantry and the British 78th Infantry were all madly jostling for space. This meant that around 450 medium tanks, 240 light tanks, 50 self-propelled guns, 320 armoured cars, 200 scout cars, 2,000 half-tracks and 10,000 lorries were jammed onto the roads in the valley.

Diadem turned into one enormous traffic jam that threatened to derail the offensive before it had even properly got underway. The Military Police trying to sort out the chaos were faced with an impossible task as tempers flared and vehicles bumped into each other. The slow-moving tanks consumed four times as much petrol as normal and the heavy traffic prevented extra fuel being brought up. It is hardly surprising that the Germans slipped the noose. On 24 May the British 6th Armoured Division was held up for several hours waiting for the Canadian 5th Armoured to clear the roads.

Hoffmeister's lead units did not kick off until 0800 hours on 24 May. The vanguard was led by a composite group of tanks and infantry made up of squadrons from the British Columbia Dragoons, each supported by carrier-borne infantry from the Irish Regiment of Canada. This was known as Vokes Force (after the commander of the Dragoons, Lieutenant Colonel F.A. Vokes) and its mission was to establish a base midway between the Hitler Line and Melfa. A second Canadian composite group, Griffin Force consisting of tanks from Lord Strathcona's Horse (CO Lieutenant Colonel P.G. Griffin) and lorried infantry from the Westminster Regiment was to pass through Vokes Force and take a crossing over the Melfa. A third leap was to be made by elements of the Westminsters, who would consolidate the bridgehead, while the 8th Princess Louise's Hussars would fight their way toward Ceprano

Hoffmeister's tanks were protected on the flanks by the British 6th Armoured Division moving on their right along Highway Six, and the Canadian 1st Infantry Division on the left whose tanks and infantry were to strike along the north bank of the Liri. It was during these operations that some of the few major tank-versus-tank battles of the Cassino campaign were fought. It was now that the Allies first came up against the Panzer V Panther in Italy. On 15 May, after urgent appeals from General von Vietinghoff, a company of Panthers had been deployed to Melfa where they arrived five days later just in time to confront the Canadians.

Shortly after midday the tanks of the British Columbia Dragoons and supporting infantry reached their objective about two miles north-west of Aquino and Griffin Force was ordered forward. At 1500 hours the Strathconas' Reconnaissance Troop crossed the Melfa. Vokes Force had brushed with the Panthers early on 24 May and remarkably had managed to account for three for the loss of just four Shermans. While A and C Companies of the Strathconas trying to cross further north managed drive the Panthers to the far bank, they lost seventeen Shermans, claiming just five panzers in return and not all these were Panthers. An infantry officer spoke of the Canadian tank crews with amazement, 'I'll never forget the way the tanks would keep coming and then one would get knocked out and then another and still they'd keep coming.'

Meantime the Canadians were unable to get any anti-tank weapons over to the Strathcona/Westminster bridgehead and the Germans launched three counter-attacks with Panthers. Three tanks almost overran their positions but PIAT anti-tank fire made the Germans lose their nerve and they wheeled away. Fortunately, by 2100 hours some 6-pounder anti-tank guns had got over the river.

In summing up the Melfa battles a staff officer in the Canadian 5th Armoured wrote:

> As for the main obstacle of the German tanks … the only reason why it was possible to make headway against their qualitative superiority was by weight of numbers … General Leese was prepared to lose 1,000 tanks. As he had 1,900 at his disposal, the Panther stood a fair chance of becoming an extinct species among the fauna of S. Italy. On our side losses had to be taken and replacements thrown in. Being somewhat up against it, the tankmen were compelled to improvise and make the most of what they had.

In the meantime, the Germans did what they were best at and conducted highly successful local defensive actions. The 90th Panzergrenadiers at Ceprano and the 1st Parachute Division at Acre managed to hold the British at bay and kept the road to Rome closed until the end of May. The Allied command despaired of their tanks ever doing what they were supposed to do. On the 29th and 30th, with Acre cleared and 13th Corps thrusting for Altari, an attempt was made to commit yet more tanks, this time the South African 6th Armoured Division. The plan was that it would replace the Canadians, but until it took over the latter's positions all it did was add a few more thousand vehicles to the existing almighty traffic jam.

Diadem cost the British and American armies 44,000 casualties, failed to destroy the Germans and condemned the Allies to another year of fighting around the Gothic Line from August 1944 to May 1945. The German 14th Army successfully conducted an orderly fighting withdrawal toward Rome. Despite this, they had lost 450 panzers, half the available armour in Italy, as well as 720 guns of various calibres. Four of Kesselring's battered infantry divisions had to be withdrawn to refit and another seven were badly weakened. Fortunately for him, four fresh divisions and a regiment of heavy tanks were on the way to help hold up the Allied advance.

The Italian capital was not taken by the Allies until 4 June 1944 and even then they failed to encircle Kesselring's withdrawing forces. South of Rome the Germans made one last desperate attempt to stop their 10th and

14th Armies losing contact. The diary of an artilleryman serving with the German 65th Infantry Division recorded:

> The whole day Tommy [British troops] is attacking. We answer until the gun barrels are red hot. At 1215 groups of enemy tanks are trying to break through at the Schotterstrasse [disused railway bed]. This attack collapses in our fire. At 1600 Tommy attacks again. Soon after that we receive orders to retreat.

His division destroyed 168 tanks in front of the Schotterstrasse and at Campoleone to the east. Yet still the Allies pressed home their attacks.

British platoon commander Raleigh Trevelyan, serving with the Green Howards, recalled:

> Sometimes a [Panzer] Mark IV tank or scout car would block main highways into Rome, and partisans would guide the Americans through back alleys. ... At about 8pm Irish Dominicans at San Clemente near the Colosseum heard a commotion like big wheels grinding and went out to investigate. A line of American tanks was drawn up close to the walls of the college. Two of the Fathers walked along the tanks, but no soldier spoke or made a noise. Suddenly from the last tank there jumped an officer, who went down on his knees and asked for a blessing.

Though badly mauled, the tough Hermann Göring Division managed to escape. Unfortunately for Kesselring the division was sent to Russia the following month. The British 8th Army, struggling up the Adriatic coast by mid-September, was resisted by elements of ten German divisions. This did not greatly deter its advance on the Senio River and by the end of the year the key armoured formations of the German 10th Army, the 26th Panzer and 90th Panzergrenadier Divisions, had suffered ever heavier casualties. Only the arrival of the 29th Panzergrenadier Division reduced the pressure on the exhausted 26th Panzer and staved off collapse.

Manned by Kesselring's 10th and 14th Armies, the Gothic Line was the last major obstacle between the Allies and the Alps. This proved to be probably the best of all the German defensive lines. The Italian landscape once more assisted the Germans, for in the valley of the upper Tiber the mountainous backbone of the country twists north-west to join the Maritime Alps in Liguria. This forms a huge natural barrier between the flat lands of the north-east and central Italy. After Cassino and Rome fell, a series of delaying battles from Trasimere to Florence brought the German engineers much-needed time. Unfortunately for the Allies the French, who were their most experienced and effective mountain troops, were withdrawn to fight in southern France.

As it was the very last line the Germans had much greater time to prepare it with the assistance of 15,000 conscripted Italian labourers. Although the Gothic Line was never finished it still presented a formidable barrier. The positions included Panther tank turrets set in steel and concrete, bunkers, air raid shelters, gun emplacements, minefields and anti-tank ditches as well as an obstacle zone stretching for 10 miles.

The Germans had done everything conceivable to stop the Allied tanks. Anti-tank defences in depth blocked the approaches to La Spezia on the west coast. From Carrara the line passed through the mountains north of Pistoia to the fortifications of the Futa Pass, which included anti-tank ditches and concrete casemates and tank turrets. Eastward to the Adriatic foothills the defences were concentrated along the Foglia to Pesaro. There deep mine-fields, a tank ditch, pillboxes and tank turrets protected the coastal belt.

The Allies launched the imaginatively-titled Operation Olive in late August 1944, with the 8th Army aiming to break through the sector of the Gothic Line held by General Traugott Herr's 76th Panzer Corps – though it did not actually contain any panzer or panzergrenadier divisions. Traugott's positions were assaulted by the Polish 2nd Corps (which included the Polish 2nd Armoured Brigade), the Canadian 1st Corps (Canadian 5th Armoured Division and the British 21st Tank Brigade) and the British 5th Corps (1st Armoured Division, 7th Armoured Brigade and 25th Tank Brigade).

The attack fell into four phases, the advance to the Gothic Line, pene-tration of its defences, the battle for the Coriano Ridge and the exploitation of this battle. The reality was that Italy was now very much a secondary theatre of operations; the battle for Normandy was at its height and the US 5th Army had lost seven divisions, which were to take part in Operation Dragoon, the invasion of southern France, at the end of August. The US 5th Army and British 8th Army had seen their strength fall dramatically from

249,000 to 153,000, leaving them just 18 divisions with which to overwhelm the 14 divisions of the German 10th and 14th Armies.

The Germans rushed reinforcements forward including the 26th Panzer Division, but this did not stop the Allies breaking through and pouring toward Rimini on the east coast. The Germans though did not give up so easily and by 4 September the 29th Panzergrenadiers and two infantry divisions had arrived to bolster the German line, causing a slowing of the Allied advance towards the Gemmano and Coriano Ridges. The fighting here was some of the toughest of the entire Italian campaign. The Coriano Ridge battle between 12 and 19 September 1944 required both the British 1st and Canadian 5th Armoured Divisions to overcome the German defences.

By this stage the Germans had been able to bring up the 90th Panzergrenadier Division and the 20th Luftwaffe Field Division, giving them ten divisions with which to oppose the 8th Army. However, the German defence was overcome and on 21 September 8th Army took Rimini and was at last in the valley of the River Po. This had been at a terrible cost to both sides, the 8th Army suffered 14,000 casualties and the 76th Panzer Corps lost 16,000. In the British sector during September the Allies lost 250 tanks destroyed by the enemy and a similar number either bogged or broken down. Losses in manpower were such that battalions had to be reduced from four to three companies. Notably the 1st Armoured Division received such a terrible mauling that it virtually ceased to exist and was disbanded on 1 January 1945. The British soon discovered that the Po valley was not the excellent tank country that they had hoped for. Instead it proved to be a boggy expanse covered in a series of watercourses that greatly suited the Germans' finely honed defensive tactics.

On the left the US 5th Army included the US 1st, British 6th and South African 6th Armoured Divisions as well as the Canadian 1st Tank Brigade. Facing them was the German 14th Army that included the 16th SS Panzergrenadier Division. By the end of the first week of September the army reserve consisting of the 29th Panzergrenadiers and 26th Panzer had been moved to the Adriatic front. On 18 September the British 6th Armoured Division took the San Godenzo Pass on Route 67 to Forli. A month later the US 5th Army gathered it strength for one last push on Bologna, however the 29th and 90th Panzergrenadiers helped put an end to any such ambitions, leaving the 5th Army stranded in the mountains over the winter.

The Allied armoured divisions were involved in one last offensive against the Germans – Operation Grapeshot. This was launched with the aim of breaking out into the Lombardy plains. The 8th Army element of the attack was called Operation Buckland and the US 5th Army's contribution was Operation Craftsman. Preparation for Grapeshot commenced on 6 April 1945 when the Germans' Senio defences were subjected to heavy artillery bombardment. Three days later 825 heavy bombers pounded the fixed positions beyond the Senio River; these were then followed by medium bombers and fighter-bombers. The latter struck anything that moved, especially exposed armoured fighting vehicles and motor transport.

The air attacks heralded the ground assault on the shell-shocked defenders, which rolled forward at dusk that day. In support of the New Zealand 2nd Infantry Division were 28 Churchill Crocodile flamethrowers and 127 Carrier Wasp flamethrowers. These scorched everything in their path and by nightfall of 10 April the New Zealanders had reached the Santerno, which they crossed the following day. The America assault, also preceded by a massive bombardment of enemy positions by heavy bombers and artillery, opened on 14 April with the US 1st Armored Division, supporting the US 4th Corps. The following night US 2nd Corps, that included the South African 6th Armoured Division, attacked towards Bologna between Highway 64 and 65.

The 8th Army had forced the Argenta Gap by 19 April 1945 and the British 6th Armoured Division swung left to drive north-west along the Reno River to Bondeno, in order to link up with the US 5th Army and encircle the Germans defending Bologna. Bondeno fell on 23 April and the 6th Armoured met with the Americans at Finale to the north the following day. Despite Hitler's instructions to stand fast the Germans had no option but fall back beyond the River Po. In the process they lost 80 tanks, 300 guns and 1,000 motor vehicles. The official unconditional surrender in Italy was signed on 2 May 1945. The remaining panzers and Italian tanks were turned over to the Allies. The Italian campaign was over.

Chapter 7

Rumble in the Jungle

During the 1930s conventional British military thinking was that the dense jungles and rubber plantations of Malaya were not at all suitable for mechanized warfare. In addition, the key choke point for vehicles heading south was some 25 miles inside Thailand north of the Malaya/Thai border. Known as The Ledge, this was a stretch of road carved along the edge of a steep hill. If it fell into Japanese hands it would allow them to invade Malaya via the interior road. If this happened, it would compromise the main British position in north-western Malaya at Jitra by opening the flank. Likewise, British defensive plans also hung on being able to cut the railway line between the Thai port of Singora and Jitra.

Although the British mindset was that Malaya was unsuitable for tanks, ironically Britain did consider sending light tanks, as it was felt the best way to stop a tank was with another tank. General Arthur Percival, commanding in Malaya, asked for two regiments – medium tanks were thought to be too heavy for many of Malaya's bridges, so some consideration was given to sending light tanks that would be manned by Australian crews. Tanks though were not available before war broke out. In the meantime, Malaya Command was not blind to the threat posed by enemy tanks and issued orders in April 1941 stating, 'All officers must be tank-minded. Against an enemy equipped with tanks movement must be from anti-tank obstacle to anti-tank obstacle.' Nevertheless, there is no evidence to suggest that combined arms anti-tank exercises were conducted in Malaya and available War Office pamphlets on tank fighting were not issued to the garrison.

To make matters worse most British Imperial forces were not equipped or trained to cope with jungle warfare. The Indian brigades sent as reinforcements in 1941 had trained to fight in the Middle East and had largely never seen a tank. All the Australian and Indian units sent to Malaya travelled light for the sake of speed. The issue of weapons such as light machine guns and field artillery was critically slow when they arrived. In the event the British

Army had to rely on about three dozen armoured cars and open-topped carriers (Universal or Bren) – neither were suitable for armoured warfare – though 2-pounder anti-tank guns and mines were available. The Japanese Type 97 tank would not have coped with the 2-pounder gun or the armour of British Matilda or Valentine tanks, but none of these were sent.

The Japanese Navy attacked the US Fleet at Pearl Harbor on 7 December 1941. The very next day Japanese troops began to land in Thailand and Malaya as well as attacking the mainland defences of the British colony at Hong Kong. The invading Japanese 25th Army had a tank corps with three regiments totalling 228 medium and light tanks, reinforced by scout regiments assigned to three combat divisions fielding 37 light tanks. The Japanese invasion of Malaya was both high and low tech with Japanese forces employing artillery, bombers, fighters, tanks and bicycles. The British 3rd Corps, headquartered in Kuala Lumpur, had its work cut out trying to defend Malaya's vast coastline. To the north defending the border with Thailand was the 11th Indian Division between Jitra and Kroh, while to the east 9th Indian Division was in the Kuala Krai area.

Alistair Urquhart, serving with the Gordon Highlanders, was stationed at Fort Canning, the British military headquarters in Singapore. In his memoirs, *The Forgotten Highlander*, Urquhart recalled how the British Army got it so badly wrong:

> Japanese troops under General Yamashita, who would later become known as 'The Tiger of Malaya,' were storming south at an unbelievable speed, relying on bicycles and the ingenuity of their engineers, who quickly restored sabotaged bridges and roads. Critically the Japanese infantry were supported by three hundred tanks. The war machines that the British Army had decided were unsuitable for conditions in Malaya cut great swathes through our lightly armed troops.

Following Japanese seaborne landings on the eastern coast of southern Thailand and northern Malaya at Singora, Patani and Kota Bharu, British forces did not move north until 10 hours after the invasion in a vain effort to block The Ledge. Elements of the 11th Indian Division, a battalion-strength battle group named *Krohcol*, crossed the border at 1500 hours on 8 December

1941 and found themselves opposed by Thai police. Having only advanced 2 miles the advance guard decided to stop for the night and await the rest of the battle group that had been delayed.

By 10 December battle group *Krohcol* were within 4 miles of their destination when they came into contact with Japanese troops led by tanks. The first one was hit by an anti-tank rifle and withdrew. Now that The Ledge was already in Japanese hands there was little prospect of taking it. The following day, while Lieutenant Colonel H.D. Moorhead sought permission to retreat, the Japanese brought forward two battalions supported by at least one tank company. The Japanese attacked on 12 December, forcing the battle group back toward the border.

The Japanese push south on Jitra opened when a spearhead of 500 troops, supported by two dozen light tanks and some light guns, drove on prepared defensive positions held nearly 14,000 men, supported by fifty field and thirty-six anti-tank guns, of the 11th Indian Division. The Japanese kept their tanks at the front and used them to blast a way through or to pin down the defenders while their flanks were turned. They brushed aside the Indian and Gurhka screening forces after two battalions were caught off guard by armour on the road and scattered. The Japanese captured Jitra on 12 December followed by Gurun three days later. To the west the town of Kroh had been taken by the 14th. Japanese tanks then converged on Taiping and advanced on Ipoh.

In the early hours of 7 January 1942 a battle group of thirty Japanese tanks, a battalion of motorized infantry and a battery of light artillery forced their way down the road at Slim River. This was a key defensive point north of Kuala Lumpur. Two tanks were lost to mines, followed by three more to anti-tanks guns and anti-tank rifles. Ultimately though nothing the defenders could do would stop them following a series of bad judgement calls. Breaking through the tanks outstripped their infantry and ran amok behind British lines.

Major W.J. Winkfield, leading a Gurkha battalion, recalled, 'Sudden sense of unease behind me and something grazed my leg. Looked to see a tank bearing down on me. Dived into ditch. After tanks passed found battalion had vanished except for a few casualties.' Wakefield only managed to round up a dozen men out of over 500. Some 25-pounder guns, that could have been brought to bear on the Japanese tanks, were caught still hitched to their tractors as their crews ate breakfast.

Further down the road an anti-aircraft battery with 40mm guns put up a fight but they had no armour-piercing rounds and could not penetrate the tanks' frontal armour. In just over five hours the Japanese pushed through two brigades and covered 22 miles. Only when they ran into a Royal Artillery unit equipped with 4.5in howitzers, which blew apart the lead tank at point-blank range and damaged a second, did they stop and await reinforcements. At Slim River just thirty Japanese tanks supported by 1,000 troops finished off the brigades. The 11th Indian Division lost 3,000 prisoners along with a month's worth of supplies, plus 50 Bren Carriers and dozens of lorries. It was not long before Japanese armour was pushing through Kuala Lumpur itself and on the road to Malacca and Singapore.

On the west coast Japanese tanks unhinged the entire British defence. With the collapse of 11th Indian Division, the 9th Indian was at risk of being cut off. Such a situation now ruled out any prospect of a counter-attack. During the retreat south from the port of Kuantan on the east coast, Eric Lomax, with the Royal Signals, feared becoming trapped:

> I knew that just ahead of us the enemy was moving with his tanks and bicycles. I had still not seen a Japanese soldier, alive or dead. That night I was lucky, and although I failed to find a truck in working order or my missing men, I also failed to meet the Japanese.

The most famous action of the campaign occurred in mid-January 1942 on the road between Muar and Bakri. Five Japanese tanks of the Gotanda Medium Tank Company ran into two Australian anti-tank guns from the 8th Australian Division, which were positioned at the side of the road at the bottom of a reverse slope. A steep cutting at this point forced the tanks to remain trapped on the road. At point-blank range all the tanks were knocked out, but three more followed and joined the firefight. The Japanese though soon moved to infiltrate the Australian and Indian positions, forcing a fighting withdrawal.

Lieutenant Colonel Tsuji Masanobu, Chief Operations Officer of the Japanese 25th Army, recorded:

> Between 16 and 23 January a desperate fight occurred. When the Gotanda Medium Tank Company lost all its tanks, the surviving

officers and men had attacked on foot, reaching the enemy artillery position and the Parit Sulong Bridge, where the last of them met a heroic death after holding up the enemy for some time ...

Thanks to the continual destruction of bridges and causeways in Johore, Japanese engineers were hard pressed to keep up with the repairs. The Japanese tank forces after losses around Gemas and Bakri had to take time to regroup. This forced the Japanese infantry to march into southern Johore initially without any tank support. Meanwhile British and other Imperial troops continued to fall back to Johore Baru and then Singapore. Japanese forces landed on Singapore Island on 8 February 1942. Nearly all their remaining tanks units were used to reinforce the Japanese 5th Division, which was task with breaching the city's defences. It attacked along the trunk road sparking heavy fighting south of the reservoirs that supplied water to the trapped population.

Captain Reginald Burton, serving with the Royal Norfolk Regiment defending Singapore, was shocked to find the Japanese had little fear of armoured vehicles. Upon hearing that some of their men were having trouble withdrawing from the racecourse Burton recalled:

> The CO [Commanding Officer] order the carrier platoon to counter-attack and rescue them. They roared into action. The carrier platoon officer was very brave, but also impetuous. We heard afterwards that he drove straight at the enemy. There was a mêlée. A Japanese officer jumped from a tree on to the carrier and severed his head with a great sweep of a samurai sword. This was perhaps our first stark indication of the Japs' barbaric lust for killing.

The Japanese 18th Division struck along the south coast of Singapore Island. Although it suffered during the first four days of fighting it was spurred on by the thought of 5th Division reaching Singapore first. The garrison's defences were strong along the southern Pasir Panjang ridge, this was held by the 1st Malaya Regiment and Australian carriers. Nonetheless, capture of the coastal guns and control of the air ensured Japanese victory. Much to the humiliation of the British Army, in mid-February 1942 General Percival surrendered with the loss of 80,000 Australian, British and Indian troops who were captured. They joined another 50,000 taken during the Malayan campaign. The Japanese victory, thanks to their tenacity, tanks and bombers, had been swift and mirrored the German Blitzkrieg in Europe.

Once Malaya was captured and Thailand occupied, the Japanese then set their sights on Burma. General Iida, commanding the Japanese 15th Army, concentrated 100,000 men on the Thai border ready to invade Burma and cut off China's supply route from Rangoon. The British garrison consisted of an under-strength division, the 1st Burma, which was reinforced in January 1942 by the arrival of the 17th Indian Division. Burma was certainly not ideal tank country by any stretch of the imagination. As big as France and Belgium combined, from north to south it is dominated by a series of mountain ranges stretching from the Himalayas and two mighty rivers. To the west a range cuts Burma from India and stretches from upper Assam to the sea. Another spur, the Arakan Yomas, runs parallel with the coast almost as far south as Rangoon. From the west this range is shadowed by the Chindwin and Irrawaddy rivers. These combine south of Mandalay and run through Magwe and Prome to Rangoon. Further east is the Sittang and Salween river valleys that lead up into the hills of the eastern Shan states and Yunnan in China.

The lack of metalled roads and the primitive railway ensured that the river valleys dominated all military movements. Burma's weather likewise severely hampered military operations. The monsoon season commences in mid-May and lasts through to October, bringing with it up to 800 inches of rain. This swells the rivers and turns the jungles into muddy swamps. Such a setting provides a fertile breeding ground for cholera, dysentery, malaria and typhus. Under such conditions the fighting tended to grind to a halt during the monsoon.

Following Pearl Harbor America began to supply China with tanks including M3 Stuarts, and later M4 Shermans and M18 Hellcats, which trickled in through Burma and formed part of the several well-equipped, well-trained armies. An estimated 812 Shermans were shipped to China under Lend-Lease, while Chinese forces in India received 100 M4A4 Shermans and employed them to some effect in the subsequent 1943 and 1944 offensives.

In the meantime, when the Japanese attack came on 15 January 1942, the only other troops available were the British 7th Armoured Brigade and a single Chinese division. In February the Japanese landed troops in Rangoon from the sea creating a critical situation for the Allies. In the face of a two pronged Japanese attack British forces deployed in Burma had little choice but conduct a fighting withdrawal northward. The Japanese intention was to protect their southern flank in Malaya, grab Burma's oilfields and sever Chinese Nationalist leader Generalissimo Chiang Kai-Shek's supply route, thereby weakening his war effort.

To prevent this Chinese forces were committed to help bolster the weak British position. During February, from Yunann province in western China, troops under General Luo Chuoying moved into southern Burma down the main road to Lashio, Mandalay, Meiktila and then Tougoo. The Chinese Expeditionary Force in Burma consisted of three armies – the 5th (under General Du Yuming), and the 6th and 66th. The first two, ironically partly trained and equipped by Germany, were considered among Chiang's best. Certainly the 5th Army was the only one that had any field guns.

General Sir William Slim, the Burma Corps commander, observed that a Chinese army actually only corresponded to a European corps of two or three divisions. He also noted:

> The rifle power of a Chinese division at full strength rarely exceeded three thousand, with a couple of hundred light machine guns, thirty or forty medium machine guns, and a few three inch mortars. There were no artillery units except a very occasional anti-tank gun of small calibre, no medical services, meagre signals, a staff car or two, half a dozen trucks, and a couple of hundred shaggy, ill-kept ponies.

In other words, exactly the sort of Chinese fighting force the Japanese expected to deal with. Crucially the Chinese lacked vital armoured and mechanized forces that could act as a mobile reserve and counter Japanese breakthroughs. It only had a single 'armoured' unit designated the 200th Motorized Infantry Division (which until the late 1930s had been a mechanized division) and supporting tank battalions. In some histories the 200th Division has been described as an armoured division, but this was far from the case.

Chiang Kai-shek, in part to ensure continued material support from Washington, subordinated these forces to an American general. Much to the senior Chinese commander General Luo Chuoying's displeasure, they came under the command of General Joseph W. Stillwell, known as 'Vinegar Joe' because of his abrasive manner. The idea was that General Luo would take orders from Stilwell, while all the other commanders took orders from Luo. Such an arrangement inevitably led to friction and resentment.

Stilwell was suspicious that Chiang was playing a duplicitous game. He hoped American equipment, supplied under Lend-Lease via Rangoon, would equip thirty Chinese divisions to fight the Japanese in Burma. Instead Chiang was more intent on using it to shore up his political position by parcelling the equipment out to his 300 divisional commanders scattered across Nationalist-held China. Many of the generals commanded little more than local militias that had no intention of tangling with the Japanese either in Burma or China. In addition, Chiang was planning a long game and stock piling much of his supplies ready to fight the communists in northern China. On top of this much of the war material gathered at Lashio was siphoned off before it ever reached Chiang's capital at Chungking. When Stilwell arrived in Chungking there was no sign of his much hoped-for thirty divisions.

At the end of January 1942 it was agreed that the Chinese 5th Army would take over the Toungoo area in the Sittang Valley to the north-east of Rangoon. This would permit the transfer of the 1st Burmese Division across the Irrawaddy Valley to join the 17th Indian Division. In the event only the 200th Division reached Toungoo. Under the command of Major General Dai Anlan it included a motorized cavalry regiment and three infantry regiments. He set about establishing defensive positions in and around the town, but crucially was left unsupported. Stilwell later noted of the Chinese tank battalion, 'They are green men in the military sense, and many of them have come from China's paddy fields to drive a motor driven vehicle for the first time in their lives.' He later went on to praise their performance in the Hukawng valley.

Stilwell urgently wanted three Chinese divisions to reinforce the 200th. However, it was to be a sacrificial lamb to Chinese politics. The three divisional commanders, under instructions from Chiang Kai-Shek, did everything in the book to delay their units move to the front. Stilwell, never one to mince his words, was so furious that he branded the Chinese generals 'pusillanimous bastards'. Chiang's real purpose was to ensure that the Japanese pushed north toward India and did not swing east into China. He had no intention of losing his best forces defending Burma for the British.

General Dai Anlan fought two Japanese divisions at Toungoo in March 1942. Despite determined resistance, by the end of the month his beleaguered 200th Division had suffered 3,000 casualties from a strength of about 7,000 men and was surrounded. They had done a professional and highly competent job of holding the Japanese at bay, but without help were doomed. The survivors were forced to abandon their vehicles and heavy equipment in order to break out the Japanese cordon. Although reinforcements from another Chinese division reached the area, they could do little but cover the retreat. It was a sorry end to the Chinese expeditionary force's only motorized force.

Meanwhile, in an attempt to alleviate the pressure at Toungoo the 17th Indian Division was ordered to counter-attack. Three infantry battalions supported by a squadron of tanks and a battery of guns were sent to drive back the Japanese. Instead this force was surrounded at the village of Schwedaung 50 miles west of Toungoo. They broke out but not before losing their vehicles, tanks and guns.

The Chinese Expeditionary Force under Stilwell then moved to save the encircled British troops at the Yenangyaung oilfields to the north-west of Toungoo. The Japanese 33rd Division had managed to trap two British brigades and a tank battalion, so Stilwell rushed a single Chinese division to the rescue. Under Lieutenant General Sun Li Jen the 38th Chinese Division, along with the British 7th Armoured Brigade, was sent to rescue the 1st Burma Division at Yenangyaung. Slim was highly impressed by General Sun and noted, 'He was, as far as I know, the first Chinese general to have the artillery and armoured units of an ally placed actually under his command ...' Together they fought for four days to free the Burma Division.

On 17–18 April 1942 after a 48-hour battle the Japanese were defeated and 7,000 British and Indian troops were saved from capture. 'I was, I confess, surprised at how he [the Chinese soldier] had responded to the stimulus of proper tank and artillery support, and at the aggressive spirit he had shown. I had never expected, either, to get a Chinese general of the calibre of Sun,' Slim recalled in his memoirs of the fighting at Yenangyaung.

The absence of this Chinese division came at a price, however, and left the right wing of Stilwell's main forces exposed. The Japanese were swift to exploit this weakness and drove the Chinese back. The Japanese seized Lashio in the Chinese rear, cutting the vital road link to the border. By June 1942 the

Japanese were in control of all of Burma, with the British in headlong retreat back into India. Part of the Chinese Expeditionary Force under General Sun also retreated into India to reorganize, while the main force withdrew to western Yunnan province to re-equip.

Thanks to superior equipment, a superior air force and a unified strategy, the Japanese with ten infantry divisions and two armoured battalions were able to defeat the combined forces of China, Britain, India and Burma and cut international communications to China in a single campaign. They lost 1,200 men killed and over 3,000 wounded, Chinese losses alone exceeded 10,000. The loss of the Generalissimo's two best armies in Burma deprived China of over a third of her strategic reserve and was to have ramifications elsewhere. What was evident was that the lack of mechanized and motorized forces cost the Allies dearly in Burma. It was a lesson they would not ignore.

After General Sir William Slim was appointed corps commander in Burma in early 1942, on inspecting the 7th Armoured Brigade he was not altogether pleased:

> Its two regiments of light tanks, American Stuarts or Honeys, mounting as they did only a two-pounder [37mm] gun and having very thin armour which any anti-tank weapon would pierce, were by no means ideal for the sort of close fighting the terrain required. Any weakness in the tanks, however, was made up by their crews. The 7th Hussars and 2nd Royal Tank Regiment were as good British troops as I had seen anywhere. They had had plenty of fighting in the Western Desert before coming to Burma and they looked what they were – confident, experienced, tough soldiers.

Slim himself had no experience of fighting with an armoured brigade. During the retreat rough Burma, he and his commanders tended to use their tanks in penny packets, with widely dispersed detachments of infantry. They saw the tanks as good for the morale of the latter rather than any sound tactical logic.

Once the British Army deployed the Sherman in North Africa it despatched around 1,700 M3 General Grant/Lee medium tanks to fight in the war in South-East Asia. This tank served as a welcome stopgap in

North Africa, having greater punch than British tank designs, but proved less popular with the Russians who were already fielding the vastly superior T-34 medium tank.

Indian forces were equipped with 900 M3s, while the Australians received 800 of them. British Army Lees and Grant tanks served with the British 14th Army from the fall of Rangoon until the very end of the war. The M3 was not used as a tank-versus-tank weapon, but rather in an infantry support role. Although it had a poor off-road capability it performed remarkably well in the hilly terrain of the region.

A British counter-attack was launched from Chittagong in September 1942 by the 14th Indian Division along the Arakan coastal region. Their advance was delayed by the weather as well as training and supply problems. Early in 1943 the offensive was halted and in April the Japanese counter-attacked driving the division back to its starting point. The British launched their second Arakan offensive in December 1943, employing the 5th and 7th Indian divisions. They were also halted by strong Japanese positions and were cut off by a counter-offensive. An attack by the 26th Indian Division forced the Japanese to retreat failing in their aim of diverting more British troops from the Imphal area.

Throughout 1944 and into early 1945 the Japanese Army's meagre tank forces faired very poorly. In contrast the Indian Army's tank brigades fought bravely with their superior armour. The Battle of Imphal in the spring and summer of 1944 involved the 254th Indian Tank Brigade equipped with Lee, Sherman and Stuart tanks. All of which were more than capable of dealing with the lightly armoured Japanese tanks. The bulk of the British 14th Army's 4th Corps holding Imphal in north-east India was made up of Indian Army infantry divisions comprising Indian, British and Gurkha troops. The jungle covering the hills around Kohima were far from ideal tank county. Beyond these mountains blocked the way to Imphal. The latter provided ideal defensive positions for the Japanese. In addition, many of the battles around Imphal were fought during the monsoon.

Supporting the Japanese Yamamoto Force, the main armoured unit was the 14th Tank Regiment with 66 tanks (comprising the Japanese Type 95 Ha-Go light tank and captured British M3 Stuart light tanks). Six Type 95 Ha-Go tanks encountered six M3 Lee tanks from the 3rd Carabiniers on 20 March 1944 with the Japanese armour succumbing swiftly to the Lees' vastly superior firepower. The following month the Japanese attacked up the main road from Tamu to Imphal. Lacking timely infantry support British anti-tank guns claimed twelve Japanese tanks exposed on the road. On 13 April Lee tanks helped drive the Japanese from the Nungshigum Ridge that overlooked the main airstrip at Imphal. The Japanese defenders were shocked when the brave tank crews drove their vehicles up the very steep incline, which the Japanese had assumed was impassable to armour.

At the same time the Japanese attacked Kohima, also in north-east India. Their objective was the Kohima ridge, that dominated the road along which supplies were ferried to the British and Indian troops of 4th Corps at Imphal. By the time the Japanese broke off from the Battle of Imphal and Kohima they had lost 55,000 casualties including 13,500 dead. Many of these losses were due to starvation and disease.

Under such conditions a single tank could make all the difference to the outcome of an engagement. This proved to be the case during the fighting at Kohima when clearing the Japanese from the area of the District Commissioner's bungalow on Garrison Hill, which they had held since early April. The 2nd Dorsets were unable to surround the enemy positions and needed some close support heavy firepower on the ground overlooking the Japanese. Artillery was considered too indiscriminate because of the closeness of the front lines. As Colonel O.G.W. White DSO, 2nd Dorsets' commanding officer, so eloquently put it, 'if we could only get a medium tank on to the tennis court, serving some pretty fast balls from the north end, the Nip would not stay to finish the set.'

On the morning of 28 April 1944 a Royal Engineers bulldozer, with a Lee M3 medium tank in front and one behind, rumbled up the Manipur road and began to clear a track up the steep hill. Once the bulldozer had completed this task it tried to drag one of the tanks up the incline, the end result being that the tank pulled the bulldozer on top of it and both crashed down the rest of the slope. They tried again on 4 May and managed to get a tank into the District Commissioner's compound, but it could not reach the tennis court higher up. Eight days later the engineers bulldozed a path straight up Garrison Hill spur.

On 13 May Sergeant J. Waterhouse of the 149th Royal Armoured Corps Regiment, supported by infantry, slid his M3 medium tank into the middle

Early production Matilda II identifiable by the Vickers machine gun mounted in the right-hand side of the turret. The smaller Besa 7.92mm was fitted in the Mk IIA. (All images sourced by author)

The British Mk VI series of light tanks were numerically the most significant armoured fighting vehicles with the British Army in 1939–40.

The Matilda I, or Infantry Tank Mk I, was much bettered armoured than the light Mk VI, but was very slow and armed with just a machine gun.

These Mk IVA (A13) cruiser tanks belong to the 2nd Royal Tank Regiment, 1st Armoured Division, deployed to France in 1940.

A Matilda II lost during the fighting at Arras. In 1940 it was the heaviest tank in British service, but was not available in sufficient numbers.

German troops pose on their prize – a captured Matilda, numbers of which were lost during both Operations Brevity and Battleaxe in North Africa in May and June 1941.

The Crusader proved mechanically unreliable, but went into battle during Operation Crusader and continued in service until the end of the fighting in North Africa.

The Valentine joined the 8th Army's tank brigades in the summer of 1941 and played a key role in Operation Crusader.

A welcome addition to the British tank inventory was the American-supplied M3 Stuart light tank. It first arrived in Egypt in July 1941.

The American M3 medium tank, while far from perfect, was an ideal stopgap remedy to the firepower of Rommel's panzers. This version is the Lee with the machine-gun cupola.

A British Sherman, which appears to be the cast hull M4A1, takes on ammunition. The British 8th Army had received about 270 Shermans by October 1942.

Grant tanks plough their way through the mud and rain in Tunisia. After the campaign ended those remaining were sent to the Far East to fight the Japanese.

M3 Lee with the 2nd Battalion, 12th Armored Regiment, US 1st Armored Division at Souk el Arba in Tunisia.

A troop of welded-hull M4A2 Shermans poised for action. Armed with a 75mm gun the Sherman first saw action at El Alamein and was a reasonable match for the panzers in Egypt and Libya.

A British Crusader II Close Support Tank, armed with a 3in howitzer, leads two Crusader IIIs (armed with the 6-pounder gun) through the town of El Hamma.

American Sherman M4A2s gathered at La Pêcherie, a French naval base in Tunisia, in July 1943 ready for the invasion of Sicily.

A veteran of the North African battles comes ashore in Sicily.

Following the German surrender in Tunisia in May 1943, British Shermans were next deployed in the invasion of Sicily – this one is north of Rammacca.

LST-77 offloading M4A2 Sherman tanks at Anzio, Italy, May 1944.

The remains of a New Zealand welded-hull Sherman. During the battles for Cassino in Italy tanks proved to be of limited value.

British Honey light tank on its way to the Sangro River from Baglieta, 9 December 1943.

Churchill tanks in Italy. After fighting against the Gustav Line, the British 8th Army captured Rimini and established a bridgehead over the Marno in mid-September 1944.

Upgunned Churchill IV (NA 75) shelling the Gothic Line in Italy. These were converted in Tunisia, North Africa (hence NA) when 120 Churchill IVs were fitted with M3 75mm guns and mantlets salvaged from damaged Shermans.

M4A4 Shermans in the town of Portomaggiore, north of Argenta, which was captured by the 8th Army on 19 April 1945.

M24 Chaffee, US 1st Armored Division, on the streets of Milan in late April 1945. Although work to develop a new light tank started in early 1943, the Chaffee was not standardized until mid-1944.

M3 Lee medium tanks supporting the Gurkhas during the Battle of Imphal in 1944.

Chinese M3A3 or M5A1 light tanks involved in the fighting at Bhamo, Burma in 1944.

Chinese-crewed Shermans on the Burma Road in 1945.

Stuart light tanks supporting Australian troops at Buna, during the New Guinea campaign fought from January 1942 to August 1945.

Disabled Sherman on the shoreline of Betio, Tarawa Atoll, Gilbert Islands, which the US Marines assaulted on 20 November 1943.

Flooded Sherman in the Tarawa Lagoon.

'Lucky Legs II' supporting US troops on Bougainville in March 1944. The island was assaulted on 1 November 1943, but the Japanese garrison held out until the end of the war.

of the tennis court and crushed one of the enemy's main defensive positions. Waterhouse said:

> We pulled to the right and found ourselves in front of a steel water tank very heavily sandbagged and small arms fire met us. My 75mm gunner dealt with this position so effectively that the Nips started to leave in hell of a hurry without even arms and equipment. ... We next paid our attention to a series of crawl trenches and machinegun posts all around the court, and had hell of a party for the next 20 minutes or so. ... The whole action lasted about 40 minutes and the infantry suffered only one casualty and even he walked out.

Under increasing pressure, the Japanese plan was that the 15th Army would withdraw beyond the Irrawaddy River, which would hold the Allies at bay. At the same time to the east the 33rd Army would carry on holding up the Americans and Chinese attempting to open a land route from India to China. Similarly, to the west the 28th Army would hold the coastal Arakan Province using the terrain to slow the Allies.

Crucially the Japanese forces were woefully understrength and lacked adequate anti-tank weapons with which to stem the tide of Allied tanks. All they could do was deploy their field artillery in a direct fire role against the enemy armour, but in doing so this deprived the infantry of indirect fire support. The expedient of using explosive suicide vests or explosive charges on a long pole (lunge mines) was only effective if the enemy tanks were not supported by infantry.

General Slim recalled a desperate anti-tank measure adopted by his enemies:

> A Japanese soldier with a 100-kilo aircraft bomb between his knees, holding a large stone, poised above the fuse would crouch in a foxhole. When the attacking tank passed over the almost invisible hole, he would drop the stone – then bomb, man, and, it was hoped, tank would all go up together. Luckily the device was not very effective and accounted for more Japanese than tanks.

In December 1944 the third Arakan offensive was launched by the 25th Indian and 82nd West African divisions and on this occasion the Japanese coastal airfields were taken. At the same time 14th Army under Slim crossed the Chindwin and marched on the Irrawaddy. In a brilliant piece of deception Slim convinced the enemy his main crossing would be near Mandalay, but instead he chose Meiktila. The sole Japanese tank unit, supporting just under a dozen Japanese divisions, was the battered 14th Tank Regiment that by 1945 only had twenty tanks.

During February 1945 the 255th Indian Tank Brigade, equipped with Shermans, fought in the Battle of Pokoku and Irrawaddy River operations, supporting the 17th Indian Infantry Division forming part of 4th Corps. During the crossing of the Irrawaddy by 14th Army, that saw Grant tanks ferried over on pontoons, opposing Japanese tanks and guns fell victim to circling Allied fighter-bombers. Meanwhile the 33rd Corps was supported by the 254th Indian Tank Brigade.

The Japanese were finally defeated during the concurrent battles of Meiktila and Mandalay in early 1945. Meiktila proved to be a tough, but ultimately highly successful battle for Slim in which mechanized forces proved their worth. Victory was far from guaranteed as the Japanese, under Major General Kasuya, numbered around 12,000 men in the Meiktila area, while in the town itself the well-equipped and dug in garrison totalled some 3,200. Japanese defences extended in an oval around three miles by four, with two large lakes protecting those positions to the north-west and south-west. They had a considerable number of heavy weaponry, including anti-aircraft guns deployed for anti-tank and perimeter defence.

At the beginning of March 1945 it fell to the 255th Indian Tank Brigade to ensure that the Japanese were cut off at Meiktila. It was also tasked with taking the airfield to the east of the town. Supported by a self-propelled 25-pounder battery and two infantry battalions, the brigade's tanks swung north-east and then westward in behind the Japanese. Slim later wrote, 'This armoured onrush was met by very heavy artillery, anti-tank, and machine-gun fire from a deep screen of mutually supporting bunkers and fortified houses.' Close to the south-eastern corner of Meiktila the 255th Tank Brigade attacked a steep hill that rose for over 500ft at the edge of South Lake. Although heavily defended once the brigade has secured it the hill gave them a clear view over the entire area.

At the same time the 63rd Brigade moved to the west to set up blocking positions in an area unsuitable for vehicles, while 48th Brigade attacked from the north, skirting around Meiktila Lake. Slim, who visited the battle, witnessed an Indian-manned Sherman tank supporting Gurkhas of 48th Brigade attacking Japanese bunkers with great effect. The garrison resisted to the bitter end with their 75mm field guns engaging enemy tanks and infantry at point-blank range.

By the end of 3 March, Meiktila had been captured, followed by its vital airfield. In some desperation the Japanese attempted to counter-attack with elements from seven different divisions. Although the fighting continued until the end of March these forces were defeated piecemeal as they tried to converge by air attacks and aggressive armoured fighting columns. Wherever they were located the Japanese were destroyed.

The tanks of Major General T.W. Rees's 19th Indian Division overwhelmed Japanese defences north of Mandalay by 4 March. A motorized column then seized Madaya the following day and three days later was pressing on the city's northern outskirts. At Mandalay artillery and air power, not tanks, were the key to victory as the defenders had to be blasted from Fort Dufferin.

Just to the west, once across the Irrawaddy, the 20th Indian Division keeping up the pressure thrust south. Notably the 100th Brigade, speared headed by an armoured and motorized column, was tasked with linking up with 4th Corps at Meiktila. On 21 March 1945 it reached Wundwin, which lay between Mandalay and Meiktila, held by administrative elements of the Japanese 18th Division. Once the town was captured the brigade then struck north destroying a few light tanks and capturing guns and lorries as well as a solitary enemy tank. In the face of this concerted attack the exhausted Japanese abandoned Rangoon and withdrew towards Thailand. Japan finally surrendered in mid-August, while the Japanese troops in China, excluding Manchuria, formally surrendered on 9 September 1945.

Chapter 8

Island Hopping

The experiences of the US 1st Armored Division in North Africa graphically illustrated just how useless the M3 and M5 light tanks were against the German medium and heavy panzers. The tank's 37mm shell simply bounced off the Panzer IV and Tiger. This led to a major reduction in light tank strength and their replacement by medium tanks in the US armoured divisions. However, in the Pacific the M3 and M5 were quite often the only tanks available. Both the Americans and Japanese were slow to adapt to the realities of armoured warfare in the region. This was in part because the conditions on the islands were not conducive for the deployment of tanks, where the restrictive terrain left them largely in a support role. The terrain in the Pacific ensured that light tanks remained of help throughout the war. Due to the poor types of anti-tank weapon possessed by the Japanese and the geography of the islands, such as New Guinea, the small size and manoeuvrability of American light tanks were often more important than heavier armour and more powerful armament.

Like the attack down the Malayan Peninsula, at Bataan the Japanese simply drove down the roads. Leading the assault was the Japanese 65th Brigade supported by the 7th Tank Regiment. The Japanese also had unchallenged air superiority, which allowed them to bomb Bataan with impunity. Although the Japanese opened their attack on 9 January 1942 it would be four months before the trapped defenders surrendered.

The M3 Stuart was the first American tank to see action against the Japanese. It equipped the US Army's 192nd and 194th Tank Battalions which were shipped to Luzon in the Philippines to form a Provisional Tank Group just 18 days before the Japanese invasion. This was established under the command of Colonel James R.N. Weaver with 108 Stuarts. The inexperienced crews, who had trained on the earlier M2A2 light tank, struggled to get their new M3s operational after the journey from America.

In response to the Japanese landings in the Lingayen Gulf on 22 December 1941, a small force from Weaver's Provisional Tank Group plus other units were sent to stem the Japanese at Damortis, by holding the coast road leading south. Unfortunately, just five of the Stuarts could be fuelled and sent forward in time. Meanwhile enemy tanks supported both the Japanese landings at Caba and at Agoo to the north of Damortis.

The first US tank-versus-tank combat occurred on 22 December, when the platoon of five M3s led by Lieutenant Ben R. Morin fought Type 95 Ha-Gos of the Japanese 4th Tank Regiment north of Damortis. While manoeuvring off the road Lieutenant Morin's tank took a direct hit and began to burn. Morin was wounded, and he and his crew were captured. The other M3s were also hit, but managed to withdraw. The M3s of the 194th and 192nd Tank Battalions continued to skirmish with the Japanese tanks as they retreated down the Bataan Peninsula, with the last tank-versus-tank combat occurring on 7 April 1942.

Following the Japanese invasion, Forrest Knox, of the 192nd Battalion, was not happy at the state of affairs, saying of the ten-day withdrawal to Bataan, 'Like any other operation at the start of a war it was totally screwed up'. However, the green Stuart crews discovered first-hand just how effective their machine guns and 37mm anti-tank gun were against Japanese infantry. Knox recalled:

> My buddy caught one Jap in his sights. He ran down the front deck and off down the trail – a 37mm at that short range was unbeliev-able. Hit him in the middle of the back and his arms and legs just flew off – kind of like shooting a gallon plastic jug full of water with an army rifle.

To combat the Stuart, the Japanese resorted to anti-tank guns, limpet mines, Molotov cocktails and sniping at the crews. In an attempt to destroy the Stuarts, the Japanese would also clamber on board and try to prise off the gas caps so they could drop a grenade into the fuel tank. In response the tanks would shoot the Japanese troops off each other. The crews tried to prevent this tactic after refuelling by using a 3lb hammer to bash the filler cap firmly on.

Knox and his fellow crewmen gained on-the-job experience of the pitfalls of the M3:

> In action we used to shut off the engine to conserve the gas. That was our shortage, not ammo. Then, without the cooling fan on the engine running, the inside quickly got like an oven. The transmission was the size of a barrel and at about 140 degrees, and the guns so hot they would cook off by themselves.

Engaging the Japanese brought other hazards inside the tank. Knox encountered another problem with the machine guns that clearly had not been thought through:

> The empty brass (cartridge cases) burnt a lot of men, so you had to wrap a towel around your neck and keep your collar buttoned tight to avoid burns. All pockets were cut off – caught brass and held it against you. You had a choice, burn your fingers getting it out or burn your ass if you left it in.

The Japanese 7th Tank Regiment played a role in defeating the trapped American and Philippine armies in Baatan, in particular the capture of the strategically important Mount Samat, which sat in the middle of their defences. The Japanese, under Lieutenant General Masaharu Homma, assumed that 25,000 men held Baatan, whereas there were actually three times as many. During January 1942 forcing the Americans from their first line of resistance, anchored on Mauban and Abucay, the Japanese suffered heavy casualties. They paused while they conducted operations elsewhere. The defenders were left besieged, hungry and disease-ridden in the face of Japanese superiority in air power, tanks and artillery.

On 3 April 1942 the newly arrived Japanese 4th Division, supported by the tanks of Akira Nara's 65th Brigade, launched the delayed offensive to finally secure Bataan. The latter unit comprising three infantry regiments included the 7th Tank Regiment, as well as attached field and mountain artillery. Elements of the 21st Division, which had arrived in late February, covered the Japanese eastern flank while the 16th Division made a feint attack to the west.

At about 0900 hours the Japanese barrage began with almost 150 guns opening the biggest bombardment of the campaign. The Americans responded as best they could, but fired blind in the face of Japanese command of the sky. The American 1st Corps on the right had around 50 artillery pieces, mainly 75mms. On the left 2nd Corps was supported by 100 guns, again mainly 75mms, but including 31 naval guns up to 3in calibre and 12 mountain guns. The Japanese artillery and aerial bombardment lasted until the afternoon and then the ground assault began. Nara's tanks pierced the line on the left of 2nd Corps and pushed southwards crossing the Tiawar River, where the Filipino defenders broke after brief resistance. Facing the 65th Brigade, the Filipino 41st Division ceased to exist and the neighbouring 21st Division fell back in disorder.

Homma, a normally cautious general, abandoned all restraint and ordered his men on 4 April to take Mount Samat. Nara's troops cut round the flank of the remaining defenders in his sector forcing them to retreat. A Japanese armoured thrust also gained control of the east-west Pilar-Bagac Road. By the night of 7 April the Japanese having reached Limay on the east coast had almost completed an offensive they anticipated would last a month. Two days later they had reached Cabcaben on the southern tip of Bataan forcing an American surrender. Following the fall of the Philippines the Japanese used captured Stuarts for garrison duty and then against the Americans in the fighting for the Philippines in early 1945. A little ironically they were the first and very last M3s to see combat in the Pacific.

While Japanese armour helped secure victory in Burma, Malaya, the Philippines and Singapore, things did not go so smoothly in the fetid jungles of New Guinea north of Australia. A combination of unfavourable terrain and unexpectedly tough opposition from Australian and American troops ensured that Japanese plans to capture Port Moresby did not go according to plan. Japanese troops were to suffer defeat at the hands of Australian tanks at Buna.

While Australian units had been helping British and Commonwealth forces against the Germans and Italians in North Africa, Japan's entry into the war brought the threat much closer to home. Initially Australian units had no armour and very few anti-tank weapons to fend off Japanese tanks, though what they had were used to some effect in Malaya. On 23 January 1942 the Japanese overwhelmed the Australian garrison at

Rabaul on the northern tip of New Britain. Then on 19 February the Japanese bombed Australia's naval and air base at Darwin, sparking an invasion scare. After the landings on northern New Guinea the Japanese tried to fight their way south over the Owen Stanley Range and down the Kokoda track from Buna.

In the meantime, Japanese landings in Milne Bay in August were intended to seize Port Moresby from the east. In their second thrust made at night the Japanese were supported by tanks using their headlights to dazzle and light up the terrain. Initially the Australian thought the lights were one of their own Bren Carriers, but actually belonged to two enemy tanks. Lacking anti-tank weapons the Australians suffered heavy casualties. Attempts to bring up an anti-tank gun failed after its tow truck became bogged down and was abandoned to the Japanese. However, the Japanese suffered heavier losses, as they did not move their tanks forward until their infantry had secured the ground. Also the tanks had to take it in turns to fight as they had to withdraw every time ammunition grew low. In the end Corporal O'Brien, using a Boys anti-tank rifle, managed to destroy both.

The victors of Milne Bay then moved east of the Japanese stronghold at Buna. They took with them four M3 Stuart tanks, but these could only operate on cleared firm ground. The peculiar terrain of such areas as New Guinea meant size and manoeuvrability were far more important than the heavier armour and more powerful armament of the Sherman. These light tanks were of great assistance while mobile, knocking holes in Japanese emplacements and protecting the infantry. In desperation the Japanese tried to light a fire under one tank, but the attackers were killed by another tank. In early January American and Australian forces supported by the tanks broke the enemy defence and captured Buna.

During the war in the Pacific the US Army committed none of its armoured divisions to this theatre of war and deployed only a third of its seventy tank battalions. Understandably the US Marine Corps employed all six of its tank battalions in the island battles. Notably the US Army only ever used its M3 medium tanks once in the Pacific. In the Battle of Tarawa US Army units were supported by a platoon of M3A5 Lee medium tanks from the 193rd Tank Battalion. The US Marines did not employ the M3 Lee, their tank battalions making do with the M3 Stuart until early 1944, when these were replaced by M4 Shermans.

The Marine tankers of Companies A and B, 1st Tank Battalion, serving with the US Marine Corps' 1st Division, were equipped with the M3 light tank. They helped spearhead the American counteroffensive in the South Pacific with the unopposed landing on Guadalcanal on 7 August 1942. Once the tanks had landed they were deployed to cover the eastern boundary of the beachhead. Initially little offensive action was seen by either of the two tank companies.

After Company A made an unopposed crossing of the Tenaru River on Guadacanal they found the vital Japanese airfield undefended. The tanks were used mainly in a defensive role and were dug-in between the airfield and the beach in a circular deployment. From these positions they could deal with any counter-attack from the sea or a paratroop landing on the airfield.

Sergeant-Major 'Vi' Viveiros recalled:

> There were two limited offensive actions. One involved a platoon of five tanks without any coordinated support, advancing from a sector of the perimeter across a large open area of thick grass. Three tanks were quickly knocked out by an anti-tank gun concealed on the far side where the heavy jungle continued. Of the two tanks that remained, one, the platoon leader's, had taken a 37mm hit dead center on the side of the turret that decapitated him. Nine of the crews of the other three tanks were killed and three escaped to safety.

The second action occurred on 21 August 1942, when Company B became caught up in an action involving up to 1,000 Japanese troops attempting to break through the American lines at the mouth of the Ilu River. The Marines crossed the river on the right flank to envelop the Japanese from behind. Five tanks crossed the sand spit at the mouth of the river and helped in mopping up enemy resistance employing high explosive and machine-gun fire on enemy positions. Gruesomely Viveiros remembered, 'More enemy were crushed and mangled than shot, as evidenced by the remains of flesh entwined in the tank suspension.' During the engagement two of the tanks were disabled, one of them by a mine, but the crews were rescued by the other tanks.

The 1st Tank Battalion was then involved in the Battle of Bloody Ridge, on 13–14 September 1942. On the 13th the tanks helped repulse a Japanese attack east of the airfield. The following morning at 0945 hours six tanks were sent to sweep the field in front of the Marines' position to prevent the Japanese hiding in the long grass. This was accomplished without incident. The tanks were then deployed at 1100 hours to destroy an enemy machine-gun position in a native hut on the eastern side of the grassy plain.

Meanwhile the Japanese moved German-made RA 37mm anti-tank guns into the wood's edge on the eastern side of the airfield. Once the tanks were within 50 yards of the hut, the Japanese knocked out three in quick succession using armour-piercing and high explosive shells. The crews of two were rescued, but the third toppled into a stream, trapping the occupants. The later was later salvaged but the others were write-offs having been smashed by the armour-piercing shells. The 1st Tank Battalion went on to take part in the bloody operations in New Guinea, New Britain, Peleliu and Okinawa.

Stuarts served with the US Marines during the liberation of New Georgia and the clearing of the Dragon Peninsula. It became evident that the Marine tanks were most effective in spearheading their attacks, because they were relatively impervious to small-arms fire and had weapons that could deal immediately with the numerous and well-hidden enemy bunkers. The tanks though needed to be protected at close quarters to prevent the Japanese from reaching them and attaching anti-tank mines. At Zanana a Japanese tank killer unit attempted to disable the tanks using flamethrowers and magnetic mines.

During the Battle for Bartley Ridge on 26 and 27 July 1943, six Marine tanks led the assault. These were deployed in two lines of three each with eighteen infantrymen armed with flamethrowers, automatic weapons, rifles and grenades providing escort. The ferocity of the Japanese fire quickly drove off the infantry and a magnetic mine was used to destroy one tank. The remaining vehicles fought from within encircling Japanese defensive positions for five hours before withdrawing. A second tank had to be abandoned after it got stuck, while a third lost its way and was destroyed. In the end American artillery had to be used to silence the determined Japanese defences.

M3A1 light tanks of the Marines' 3rd Tank Battalion fought at Bougainville in November 1943; the battalion also participated in the Battles of Guam and Iwo Jima. The 4th Tank Battalion of the 4th Marine Division was equipped with the newer M5A1 when they were involved in the battles of Kwajalein on 1–2 February 1944, Saipan on 15 June–9 July 1944 and Tinian on 24 July–1 August 1944. The M5A1 was capable of combating Japanese light and medium tanks and provided welcome support both in the gun tank role and when fitted with other weaponry.

In January 1944 the US Fifth Amphibious Corps shipped 20 Ronson M3 flamethrowers to the Pacific. The Canadian Ronson flamethrower had been intended for the Universal Carrier. After trials it was decided to mount the weapon in a medium tank, but few were available and as the M3 light tank was being replaced by the M5 light tank it was decided to use the M3 and M3A1 instead. The Ronson replaced the 37mm gun and was protected by a howitzer-like shroud and had a traverse of 180 degrees. Four specially built fuel tanks were added that had a total capacity of 175 gallons, giving two minutes of sustained fire. Produced in Hawaii this system was aptly dubbed the Satan Flame Gun.

The Satan's role was to clear enemy bunkers, buildings, caves, canefields and dugouts. The 2nd and 4th Marine Divisions were issued with twelve of these flamethrowers when they landed on Saipan on 17 June 1944 (D+2). Four flame tanks and one light tank formed a platoon normally assigned to a medium tank company. They were employed continuously until 13 July and eleven days later were shipped to Tinian and were deployed with the assault wave. After the Tinian landing, 400 burned bodies were counted on the beach. Due to the vulnerability of the light tank to Japanese artillery and anti-tank guns, it was decided that medium tanks would be used in future flamethrowing roles, thus ending the Stuart's flamethrower career.

The M4 Sherman medium tank was used extensively by the US Army and the US Marine Corps from late 1943 onwards, and was involved in almost every island hopping battle fought in the Pacific. The Sherman was vulnerable to the Japanese 47mm anti-tank gun which could penetrate the tank's side armour. To counter this threat, the crews made various field modifications using spare track blocks, bogey wheels, oak planks and sandbags. The frontal armour in contrast could withstand such punishment. The 47mm Type 1 anti-tank gun was the most modern in the Japanese inventory, but retained the driven trail spades that hampered manoeuvrability of the previous 37mm. While it could penetrate the side armour of American medium tanks, the small bursting charge inside the round often failed to explode.

Serving as a driver in a Sherman equipped with a dozer blade, Nile E. Darling, a USMC tanker, remembered:

> We took a direct hit from an enemy 47mm anti-tank gun. It hit the front slope plate of the tank and right in front of me. Since they were using smokeless powder and leaving no dust, we had trouble spotting their emplacement. My tank commander gave me the order to put the tank into reverse gear, my hand on my lap and not touch the brake lever, which I did and we backed up a few feet and then they hit us again. We then moved straight forward a few feet and they hit us a third time. We took five hits – none of which penetrated – before we could locate their gun and destroy it.

The Japanese garrisons in the Pacific turned every island they occupied into fortresses defended by mines, barbed wire, bunkers, pillboxes, weapons pits, tank traps, trenches, anti-tank guns and heavy artillery. The beaches were sown with mines and artillery shells and littered with obstacles. On the larger islands they also burrowed into and fortified the inland hills and mountains to create stop points and bunker networks from where they could continue to resist. Umurbrogol Mountain on Peleliu and Mount Suribachi on Iwo Jima were prime examples of this. Under such conditions the Stuart and Shermans' role was to help the troops get off the beaches and engage enemy strongpoints.

During the attack on Guadacanal the amphibious Landing Vehicle Tracked (LVT) was mainly used for logistical support. The development of the LVT-4 allowed for disembarkation by a rear ramp which greatly enhanced its combat utility. It was bloodied in this second role during the amphibious assault on Tarawa when 125 were committed to the attack. They were to ferry men across the coral reef and through the shallows to the beach,

At Tarawa the Marines found that the tide had not risen sufficiently to clear the reef when the island was assaulted in Operation Galvanic on 20 November 1943. Only the LVTs got over, leaving the landing craft stranded. On the way in the LVTs suffered from the intense Japanese fire and those that made it ashore were unable to clear the log sea wall. The return trip to the reef proved equally hazardous. As a result, only thirty-five remained operational by the end of the opening day of the invasion.

Similarly, the tank landing craft were hampered by the reef and suffered in the Lagoon. On the east end of the beach two Stuart light tanks got ashore only to be knocked out. Six Shermans disembarked from their landing craft and climb over the reef to be guided inland by marines on foot. Several were lost in sink holes and their engines drowned, but those reaching the western end of the island pushed forward nearly 300 yards inland. One became stranded in a tank trap while another detonated a magnetic mine. A third tank had its 75mm gun damaged by an incoming Japanese shell, so acted as a mobile pillbox. Four further tanks came ashore at noon, by which time the Marines had secured the beach up to the first line of Japanese defences. By the end of the day only one tank remained in action. In the mid-afternoon the Japanese garrison commander ordered two Type 95s to cover his withdrawal from the concrete command post at the western end of the airfield. But as he and his men gathered outside the bunker American naval gunfire landed in their midst and killed them all.

As a result of the lessons learned at Tarawa it was very evident that the LVT was too lightly armoured and too poorly armed. Some were converted into 'amtanks' or amphibious tanks armed with a 37mm gun or 75mm howitzer mounted in the M3 light tank turret to provide close fire support. LVTs subsequently played a key role in the Leyte landings and the Battle of Okinawa.

After the Marines came ashore on Guam, either side of the Orote Peninsula, on 21 July 1944 those on the northern beach met stiff resistance until the arrival of the tanks improved the situation. On the southern beach the Japanese counter-attacked around Hill 40 on numerous occasions. The attacks, resulting in heavy Japanese casualties, were supported by four Type 95 Ha-Go tanks, which were easily destroyed by the Marines' bazookas or Shermans. In total the Japanese were to lose ten Type 95s on Guam. General Takashina, the garrison commander, was killed by machine-gun fire from a Sherman as he was overseeing the withdrawal in the Fonte area. Shermans of the 3rd Marine Tank Battalion were also involved in the fighting around Agana east of the northern beachhead.

The amphibious assault on Peleliu Island on 15 September 1944 was the first time that the US Marines had armoured support for a landing. The plan was that the waterproofed Sherman tanks of the 1st Tank Battalion would disembark from their landing craft half a mile from the beach and cross the shallow waters while providing close gunfire support. The presence of a reef around the island meant that the Marines' Amtracs had to conduct a very exposed ferry service from the reef.

The right-hand brigade was allocated six Shermans, nine to the one in the centre and fifteen to the left hand brigade. The other sixteen of the US 1st Marine Division's forty-six tanks had to be left behind due to lack of shipping space. The well dug-in Japanese garrison numbered 11,000 veteran troops, supported by the Type 95 Ha-Go armed with a 37mm gun (other sources state they were the tiny two-man light Type 94 tankette – either way they were wholly inadequate).

Within minutes of the first waves hitting the beach twenty-six Amtracs were hit by accurate Japanese artillery and mortar fire. Some of these were carrying the assault force's communications equipment. The fourth wave included some thirty waterproofed tanks that waded ashore in six columns of five tanks each led by an Amtrac. Japanese artillery and mortar fire was so intense that seventeen of the tanks were hit up to four times each, though only three were lost before reaching the beach. The Japanese responded to the invasion by launching a counter-attack across Peleliu airfield with up to nineteen tanks. In an effort to close with the Marines as quickly as possible the tanks quickly left the assaulting infantry behind.

Marine Robert Leckie was caught right in the firing line, 'Their tanks swooped suddenly upon us. They came tearing across the airfield, a dozen or so of them. It was startling. They came out of nowhere, and here were only riflemen and machine gunners to oppose them.' Leckie and his comrades were trapped in a bomb crater as, 'The enemy tanks whizzed past, their little wheels whirling within their tracks.'

The 75mm guns of three Shermans, 37mm anti-tank guns, bazookas and anti-tank grenades met the Japanese tanks. One Marine said, 'A tank rushed for the machine-gun on my right. "Stoney" stands up in his foxhole (he's a lad with guts) and lets go a burst of automatic fire. The tank was not ten foot away when it burst into flame, leaving a trailing fire as it still rolled forward.' The vehicle forced the machine gunners to flee for their lives as the burning tank rolled over their position and crushed their weapon.

When the Japanese tanks were approximately halfway across the airfield four Shermans appeared to the south. The US Marine Corps tankers found that their armour-piercing rounds went straight through the tanks' thin armour so resorted to using high explosive which blew them apart. While the marines opened up with everything they had, a US Navy dive-bomber also swooped in and dropped a bomb. Taking up the story again Leckie says, 'Once a torpedo plane flashed by, so low its belly might have scraped the coral. To my right, I saw a line of our tanks advancing firing as they came, seeming to stop each time their guns stuttered. Then it was over.'

Corpsman Jack McCombs witnessed a bazooka team destroy one of the attacking force:

> A Jap was cut in half by machine gun fire as he tried to get out of his tank. As a joke the guys carried his pants with the parts of his legs in them and threw them to one another. I know it sounds gruesome but it helped break the tension.

Marine Eugene Sledge noted this change in Japanese tactics:

> Rather than a banzai, the Japanese counterthrust turned out to be a well-coordinated tank-infantry attack. Approximately one company of Japanese infantry, together with about thirteen tanks, had moved carefully across the airfield until annihilated by the Marines on our left. This was our first warning that the Japanese might fight differently than they had elsewhere.

In fact, the Battle of Saipan, fought in June 1944, witnessed the largest Japanese tank battle of the Pacific War, when the Japanese committed a much larger number of Type 97 medium tanks and Type 95 light tanks. Likewise, the Battle of Okinawa fought in the first half of 1945 saw the Japanese commit just under thirty tanks.

As the situation deteriorated for the Japanese in the Pacific, in April 1944 the 9th Armored Regiment of the Japanese 1st Tank Division was reassigned to 31st Army, and dispatched to Saipan – where it was annihilated at the subsequent Battle of Saipan and Battle of Guam. Its remaining three regiments participated in Operation Ichi-Go in mainland China. The surviving units of the 2nd Tank Division were reassigned to the Japanese Fourteenth Area Army, and sent to the Philippines in July 1944, they were annihilated at the subsequent Battle of the Philippines.

For the invasion of Okinawa in April 1945 Lieutenant Colonel Bob Denig, commanding the US Marines' 6th Tank Battalion, trained to provide divisional level support rather than regimental. This was on the grounds that when a regiment was in reserve the attached tank company was left kicking its heels. By late May Denig noted:

> The main thing about the show so far is the anti-defenses that the Nips have set up against the tanks. Their mainstay is the 47mm gun but we are and have devised means to take most of the sting out of it. The next worry are the mines and those jokers have put them all over the place. We have run over about 25 of them but only one tank was destroyed because of a mine. The remainder just blew off the track or something and we fix them up when we can work on them without fear of artillery fire. The Nips even shoot single 150mm guns at the tanks, sniping at them if you will. So far they have only hit one and that was on the front slope where it is thick and only one man was wounded and they drove the tank away and back to the park.

Chapter 9

D-Day Tanks

The Americans, British, French, Canadians and Poles committed about a dozen armoured divisions and numerous independent armoured brigades to the Battle for Normandy. Their accumulated strength for the campaign amounted to almost 8,700 tanks. Easily the most common Allied tank in Normandy was the American M4 and M4A1 Sherman. While mechanically reliable it was handicapped by thin armour and a gun lacking sufficient punch. Its good cross-country speed and high rate of fire could not make up for these two key shortcomings. Tank crew protection was paramount: tanks could be replaced relatively easily but not experienced crews, but the Sherman had a very nasty habit of burning when hit and if this happened the crew only had a 50 per cent chance of survival.

The naval element of Operation Overlord, or D-Day, came under the designation of Operation Neptune. Implementing this on 6 June 1944 required one the largest seaborne invasion fleets in history, comprising 1,213 warships, 4,126 landing ships and landing craft and 1,600 other vessels – almost 7,000 in total. The key craft for getting the tanks ashore was the Landing Ship Tank or LST, which was capable of carrying 60 vehicles or 300 troops. In total 1,051 of these were built during the Second World War, seeing action in the Mediterranean, Pacific and the English Channel. In total 236 were committed to D-Day along with 768 smaller Landing Craft Tank and 48 Landing Craft Tank (armoured). The LCTs could carry five Sherman DD tanks.

Once all these craft had been assembled the really big headache for the planners was the loading and landing schedule. General Francis de Guingand, Chief of Staff of General Bernard Montgomery's 21st Army Group, recalled:

> Many of the ships carrying vehicles and equipment, although not required at once, had to be loaded before D-Day. Relative priorities so much depended upon the course of the campaign, and therefore

decisions at this early date were not easy. For instance, by what date would another load of bridging be required? This depended, of course, upon our rate of progress. When would the 12th US Army Group take over? If we shipped over all their vehicles too soon, valuable space might be wasted. Such problems came up each day.

Having learned a very nasty lesson from the disastrous Dieppe raid in 1942 – where armour was unable to penetrate inland – the British military realized it was vital to have specialized armoured fighting vehicles that could punch right through the hard crust of Hitler's Atlantic Wall defences. The Allied assault on his *Festung Europa*, or Fortress Europe, saw British military ingenuity at is best, resulting in a unique armoured division.

Major General Sir Percy Hobart was first tasked with developing novel ways of assaulting *Festung Europa* in April 1943. De Guingand was delighted about 'Hobo' Hobart's appointment, for it was his drive and personality that was largely responsible for the success of the project. 'Some of the staff under me would become terrified when they knew General Hobo was about,' recalled de Guingand with amusement, 'He was such a go getter that they never really knew until he had left what new commitment they had been persuaded to accept.'

From its creation in 1942 the British 79th Armoured Division was a regular armoured unit, but the following year with the impending invasion of Nazi-occupied France it was earmarked for a specialized role. In fact, its task was so secret that the existence of the division was not publicly acknowledged until after the Rhine crossing in March 1945. Even then specifications of some of the vehicles, such as the swimming DD tank, were withheld until September 1945. Hobart's 79th became affectionately known as the 'Funnies' because of its unique armour. It was the largest division in the British Army and by the time of the Rhine crossing consisted of five brigades operating 1,916 specialized vehicles and gun tanks (compared to a normal armoured division's compliment of 350 armoured fighting vehicles and 4,762 soft-skin vehicles). While it never fought as a whole, it has the distinction of being the only armoured formation to have units fight with every brigade, division and corps of the British and Canadian armies in North-West Europe from June 1944 onwards.

Initially Hobart's 'Funnies' were equipped with just three principal types of specialized armour. The most immediate problem facing the Allies was to get their armour ashore as quickly as possible to support the assault infantry; landing craft were vulnerable and the larger landing ships could only offload once the beaches were secure. The solution was the amphibious Sherman Duplex Drive (DD) or swimming tank, designed by Nicholas Straussler, who found waterproofing the vehicle's hull and raising the freeboard could make a tank float without cumbersome buoyancy aids. This was done by erecting a canvas screen round the hull and initially was produced as a Valentine tank conversion in 1943–4, a few of which saw service in Italy. The crews were not keen on the newer Sherman, as they were larger and heavier than the Valentines. Although the freeboard was higher on the Sherman, this did not prevent it shipping alarming amounts of water in choppy seas.

Once ashore, the Armoured Vehicle Royal Engineers or AVRE, consisting of various equipment mounted on the Churchill tank chassis, was designed to deal with the Germans concrete sea defences. Churchill Mk III and IV tanks were equipped with a massive 290mm Petard spigot mortar for 'bunker busting'. The third specialized tank was the Sherman Crab flail tank designed to clear defended minefields and barbed wire.

In the run-up to the landings copies of German coastal defences were built at the Orford training area in Suffolk, where the various vehicles were put through their paces and techniques refined. DD tank swimming training was undertaken at amongst other places Osborne Bay, Isle Wight, Stokes Bay, Gosport and Studland Bay, Dorset. Some 30,000 DD launches were made during the exercises and officially there was just one death. Nonetheless, rumour amongst the tank crews was that the 4th/7th Dragoon Guards lost six tanks with six fatalities off Poole. 'On one occasion,' recalled Lieutenant Stuart Hills of the Sherwood Rangers Yeomanry,' I received orders from the squadron leader by radio to launch in conditions I deemed suicidal.' Luckily good sense prevailed.

As well as punching through the sea defences Hobart's forces were also tasked with helping to deal with the various man-made obstacles that obstructed the shoreline. The best methods devised were to blow them up with demolition charges or simply drag them out of the way. 'I paid a visit to see these activities,' says de Guingand, 'and returned feeling that yet another "horror" had been laid low.'

The first formal rehearsals involving the 'Funnies' were conducted at Studland in front of a very senior audience including the King, General Bernard Montgomery and the Allied Supreme Commander General Dwight Eisenhower. De Guingand recalled:

> It was agreed at this conference that the DD tanks would be the first to land, and that the self-propelled artillery would be positioned in the rear, firing over the leading waves. Naval ships would support the assault from the flanks. No fixed rule was made for the different gun devices [i.e. the Funnies]. A 'menu' would be selected to suit the problem presented by the particular beach in question. This arrangement worked very well.

By the summer of 1944, after much hard training and absorption of this new kit, the division consisted of four brigades, 27th Armoured (DDs), 30th Armoured (Crabs), 1st Assault Royal Engineers (AVREs) and 1st Tank (CDL – Canal Defence Light, which was not used during D-Day). The Americans declined such vehicles except for the DD tanks and this was to have ramifications for the American troops assaulting Omaha Beach.

Due to varying tide times and bombardment lengths the invasion beaches, stretching from La Madeleine in the west to Ouistreham in the east had their landings staggered. The American Utah and Omaha Beaches were assaulted at 0630 hours on 6 June 1944, while the British Gold and Sword Beaches at 0725 hours and lastly the Canadian Juno Beach at 0745 hours. Utah, forming the far western flank, centred roughly on La Madeleine, was assaulted by Major General J. Lawton Collins' US 7th Corps, led by the US 4th Infantry Division. Their job was to link up with the US 82nd and 101st Airborne Divisions, establishing a bridgehead over the River Vire and the nearby canal ready to link up with Omaha to the east.

Due to the tide the American GIs went ashore 1,000 yards south of their landing zone. Twenty-nine Sherman DD tanks spearheaded the assault and were launched 5,000 yards from the shore. Little resistance was encountered, consisting mainly of small-arms fire. Around 0800 hours Pouppeville was attacked, and the US 4th Infantry managed to push four miles inland brushing aside most of the German resistance. By the end of the day the

Americans had successfully put ashore 23,000 men, 1,700 vehicles and 1,700 tons of stores.

Major General Leonard T. Gerow's US 5th Corps, led by the US 1st Infantry Division, attacked Omaha Beach bordered by Vierville-sur-Mer and Ste-Honorine. The preliminary bombardment lasted only 40 minutes and consequently many of the German defences remained intact. Also the shingle beach was bordered by marshland and a high bluff, making it an ideal killing zone. Thanks to the rough seas and enemy fire, out of thirty-two DD tanks only five cleared Omaha Beach, while out of the fifty-one tanks landed dry-shod by the assault craft eight were knocked out before even clearing the sea. Under heavy machine-gun, mortar and artillery fire the Americans were cut to pieces as they staggered from the water. Denied armour support, they were unable to quickly clear the beach.

The Americans had declined the offer of British 'Funnies' and German fire was so intense that of the engineers' sixteen bulldozers put ashore on the right side of the beach, only two were serviceable. By 0900 hours a few Americans had reached the top of the bluff and were beginning to move inland towards the villages. However, the GIs suffered an appalling 2,500 casualties and only managed to get two miles inland, though by nightfall 33,000 men were ready for the offensive.

The British and Canadian eastern task force attacked a broad 25-mile front, between Port-en-Bessin and Ouistreham. Gold Beach, centred on Le Hamel and La Rivière was assaulted by Lieutenant General G.C. Bucknall's British 30th Corps, led by the 50th Infantry Division. Their task was to take Port-en-Bessin in order to link up with Gerow's US 5th Corps, thrust for St Leger on the Caen-Bayeux road and seize Bayeux. At 0725 assault units of the 79th Armoured Division, consisting of Sherman Crabs and Churchill AVREs, went in. Once again due to the rough sea the DD tanks had to be landed dry-shod; also adding to their problems the tide rose 30 minutes early.

The AVREs were late and Le Hamel proved to be heavily defended: the sanatorium had been converted into a German strongpoint and German artillery was sweeping the beach. Nevertheless, by the afternoon Port-en-Bessin had been taken. By 2100 hours Arromanches had fallen, but the drive on Bayeux had stalled, even though the Germans had largely abandoned it. Also the route west from Caen had been captured, but at the end of the day a six-mile gap existed between Gold and Omaha Beaches. About 25,000 men were put ashore and 50th Division punched six miles inland.

At Juno the assaulting formation was the Canadian 3rd Infantry Division under Lieutenant General J.T. Crocker's British 1st Corps. The beach was centred on Courseulles and Bernieres. The Canadians were to seize the two towns and drive their tanks flat out for Carpiquet airfield west of Caen. In order to ensure the sea carried their landing craft over the reefs, the assault was timed for 0745 hours, but because of the rough sea it went in at about 0800 hours. While they did get over the reefs and most of the beach obstacles, the return trips were disastrous. Only twenty-nine DD tanks were launched, twenty-one reaching the shore, the rest had to be landed dry-shod from the landing craft. The 1st Hussars Regiment B Squadron, supporting the Regina Rifles, landed at Courseulles at 0755 hours with fourteen of nineteen tanks. Seven A Squadron tanks landed a few minutes after the Winnipeg Rifles, on the beach west of Courseulles. Five more tanks were landed by a LCT that earlier had had problems with its ramp.

Arriving before their armour, the Canadian infantry found many of the German positions intact. Under heavy small-arms fire they could not get off the beach and many Canadians were mown down trying to reach the shelter of a sea defence wall at the rear of the beach. Lacking armour support the Canadian infantry faltered, but an AVRE managed to blow a hole in the 12ft-high sea wall, and they began to move inland. By the end of the day 21,500 men had been landed, and the beach linked up with the British 50th Division at La Rivière.

Crocker's 1st Corps, led by the British 3rd Infantry Division, assaulted Sword Beach, centred on Lion-sur-Mer. Their key objective was to take the city of Caen, the Germans' regional headquarters, and link up with the airborne bridgehead over the River Orne to the east. H-Hour was 0725 hours and the spearhead DD tanks were launched 5,000 yards from the shore, out of thirty-four successfully launched only three were lost. By the evening 29,000 men were ashore in the Sword area.

Just four LCTs were lost during Neptune and the Landing Ship (Infantry) *Empire Broadsword* was sunk by a mine off Normandy on 2 July 1944. The LSTs continued to support operations and by the end of September they had brought 41,035 wounded men back across the English Channel as well as thousands of PoWs.

While 21st Panzer Division moved to secure the Caen area during the night of 7 June the British 50th Infantry Division took Bayeux. The following day the US 1st Infantry Division captured Tour-en-Bessin and Le Coudrai on the Bayeux-Isigny road. Fortunately for the Allies the powerful Panzer Lehr Panzer Division was unable to attack toward Bayeux until the 9th. Running into Bucknall's 30th Corps it suffered heavy losses and only got to within three miles of the city before going over to the defensive.

This forced the British to shift their efforts west of Caen to the flank of Panzer Lehr and the high ground beyond Villers-Bocage. The idea of a right hook was Major General G.W. Erskine's, commander of the 7th Armoured Division, and it was hoped the move would break up the resistance in front of the 50th (Northumbrian) Division. It was also hoped to encircle the troublesome Panzer Lehr and break the logjam around Caen.

On D-Day the Allies successfully landed 155,000 troops, 6,000 vehicles including 900 tanks, 600 guns and about 4,000 tons of supplies. Quite remarkably within five days 326,547 troops, 54,186 vehicles and 104,428 tons of supplies had been brought ashore. This momentum was lost once the weather deteriorated and on 19 June a storm halted all shipping in the English Channel for three vital days. The two Mulberry artificial harbours began to disintegrate and the one off Omaha was written off and used to repair the British one at Arromanches. The build-up virtually ground to a halt, delaying 20,000 vehicles and 140,000 tons of stores; however, by the end of the month over 850,000 men, 148,000 vehicles, and 570,000 tons of supplies had been landed taking the battle far into the Normandy countryside.

By the time of Operation Goodwood, the Allies' tank strength stood at almost 5,900 and continued to rise, reaching almost 6,760 a week later when Operation Cobra was launched. When the Germans commenced their Avranches/Mortain counter-attack in early August, the US Army could muster almost 4,000 tanks. Allied industrial muscle meant that losses were quickly replaced; for example, three British armoured divisions were able to shrug off the loss of 400 tanks following two days of heavy fighting during Goodwood; replacements arrived within 36 hours.

After D-Day both the Allies and the Germans knew the strategic ground lay in the east where the British 2nd Army was fighting around the city of Caen. Just to the south-east lay open tank country that could facilitate the Allies breakout. After the Germans had successfully blunted Montgomery's initial advances, rather than fight a bloody frontal battle for Caen, he decided 2nd Army would launch its main effort to the west towards Villers-Bocage and Evrecy, then south-east towards Falaise.

Of all the frustrations the Allies suffered during the Normandy campaign, the failure of Operation Perch on 13 June 1944 has to be one of the worst. Just a week after D-Day in the space of five minutes a handful of Tigers destroyed the spearhead of 7th Armoured Division, saved the Panzer Lehr Division from encirclement, prevented the German line from being rolled up and stopped the Allies from breaking out to the south-west of Caen. In short this engagement could have speeded the conclusion of the Normandy campaign, instead poor planning and bad luck resulted in a major setback.

Montgomery committed his two veteran divisions, the 51st Highland and 7th Armoured, for two main flank attacks. The 51st were to attack through the British 6th Airborne Division, east of the Orne and the 7th Armoured would attack to the south-west. The 51st's attack on 11 June was crushed and two days later their assault had petered out. The 7th Armoured's advance was slow, but a hole in the German line between Villers-Bocage and Caumont was detected. Greeted by joyful locals, the advance elements of Major General G.W. Erskine's 7th Armoured entered Villers-Bocage on 13 June.

The gap between the British tanks and supporting infantry proved too great, allowing the German infantry to hold up the armour. The 4th County of London Yeomanry, known as the Sharpshooters, was over confident with poor tank-infantry cooperation and inadequate dispersion. While the Tiger was a vastly superior tank to the light Cromwell, this was no excuse for the shambles that SS-Lieutenant Michael Wittmann inflicted at Villers-Bocage. In short it was an intelligence disaster.

Wittmann's prompt action in thwarting the British enabled Villers-Bocage to be retaken later in the day (by Panzer Lehr and units of 2nd Panzer battle group) thus plugging the gap. The only consolation for the British was that by 18–19 June Panzer Lehr had lost about 100 of its 260 tanks in the fighting in the Villers-Bocage area. Its commander General Fritz Bayerlein claimed this weakened his division so much it was incapable of launching an armoured thrust towards the sea. By 1 August 1944 Panzer Lehr had just twenty-seven tanks.

The Germans' successful defensive action forced Montgomery to launch two more costly enveloping attacks with Operation Epsom to the west of

Caen on 25 June and Goodwood to the east on 18 July. It seemed that Epsom could not fail; but directly its path lay the 12th SS Panzer Division (supported by the 2nd Heavy Tank Company with Tiger tanks). Bucknall's 30th Corps was to jump off first followed by Lieutenant General Sir Richard O'Connor's 8th Corps. The latter had 60,000 men, 600 tanks, 300 guns and the support of another 400 guns from 30th Corps, plus naval and air support.

The plan was for 8th Corps to break through between the 47th Panzer Corps and 1st SS Panzer Corps, force a bridgehead over the Odon River and take the strategic height of Hill 112. For the British it was a race against time as the 2nd Panzer Corps and 2nd SS Panzer Division were heading for the sector; even if the attack pierced the in-depth defences of the 12th SS the intervention of German armoured reinforcements could kill Epsom.

On 25 June 30th Corps conducted Operation Dauntless, a subsidiary attack to secure 8th Corps western flank before the main offensive carried out by the 49th (West Riding) Infantry Division supported by the 8th Armoured Brigade. The 49th also conducted Operation Martlet, intended to capture Fontenay-le-Pesnil. By 30 June 30th Corps had fought its way to Rauray and Tessel, but in the face of determined resistance from 2nd SS could not maintain its momentum and failed to reach the Odon. In contrast 8th Corps forced its way over the river, creating a narrow bridgehead between Gavrus to the west and Baron to the east. Although the Epsom offensive toward Evrecy south of Caen was a tactical failure, the Orne was crossed, Hill 112 taken and a deep salient driven into the German defences west of Caen.

In countering Epsom, the panzers of the 10th SS attacked the Gavrus bridgehead on the flank of Major General G.P.B Roberts' 11th Armoured Division on Hill 112. The usual problem, shortages of fuel, greatly limited the number of panzers the division could initially throw at Roberts. Nonetheless, the 12th SS attacked Hill 112 from the east and by midday on the 30th were on the summit. Epsom cost British 8th Corps 4,020 casualties; the 11th Armoured Division alone lost 100 tanks and suffered 1,000 casualties during 26–29 June. While the Germans succeeded in containing Epsom, it was at a cost 12th SS over 2,600 casualties, while 9th SS suffered 1,145 casualties and lost sixteen Panzer IVs, six Panthers and ten StuG III assault guns.

Chapter 10

Monty's Armoured Charge

In late 1943 Montgomery said goodbye to the officers and men of the 8th Army in Italy. His place in the history books was firmly secured thanks to his victories in North Africa and Sicily, and now he was going on to bigger and better things. He was to command the 21st Army Group tasked with liberating Nazi-occupied Europe. Monty took with him Major General 'Bobby' Erskine's veteran 7th Armoured Division, the famed 'Desert Rats'. He also took the 50th (Northumbrian) and 51st (Highland) Divisions; along with 7th Armoured they had formed the backbone of the 8th Army.

In the days following D-Day before Caen Montgomery was like a prizefighter. First he launched a series of right jabs to the west of the city. These were followed by a head blow with a direct assault and then a very heavy left hook. For the later 7th Armoured were ordered to deliver the coup de grâce. Such was its reputation that some thought that it was unstoppable.

Field Marshal Rommel always knew that the battle for Normandy hung on the defence of the city of Caen. More specifically the strategic high ground just to the south and south-east formed by the Bourguébus Ridge. Beyond this was good tank country that would offer the Allies an easy ride to the Seine and Paris. While D-Day had gone remarkably well the American breakout in the west had been slowed by the need to clear the Cotentin Peninsula and secure Cherbourg. To the east Montgomery with the British and Canadian forces had struggled to evict the Germans from Caen. Frontal attacks and the push to the west had achieved very little. Monty now decided to try and break through Rommel's thick defences to the east of the city, then head for Falaise 20 miles due south.

To achieve this, he massed three armoured divisions, the Guards, 7th and 11th. While the Guards and 11th Armoured were newly arrived, 7th Armoured had been in Normandy since just after D-Day. The 'Desert Rats' were considered tough combat veterans, and as a result great things were expected of them. 'The 7th Armoured Division were very experienced fighting men,' said Sergeant Harry Ellis with pride, 'and we felt we had been selected to take part in the coming invasion in Europe because of our experiences in battle.' Instead its first major engagement in Normandy at Villers-Bocage proved a severe embarrassment when its spearhead was mauled unexpectedly by German Tiger tanks.

The 'Desert Rats' morale had been dented when they left Italy without their heavy equipment. 'In early November [1943], word got round that were going home,' recalled Sergeant Ellis. 'We handed all our guns and vehicles over to the 5th Canadian Armoured Division and made for the Sorrento Peninsula to await a convoy to take us to Blighty.' Many of the veterans had been at war for three years and for them, unlike a fresh unit, there was no sense of adventure. Furthermore, despite its veteran status North Africa and Italy had not prepared the division for what was to come in France. 'Three years in the desert was not the best preparation for the bocage [Normandy hedgerows],' grumbled Sergeant Bobby Bramall of the 4th County London Yeomanry,' We'd had no training for this jungle country ... it was that close and not tank country at all.'

Crucially the 22nd Armoured Brigade had surrendered all its Sherman tanks in Italy. When the crews got home they were equipped with the new British-built Cromwell tank. Although faster than the Sherman, it had the same inadequate 75mm gun and similar armour. This meant this it was inferior to German tanks such as the Panzer IV, the Panther and the Tiger, although each troop of three Cromwells was beefed up with a Sherman Firefly armed with a 17-pounder anti-tank gun. Some Cromwells were produced as a close support variant armed with a 95mm howitzer, but this was intended to fire high explosive only.

Trooper Duce, with the 8th Hussars, while not blind to their new tank's shortcomings was still impressed. 'The Cromwell's strongpoints were its speed and reliability,' he said, 'and once these factors could be taken advantage of, the slow, ponderous enemy would be taken care of in other ways.' In contrast Sergeant Bramall was of a completely different opinion, 'they were atrocious tanks, fast enough but thin skinned and somewhat undergunned'. He commanded a Firefly which he thought was a good tank. However, he was alarmed that prior to D-Day, apart from firing their guns, they had no tactical training.

During May 1944, while the division was undergoing its Operation Overlord refit, the rumour circulated that their destination was the Dutch coast. The 22nd Armoured Brigade moved from Norfolk to Ipswich, while the others headed for Tilbury docks in east London. General Erskine gathered his officers in a cinema in Brentwood, Essex to give them a final briefing. The division embarked on 6 June and sailed that night for Normandy in fairly rough seas.

The advance elements of the division came ashore on Gold Beach on 7 June 1944. 'We crossed in daylight and hit the beach about mid-afternoon,' recalled Sergeant Bertram Vowden with the 8th Hussars. There was no opposition but disturbingly they saw the bodies of dead British soldiers bobbing up and down with the tide. 'Once on the hard-packed, wet, shiny sand, the Beachmaster directed us to the white taped lanes,' recalled Trooper Duce, 'which had been swept by the Mineflailer Shermans. What a Godsend they were, and what high calibre men crewed them.'

The 'Rats' suffered their first casualties on 9 June after running into German anti-tank guns. The following day those units that had landed were sent toward Tilly-sur-Seulles. Five miles south of Bayeux they destroyed a Panzer IV. The division was finally in the fight. On 12 June General Erskine was ordered to secure the town of Villers-Bocage and the high ground to the east. Here the division soon became embroiled in heavy fighting with elements of two German armoured divisions, 2nd Panzer and Panzer Lehr plus two companies of powerful Tiger tanks.

The advance guard from 4th County of London Yeomanry pushed through Villers-Bocage at 0900 hours on 13 June and reached Point 213 to the north-east. Unknown to them part of 2nd Company from the 101st Heavy SS-Panzer Battalion was in the area under panzer ace SS-Lieutenant Michael Wittmann. The 1st Company under SS-Captain Mobius was on their right. What followed was a disaster for the 'Desert Rats'. Wittmann and a handful of Tigers made short work of 7th Armoured's advance guard.

Sergeant Bramall recalled, 'A Tiger came into the village ... First it wiped out the Artillery observer tanks ... poor devils. Then it got to the Recce Troop.' This was Wittmann, who got between A and B Squadrons deployed either side of the town. When he reached the western outskirts he was driven off by Sergeant Stan Lockwood's Firefly, which achieved at least one hit but did no damage. On the hill, A Squadron were trapped on the road by

Wittmann and the other Tigers and systematically knocked out. Once the Fireflies were destroyed the Cromwells were helpless.

A British tank commander, J.L. Cloudsley-Thompson, watched as A Squadron were just leaving the town when the rear tanks were hit and burst into flames. 'Then an armour-piercing shell whizzed between my wireless-operator's head and mine,' he said. 'It passed so close that although I was wearing headphones it made me slightly deaf for 24 hours afterwards.' His tank was suddenly confronted by a Tiger and alarmingly his 75mm rounds just bounced off it. 'Wham! We were hit.' Cloudsley-Thompson and his crew bailed out taking shelter under a currant bush. He noted that, 'The Tiger drove off undamaged, its commander waving his hat and laughing. Its armour was so thick that none of our Cromwell tanks had been able to knock it out.'

At 1300 hours Mobius, with eight more Tigers supported by infantry, arrived to mop up British survivors between Point 210 and 213. Wittmann likewise reappeared to cause more mayhem. Eventually he was ambushed by B Squadron and two Tigers and a Panzer IV were lost in the town centre. Lieutenant Bill Cotton's Cromwell was only armed with a 95mm howitzer so let Wittmann pass unmolested. His Tiger was then successfully hit and disabled by a British 6-pounder anti-tank gun. Sergeant Bramall's Firefly knocked out the second Tiger. The Panzer IV was hit in the rear at close range. However, Wittmann and most of the crews managed to escape on foot to fight another day.

In total this opening battle cost the 'Desert Rats' twenty Cromwells, four Fireflies, three light tanks, fourteen half-tracks and fourteen Bren carriers. The Germans lost about fifteen tanks. A very shaken 7th Armoured was forced to abandoned Villers-Bocage. 'We felt bad about getting out,' said Sergeant Lockwood. 'It made it seem as if it had been such a waste.' What was worse was the way they had blundered into the Germans.

The debacle at Villers-Bocage was a blow to the division's morale and General Erskine knew it was likely to cost him his job. Afterwards the division was deployed east of Caumont. Living in trenches next to their tanks the 'Rats' stayed there until the end of June. In the face of roving Tiger tanks and Panzerfaust teams their losses mounted. The division's first three weeks in Normandy cost it 1,100 casualties. During this time the division made the most of the opportunity to resupply. Jack Geddes, a Sherman Firefly gunner, noted with some irritation, 'You would be surprised at the amount of wood, wire and canisters the factory bods used to wrap a shell or two.'

The 'Desert Rats' expenditure of ammunition during the Normandy battles was, not surprisingly, very heavy. For example, the Sherman Fireflies averaged 3,250 rounds a month, 4.2in mortars 1,313, .303 rifle ammunition some 76,575. Around 300 tons of ammunition had to be resupplied every day along with 150 tons of petrol. This was a major logistical undertaking with the supply lorries being regularly shelled and shot at by the Germans.

The 7th Armoured was not closely involved with Monty's next attempt to break through German defences west of Caen. This time the honour fell to three fresh divisions under 8th Corps, that included 11th Armoured. Operation Epsom ran from 26 June to 1st July with the loss of over 4,000 men. The 'Desert Rats' next went into action as part of Monty's controversial Operation Goodwood. Publicly at least the intention was to help the Americans, ready for their breakout to the west, by tying the panzers in the Caen area and cutting through to Falaise.

Rommel, having walked the ground before D-Day, had made sure that the Bourguébus Ridge was heavily defended and to a great depth. Monty's intelligence assessed the German defences to be three miles deep, but in reality they were three times this consisting of five defensive zones. The first consisted of infantry, then tanks from the 21st Panzer Division, behind these were a chain of fortified villages and farm houses, then a gun line that encompassed the Garcelles-Secqueville woods and the Bourguébus ridge backed by panzergrenadiers and Panthers from the 1st SS. The last zone consisted of two battle groups from the 12th SS. The gun line on the ridge included 88mm guns, field guns, heavy flak guns and rocket launchers. German tanks and other armoured fighting vehicles totalled around 400.

To convince the Germans that Monty would attack to the west again, on 15 July operations were conducted by the 12th and 30th Corps. To the east the problem Monty faced was that he first had to get his armoured divisions, 11th, Guards and 7th over the Orne. Although the country to the east was suitable for tanks there were not enough bridges over the river and Caen canal. As a result, the divisions could only advance in columns of brigades one after another. Although General O'Connor's 8th Corps could pitch 870 tanks against 230 panzers, he simply could not bring them all to bear at once. In addition, there was a shortage of infantry support as they were deployed on either flank.

Lieutenant Colonel Rankin, with 7th Armoured, and other officers who attended the 8th Corps planning conference came away with a deep sense of gloom. 'No-one felt that passing three Armoured Divisions over one bridge could lead to anything except chaos,' he said, 'and we knew the bulk of the German armour had been concentrated in the area S and SE of Caen.' Afterwards Corporal Norman Habetin, serving with 11th Armoured, recalled, 'We were briefed for Operation Goodwood, which was going to be the attack to end all attacks.' General 'Pip' Roberts, commanding 11th Armoured, had every confidence in his division and the Guards. 'They had a view on the battle very much the same as ours,' he said, 'they were raring to go and show what they could do.' In contrast he characterized 7th Armoured as, 'a little too wary … and a little too canny'. This did not bode well for the coming operation.

The Germans were stunned by a massive artillery and aerial bombardment before the British tanks surged forward in 18 July. At 0745 hours 11th Armoured, with the British 3rd Division on their far left heading for Troarn and the Canadian 2nd Division on the immediate right pushing on Colombelles, charged the German defences. Their target was the village of Le Mesnil-Fremental followed by Verrières and Rocquancourt. The Guards on the left met stiff resistance at Cagny. When the lead elements of 11th Armoured cleared the enemy minefields they found themselves exposed. 'The Germans knew the exact yardages and they could knock you out quite easily,' observed Corporal Bill Scott, 'and they did – from both flanks.'

In the meantime, the 7th Armoured found itself snarled up in the bottleneck caused by congestion on the bridges and was unable to join the battle until the afternoon. 'All I remember of Goodwood is sitting for most of one night in a traffic jam waiting to cross a bridge,' said Private Robert Boulton, 'and the non-existent Luftwaffe being very existent.' The delay in the 'Desert Rats' 22nd Armoured Brigade joining the battle did not go unnoticed by General Roberts. He wanted them to take over the space between his 11th Armoured and the Guards. Roberts grumbled that, '7th Armoured did not put in an appearance before 5pm.' Six hours earlier Roberts had met Brigadier 'Looney' Hinde commanding 22nd Armoured Brigade. Hinde had not been happy about the battlefield saying 'There are too many bloody tanks here already.' Roberts was about to point out that many of these were wrecks but Hinde had gone.

Once across the Orne the 'Desert Rats' came into contact with the enemy at Cuverville. The 5th Royal Tank Regiment destroyed two Panzer IVs, but this cost them six tanks and twelve men. In contrast 11th Armoured lost over 100 tanks. The casualties for the day showed that Roberts' division had borne the brunt of the battle having suffered 336 casualties; the Guards lost 137 and 7th Armoured 48. Roberts was not impressed with the 'Rats', noting rather caustically 'they certainly did not have the same enthusiasm for this battle as ourselves and Guards Armoured Division'. This perhaps was a little harsh in light of them being late to the fight, but they did seem to lack drive and aggressiveness.

On the morning of 19 July 5RTR took Grentheville along with eighty prisoners. The 7th Armoured fought its way through Panther and Tiger tanks and their supporting infantry. For the crews it came as a shock to see the battlefield littered with so many knocked-out tanks. Major Bill Apsey, who was wounded by German mortar rounds, observed, 'In the ambulance were two tank boys horrendously burnt, both died on the way back.' At 1700 hours 5RTR commenced clearing the Germans from Soliers, while 1RTR took Fours. Their objective was the heavily defended Bourguébus ridge.

The following day Captain Bill Bellamy recorded, 'On 20 July Ifs, Bras and Hubert-Folie were occupied and patrols pushed on as far as Verrières, held by up to 100 tanks of 1 SS PZ Div, a battle group of 2 Panzer and 272 Infantry Division.' At 1800 hours on 20 July 5RTR took the village of Bourguébus. Remarkably for the loss of just one Cromwell they claimed two Tigers and a Panther. All three panzers were destroyed by a Firefly commanded by Sergeant 'Pluto' Ellis. One of them he knocked out by shooting it through a haystack. The following day they captured two Panthers, set another on fire and destroyed a Tiger without loss. Also on the 20th the 4CLY got to the Caen-Falaise road near Bras.

On the 21st the weather broke and there was torrential rain that turned the battlefield into a quagmire. Although Monty had taken Caen and 30 square miles of territory, Goodwood had run out of momentum. The Germans remained entrenched on part of the Bourguébus ridge. In three days of fighting he lost in excess of 400 tanks. The Allies were easily able to replace these, but the tank crews and supporting infantry were irreplaceable. The

7th Armoured alone suffered 200 casualties. 'After Goodwood,' recalled Private Bill Hinde, 'Jerry made a couple of counter-attacks but Div and Army Arty [artillery] made short work of them. He got nowhere near our positions ...'

There was to be little respite for the 'Desert Rats'. On 25 July they came under the Canadian 2nd Corps for Operation Spring. This was a continuation of Goodwood that saw another attack toward Falaise. At the end of the month 7th Armoured were committed to Operation Bluecoat, which pushed toward Mont Pincon. By mid-August the division was triumphantly heading for the Seine.

Rather unfairly Goodwood was chalked up as a failure. Monty's armoured fist had been fought to a standstill. Strategically though, the 'Desert Rats' and the others had contributed to a victory. Goodwood forced the Germans to deploy the bulk of their panzers facing the Allies eastern flank leaving less than 300 facing the Americans. On 25 July 1944 the Americans launched Operation Cobra that heralded the German collapse in Normandy.

Chapter 11

Battle of the Hedgerows

Immediately after D-Day tanks from the US 2nd, 3rd and 4th Armored Divisions pushed west, with 2nd Armored linking up with the 101st Airborne near the city of Carentan. Thrown into combat on 10 June 1944, the reconnaissance battalion of the 17th SS Panzergrenadier Division set about the American paratroopers – who were only saved by the timely arrival of the US 2nd Armored's tanks. The presence of the 17th SS helped persuade the Americans that they should first clear the Cotentin peninsula and capture the vital port of Cherbourg, before making further efforts to strike southward. While Montgomery's forces were struggling west of Caen, Major General Collins' US 7th Corps fought its way up the Cotentin to Cherbourg and attacked the city on 22 June. After four days of fierce fighting the garrison, some 21,000 men, surrendered.

The US 2nd Armored Division began to land on Omaha Beach just three days after D-Day on 9 June. Its arrival did not go without mishap as a LST struck a mine, with the loss of sixty-six men, thirty-one tanks and fifteen other heavy vehicles. The division came ashore in three groups comprising Combat Commands A and B plus the support units. General Omar Bradley, commander of the US 1st Army, initially deployed them to the American left where they clashed with the 17th SS. This engagement gained them the German nickname 'Roosevelt's Butchers'. The 2nd Armored was then placed in reserve to await the rest of those units that had to cross the English Channel. On 30 June, now under General Charles Corlett's 9th Corps, the division moved south-west of Bayeux to support the British flank.

By 1 July the Cotentin had been cleared, with US forces having entered Auderville on the Cap de la Hague to the west of Cherbourg and Barfleur to the east. However, thanks to extensive German demolition efforts the port was not serviceable until mid-August. In the meantime, to the south a German defensive line took shape between Lessay and St Lô, which was held by the German 7th Army anchored on two panzer divisions and a panzergrenadier division.

While for American armour the battle of the hedgerows or Bocage was a bloody affair, for the infantry it was a gruelling ordeal. St Lô was scheduled to be captured on 11 June, but it did not fall until a month later on 18 July. Taking the town cost the 29th and 35th Infantry Divisions 5,000 casualties. To the west the Germans still held the Lessay to Periers road and were able to shell St Lô. The seventeen-day push seven miles west of Vire and just four miles east of it came at a cost of 40,000 American casualties, 90 per cent of whom were infantry. By mid-July the shortage of infantry meant that 25,000 reinforcements had to be shipped from America. Total German casualties had risen to about 100,000. The breakout could not be launched before 20 July because of the necessary build-up of supplies. The plan was to sweep south-east through Avranches and Mortain thereby cutting off the panzers in Normandy.

While Montgomery was battling it out, Bradley's plan for Operation Cobra involved fifteen American divisions under Middleton's 8th Corps, Collins' 7th Corps and Corlett's 9th Corp respectively; with Collins' 4th, 9th and 30th Infantry Divisions opening the attack followed by the 1st Infantry, 2nd Armored and 3rd Armored. The intention was to break through and swing right, trapping five or six enemy divisions. As well as fighter-bomber and bomber support, a barrage was to be laid down by 1,000 guns. To fend off Cobra the Germans had eleven very weak divisions, only two of which were armoured – the Panzer Lehr and 2nd SS. The Panzer Lehr Panzer Division could muster barely 2,200 men and just 45 operational armoured vehicles.

Hitler prevailed upon von Rundstedt and Rommel that they should wear the Allies down, missing the point that this was the very thing happening to his panzer forces thanks to Montgomery's sledgehammer blows around Caen. After the 20 July bomb plot he took personal command of operations in the West. Following the initial American breakthrough, Hitler ordered six infantry divisions to replace the panzer divisions facing the British and Canadians so they could retake Avranches. However, there were no mobile reserves to help 7th Army contain an Allied breakthrough and reinforcements lacked combat experience and were short of artillery and anti-tank weapons.

Fed up with the dangerously confining Bocage, which lined all of Normandy's roads and fields, for Cobra, the US Army deployed a simple but effective secret weapon. Up until this point the hedgerows had helped German defensive operations no end and they were proving lethal to American tanks; it seemed behind every hedge lurked a panzer or an anti-tank gun. That is until the 'Rhino' steel tusks were welded to the front of many American tanks.

While Sergeant Curtis C. Cullin of the 2nd Armored Division got the credit for devising a plough that effectively tore out the hedgerow's earth bank obstructing a tank, it was really a team effort. To be fair by this stage many American armoured units were experimenting with field modifications that did not require the services of an armoured bulldozer or indeed the Sherman fitted with a bulldozer blade. The 17th Armored Engineer Battalion's 'tank-dozers' (tanks fitted with bulldozer prows) had been deployed at Carentan as an ungainly solution.

Ironically the steel for the ploughs came from Rommel's beach obstacles. While the Rhinos were of great practical value the psychological impact was also immense because they encouraged American tankers to get off the roads and outflank the panzers. It would soon become the panzers' turn to become trapped in ever-greater numbers amongst the Normandy hedgerows.

Three US infantry divisions of Collins' 7th Corps were assigned the task of spearheading the break-out, drawing up on the Lessay-Periers-St Lô line. Initially scheduled for 24 July it had to be called off due to the bad weather. The following day the Americans withdrew 1,200 yards, while bombers dropped over 4,000 tons of bombs on the German defences, in an area four miles long by one and a half miles wide just south of the St Lô-Periers highway. At 0230 hours the assault troops moved off only to meet determined German resistance. The 116th Panzer Division was thrown into the struggle to stabilize the German line. Two days later General Collins decided to launch his own armour into the thrust. The US 2nd Armoured Division lost one tank as they moved off and little serious opposition was met, 7th Corps armour then fanned out.

It was not until Patton's breakout 30 miles further south at Avranches, a week after Cobra commenced, that the pursuit really got underway. While Patton waited for his US 3rd Army to become operational, he took command of 8th Corps and drove southwards along the coast into Brittany, ready for the sweep into line for a thrust towards the Seine. He took Coutances and on

30 July the US 4th Armored Division, hurtling down from 8th Corps, seized Avranches on the Atlantic coast. The town's bridges were found to be intact.

On 1 August, ignoring Bradley's orders to secure a wide corridor, Patton squeezed six divisions down the coast through the gap at Avranches in twenty-two hours. He was now poised to sweep south-eastwards into the open plains in order to trap the Wehrmacht in north-western France. At this point, if not earlier, Hitler should have authorized a withdrawal beyond the Seine to the comparative safety of the German 15th Army. Instead he insisted that no inch of ground be given, denying his generals any initiative.

Now in an effort to seal the American breakout, Hitler disastrously ordered a counter-attack to isolate Patton's 3rd Army. He wanted eight panzer divisions to assemble near Mortain, and to strike towards Avranches. In reality Hitler's forces were simply driving themselves deeper into the noose. When Captain Harry C. Butcher, Eisenhower's naval aide, pointed out to his boss that the Germans had about 500 tanks in the Mortain area, Eisenhower responded, 'We've got 3,500; what are we scared of?' The sentiment was right, but not the intelligence.

Panzergruppe West was renamed 5th Panzer Army on 5 August with responsibility for 7th Army's right flank. General Eberbach considered a counter-attack a hopeless cause; his forces were too weak, Allied air power too strong; any success would be short-lived as it would be impossible to fend off the Americans once they caught their breath. In addition, supplying the four panzer divisions available for the attack would have to be conducted at night.

Nonetheless, Hitler ordered Operation Lüttich to close the developing American breach. The panzers in Normandy were down from 1,400 tanks to 800, of which 120 were allotted to Liege (belonging to the 2nd and 116th Panzer Divisions as well as elements from Panzer Lehr, and 2nd SS), supported by two infantry divisions. Only eighty panzers crossed the start line on 7 August, but the tired Germans drove hard taking Mortain and advancing seven miles before the US 30th Division held them until reinforcements arrived. Then with the help of Allied air strikes Hitler's German counter-attack ran out of steam. RAF Typhoon fighter-bombers pounced on some 300 armoured vehicles, destroying 80, and other squadrons followed up to take their share of the kills. German troops dubbed it the 'Day of the Typhoon'.

Hitler's panzers got to within nine miles of Avranches, but could get no further. The US 2nd Armored Division found itself slugging it out with depleted elements of 2nd Panzer, 2nd SS Panzer and Panzer Lehr in the vicinity of Barenton, and 116th Panzer around Vire. On 8 August 7th Army received orders to postpone the attack following a British breakthrough south of Caen, which had shaken 5th Panzer Army.

Hitler demanded the counter-attack in the American sector be renewed and instructed Eberbach to assume command of the newly activated Panzergruppe Eberbach on 10 August, while General 'Sepp' Dietrich took command of 5th Panzer Army. The Allied pressure on both the American and British sectors was such that despite the panzers' best efforts the dam was about to burst in a very spectacular fashion. In reality for the renewed attack Eberbach could only gather 124 tanks, 77 Panzer IVs and 47 Panthers, roughly the same inadequate numbers that had been launched in the initial attack. His efforts though were stillborn once the Americans were south of Argentan. All thoughts of counter-attack were abandoned in favour of trying to extricate as many units as possible from the American, British, Canadian and Polish pincer movement now forming.

Eberbach blamed the failure of the German attack on Avranches squarely on the High Command. Referring to the transfer of Panzergruppe West's armour to 7th Army for the operation he commented, 'The failure was caused by the fact that the panzer divisions of Panzergruppe West (5th Panzer Army), committed at the front, were not relieved by infantry divisions in due time. The Armed Forces High Command is to blame for this. It did not authorize CinC West to act freely, and delayed the transfer of the divisions.'

Patton, sweeping south of Le Mans, knew that if the Germans persisted with their attack they would ultimately not be able to get away. Slowly but surely, 7th Army and 5th Panzer Army were being wedged in a giant vice. In trying to stop Patton's tanks, 9th Panzer Division was reduced to a dozen panzers. The Allies could see their plans coming to fruition. The Canadians drove through the south of Caen and headed for Falaise, while the Americans sped eastwards, creating a gigantic trap. Montgomery ordered the Americans to make a long hook, in order to envelop as many of the enemy as possible and prevent them escaping over the Seine. The developing pocket could not be closed because the Germans dug in north of Falaise and the Canadian advance was slower than expected.

The US 5th Armored Division entered Sees on the Orne on 12 August and headed north for Argentan, which lies south-east of Falaise, tightening the noose around over twenty German divisions. Trapped in the pocket were the cream of the German tank forces including elements of seven panzer divisions.

At Argentan the Germans had just 70 tanks with which to fend off 300 American Shermans. General Bradley, fearing his troops might be trampled by the fleeing enemy, refrained from driving on to Falaise. This meant the two German armies caught in the Falaise Pocket were able to struggle eastward for another week. To the north the Germans held up the Canadian advance, known as Operation Tractable, for two days before they reached Falaise.

Hitler's position in France became impossible to maintain after 15 August 1944 when the Allies landed in the Riviera. Hitler grudgingly agreed to let the German army withdraw through the Argentan-Falaise Gap on 16 August. The 2nd SS Panzer Corps were to hold the northern flank against the British and Canadians. At the same time 47th Panzer Corps were to defend the south against the Americans, while 7th Army and Panzer Group Eberbach/5th Panzer Army conducted a fighting retreat eastward.

Patton's US 3rd Army and Crocker's British 1st Corps were slowly heading for each other and the Falaise Pocket was steadily squeezed from all sides as the Germans fought to hold open the neck. By 17 August the pocket was only 20 miles wide by 10 miles deep, containing about 100,000 men, remnants of 15 divisions with elements from at least 12 others, all trying desperately to extricate themselves. The panzer divisions managed to hold the Americans and Canadians at bay, but the vast retreating columns were decimated by Allied fighter-bombers and artillery, the roads becoming choked with burnt-out vehicles which added to the chaos.

Montgomery demanded the Trun-Chambois gap be closed and on 17 August issued orders stating, 'It is absolutely essential that both armoured divisions of 2nd Canadian Corps, i.e. 4th Canadian Armoured Division and 1st Polish Armoured Division, close the gap between 1st Canadian and 3rd US Army. 1st Polish Armoured Division must thrust past Trun and Chambois at all costs and as quickly as possible.' The Canadians and Poles were soon pressing hard on the Germans' flanks.

Canadian troops burst into Falaise on 16 August and three days, later supported by Sherman tanks, seized St Lambert-sur-Dives right in the path of the fleeing Germans. They held out for three days withstanding efforts by the remains of 2nd Panzer to dislodge them. Germans escaping over the river came under constant fire and at one point the Canadians called artillery fire down onto their own positions. Canadian soldier Duncan Kyle recalled the carnage, 'Germans charred coal-black, looking like blackened tree trunks lay besides smoking vehicles. One didn't realize the obscene mess was human until it was poked at. ... The road to Falaise was nauseating. I felt like puking many times, what butchery.'

The escape route was just five miles wide by 19 August, though it would not be completely sealed for another two days, and the rapidly shrinking pocket measured just seven miles by six. Under pressure from German paratroops within the pocket the Polish tanks were forced to relinquish control of some of the roads and up to 4,000 paratroops supported by three panzers from 2nd SS escaped. Outside the mouth of the pocket on 20 August the 2nd SS Panzer Corps attempted to reach the remnants of 7th Army, but with just twenty tanks they were unable to break through and the 9th SS were halted by the 2nd Polish Armoured Regiment.

Inside the corridor 2nd Panzer with their remaining tanks attacked toward Canadian-held St Lambert and found the bridge intact. Their commanding officer, General Heinrich Freiherr von Lüttwitz recalled, 'The crossing of the Dives bridge was particularly horrible, the bodies of the dead, horses and vehicles and other equipment having been hurled from the bridge into the river formed a gruesome tangled mass.' The 10th SS and 116th Panzer managed to cross the river Dives via the St Lambert bridge and drove the encircling Allies away.

The 9th SS tried to break through again on 21 August using two massive Tiger II tanks, but these were swiftly knocked out. The Allies began to mop up the remaining Germans trapped west of the Dives and about 18,000 men went into the 'bag' that day. In total the Germans lost 10,000 killed and 50,000 captured. They claimed that 40,000 troops escaped, although many of them were lost before they crossed the Seine.

When the Allies finally overran the panzers in the Falaise Pocket the debris was quite phenomenal. In the American zone alone there were 540 tanks and self-propelled guns as well as 5,000 vehicles. The British, Canadian and Polish zones were littered another 344 armoured vehicles. While the 2nd SS Panzer Corps lost 120 tanks during the counter-attack at Falaise, it managed to withdraw to fight another day.

Chapter 12

The Champagne Campaign

During the Allied naval build-up in the Mediterranean prior to Operation Dragoon and the landings on the French Riviera, the Luftwaffe kept General Friedrich Weise, commander of the German 19th Army, informed of developments. He and his boss General Johannes Blaskowitz did not know exactly where the blow would fall and had insufficient forces to defend the entire coastline. The heavy Allied bombing of Toulon and other targets in the days before the invasion alerted Blaskowitz that something was likely to happen. By 14 August 1944, suspecting an attack in the Marseilles–Toulon region, he moved 11th Panzer and two infantry divisions east of the Rhône. The Germans' lack of panzers in southern France meant that armoured divisions were not a priority for the Allies in this campaign.

The Allied assault was scheduled to commence the following day at 0800 hours. The US 3rd Infantry Division were to land on the left at Cavalaire-sur-Mer, the 45th in the centre at St Tropez and the 36th on the right on at St Raphel. The 3rd was to strike the boundary of the German 62nd Corps' 242nd and 148th Infantry Divisions. French commando units were also to land between Cannes and Hyères, flanking the assault beaches. Armoured support was provided by Sherman DD tanks of the US 191st, 753rd and 756th Tank Battalions and the 1st Combat Command from the French 1st Armoured Division. The US 14th Armored Division was not due to land at Marseilles until late October. It was subsequently joined by the US 10th and 12th Armoured in central France the following year.

On the evening of 14 August transport aircraft and gliders had been gathered to ferry the airborne assault force to the Riviera. Le May, sited inland from the landing beaches, provided protection for the invasion area and access to the Argens valley corridor, it was therefore to be secured by Allied airborne troops. While the airborne landings suffered heavy losses, the seaborne landings themselves were largely unopposed. There was no firing on the Allied fleet and 40 per cent of the prisoners taken were anti-Soviet Russians who had volunteered to fight Stalin, but had found themselves in the south of France. Those who did offer token resistance were swiftly dealt with.

Captain Harry Butcher, Eisenhower's naval aide, recalled,

> Today is D-Day for Anvil. … We have just heard from Major General Alexander M. Patch, veteran of Guadalcanal, who commands the US 7th Army in the southern landings. He says the operation seems successful.
>
> Our old friend Lucian Truscott is commanding the 6th Corps, which is comprised of the 3rd, 36th, and 45th Divisions, which were the assault divisions. These were supported by airborne troops, Rangers, Commandos, French Commandos, and the 1st Special Service under Major General Robert T. Frederick (formerly of Operations Division). All assault divisions reported successful breaching of beach defences in target area and the attack was proceeding according to plan.

Churchill, with his eye on history, accompanied the fleet on HMS *Kimberley* but slept through the initial landings. Later, standing on deck, passing American troops yelled 'Winnie, Winnie!', unaware that he had done everything in his power to stop Dragoon. Unimpressed, he retired to his cabin to read. He later noted bitterly, 'One of my reasons for making public my visit was to associate myself with this well-conducted but irrelevant and unrelated operation.'

Over 94,000 men and 11,000 vehicles came ashore on that first day. The US 3rd and 45th Infantry Divisions were soon pressing toward Marseilles and the Rhône, while the 36th made toward the Route Napoleon and Grenoble. The follow-up forces including the US 7th Army headquarters, US 6th Corps headquarters, and the French 2nd Corps, comprising the French 1st Armoured, 1st Motorized, 3rd Algerian and 9th Colonial Divisions, came ashore the following day and passed through 6th Corps on the Marseilles road. Due to the rapidity of the advance, lack of fuel became a greater impediment than German resistance. What followed was dubbed 'the champagne campaign'.

General Weise tried to establish a defence line using the 242nd Infantry Division in the Toulon area, the 244th guarding Marseilles and elements of the 189th and 198th as they came across the Rhône. The failure of the German Mortain counter-attack in Normandy and the developing Falaise Pocket meant that by 16 August it was imperative to save Blaskowitz's Army Group G before a wider spread collapse occurred in France.

Blaskowitz received his orders and abandoned Toulouse, withdrawing north. General Ferdinand Neuling's 62nd Corps at Draguignan, a few miles north-west of Le Muy, was not so lucky and found themselves surrounded by enemy paratroopers, his two infantry divisions trapped at Marseilles and Toulon. Weise sent the 189th Infantry Division to clear Le Muy and relieve 62nd Corps, but the Americans easily fended off the feeble counter-attacks by elements of the 189th and 148th Divisions.

Blaskowitz was ordered to move his forces north-east, except for the 148th Division in the Cannes-Nice area and a reserve mountain division at Grenoble, which were instructed to move into Italy. Marseilles and Toulon were to remain German fortresses. Overseeing the retreat up the west bank of the Rhône was General Petersen's 4th Luftwaffe Field Corps, while Kniess' 85th Corps was to manage things on the east bank. The plan was to co-ordinate their march on Lyon with the 64th Corps heading from the Atlantic Coast via central France with the remains of two infantry divisions. This combined force would then move north toward Dijon and make contact with the retreating Army Group B. Blaskowitz must have looked at his situation maps with an air of exasperation, as all this had to be achieved with Patton's US 3rd Army on the verge of seizing Lyon or Dijon and the US 7th Army pushing up behind from the Riviera.

In addition, both 4th Luftwaffe Field Corps and 85th Corps had to shepherd vulnerable retreating support personnel numbering about 100,000, including 2,000 women, all of whom had little or no combat value. These units had no more than rifles with which to protect themselves and were at risk from the vengeful French Resistance or Maquis. Indeed, the presence of the resistance ensured they could not flee north-east via the Massif Central, but had to detour via Poiters and Bourges to Dijon.

Giving the withdrawal order to 19th Army was easy as it shared Blaskowitz's Avignon HQ, but 64th Corps could not be raised on the radio so a liaison officer was sent to Toulouse by car from where radio and courier messages could be sent out. Just to be on the safe side a plane was also despatched to Bordeaux. After all this none of the messages got through, though by good fortune the naval station at Bordeaux received the order via Berlin. Frustratingly, before its departure 64th Corps was obliged to leave behind the better elements of two infantry divisions to hold the fortresses of Bordeaux-Gironde and La Rochelle. In the meantime, the 159th Infantry Division formed the vanguard and the southern flank of this retreating corps, while the 16th Division acted as rearguard and screened the northern flank.

On 20 August the French 3rd Algerian Infantry Division reached Mont Faron on the outskirts of Toulon, where General de Lattre ordered de Monsabert's forces to Ange Pass in preparation for an assault on Marseilles to the west. By the 21st the German garrison at Toulon was completely surrounded and in the evening the Algerians moved from the suburbs into the city itself and street fighting broke out. The last of the German units had surrendered by the 26th. The week-long battle for Toulon cost the French 2,700 casualties, but Blaskowitz's forces needlessly lost 17,000 men.

In Marseilles the Resistance did not stand idly by. The Communists took over the city's prefecture on 23 August as de Lattre's troops closed in on the suburbs. The garrison could have easily overwhelmed them but was more concerned with the approaching regular French Army. Just two days after the fall of Toulon and following an attack by the Algerians on the Notre Dame de la Garde feature, the Marseilles garrison also officially surrendered. Some 11,000 German troops laid down their weapons. The American and French armies found Marseilles already in the hands of a Resistance-led left-wing administration. Initially cooperation between the American military and the French preceded smoothly, but American plans for the port and a long-term presence soon strained relations, causing problems for the pursuit northwards.

Remarkably French and American forces had captured both Toulon and Marseilles in just fourteen days. The planners, erring on the safe side, assumed that they would not be secured until D plus 40. With all his formations ashore de Lattre's Army B became the French 1st Army consisting of 1st Corps under General Béthouart on the right and 2nd Corps under de Monsabert on the left. They would soon be snapping on Blaskowitz's heels.

Even as the Allies' bridgehead was being consolidated, in order to avoid the errors of the Anzio landings in Italy, it was decided that it was imperative for General Truscott's US 6th Corps to thrust northward as quickly as possible. The Gap of Montélimar provided him with the best way of blocking the Route N7 and trapping Wiese's escaping 19th Army.

The River Rhône flows in an almost straight north-south route over 124 miles between Lyon and its entrance to the delta at Avingnon. Beyond Orange it narrows greatly, 43 miles north of Avingnon at Montélimar the Montélimar Plain and the Valence Plain are divided by the Cruas Gorge also known as the Gap or Gate of Montélimar. The west bank of the river is bordered by cliffs while on the east deeply forested hills slope up to some 1,300ft. To exploit his breach, at the town of Gap, Truscott ordered his deputy corps commander Brigadier General Frederick Butler and his task force consisting of the US 753rd Tank Battalion, 2nd Battalion 143rd Infantry from the 36th Division, 59th Armoured Field Artillery Battalion, 117th Reconnaissance Squadron plus tank destroyers and supporting combat engineers, to spearhead the push.

The US 36th Infantry Division was to follow up toward Grenoble through Castellane and up the N85, while the 3rd and 45th Divisions pushed up the Argens corridor toward the Rhône. The 3rd rumbled along the N7, triumphantly forcing its way into Aix-en-Provence on 21 August. Everywhere the Germans seemed in disarray or had already vanished. The 45th secured the crossings over the Durance by clearing Barjols, which enabled the 3rd to shift right to join the march on Grenoble. Their job, if all went well, was to herd the fleeing Germans into the arms of Task Force Butler and the 36th Division at the Gate of Montélimar. A trap was being set to foil Blaskowitz's orderly withdrawal.

Futile German attempts to reinforce their troops facing the beachheads were soon thwarted once Task Force Butler had taken the Col de la Croix Haute mountain pass, 3,868ft up on the N75 north of Apres. Similarly, with the aid of the Free French forces Gap was taken along with 1,000 German prisoners. This meant that the German 157th Reserve Division at Grenoble could not despatch further troops south.

Butler swung west to block the Germans' escape routes up the Rhône Valley. North of Livron they caught a German convoy of thirty vehicles with devastating results, but around La Coucourde ran into superior German forces. By this stage the Germans had established themselves on the hills dominating the roads heading north and east, namely Ridge 300.

However, on the 21st the Americans reached the high ground overlooking the Rhône Valley north of the Gate of Montélimar. A desperate battle was now imminent.

From the hills lining the Rhône Valley, north of Montélimar, the Butler Task Force's reconnaissance units watched enemy traffic stream up the main valley road, and blocked the enemy armour trying to get there through Puy-St. Martin. Along the floor of the valley itself, the Germans had grouped round the 11th Panzer Division. Obstructing them were the US 636th Tank Destroyer Battalion, and the 753rd and 191st Tank Battalions. The first real tank battle of the campaign now commenced.

Butler's men opened up on the shooting gallery presented by the fleeing Germans below. A tank crewman attached to the 143rd Infantry Regiment recalled:

> We fired our guns continuously without stopping, and the recoil system got so hot that the system was slowing down. Norris, my loader, was pushing shells into the breach with his fist, and due to the fast fire, his skin began to peel off his hand. I exchanged places with Norris for a while, and I also lost some skin. We fired until we were out of ammunition and had to order more.

Just seven days after the landings the US 36th Infantry Division had penetrated 250 miles to Grenoble. Truscott instructed the division to obstruct the German withdrawal up the Rhône, as well as counter any German reinforcements that might be pushing south. However, the 36th Infantry was spread over four widely separated sectors at Grenoble, Gap and Guillestre, Digne, and in the beachhead.

This meant that to escape Wiese's German 19th Army would have to barged the GIs of the 36th Infantry out of the way. By 1700 hours on 23 August a battalion from the 141st Infantry Regiment had got to within a mile of Montélimar before small-scale counter-attacks developed along its flanks. By midnight, enemy infiltration threatened its supply lines and the battalion was forced to withdraw. The following day the entire division deployed to the region. The 142nd Infantry Regiment moved swiftly from Gap and Guillestre to defensive positions, while the 143rd hurried down from Grenoble.

Behind 11th Panzer, reinforced and backed by fresh units, came the entire 198th Infantry Division determined to break the American cordon. Just as the 198th mounted a full-scale attack to drive the 141st from its positions north-east of Montélimar and force their artillery to withdraw out of range of the highway, the 142nd and 143rd Regimental Combat Teams raced up from the south. On 24 August, the 142nd reached the battleground and occupied defensive positions 25 miles long, followed by the balance of the 143rd.

From 25 to 30 August the 36th Division was attacked daily, with the main German effort pushing along a spur valley which ran north-east from Montélimar, in an attempt to cut the 36th's supply routes and encircle the defenders. In addition, the Germans constantly subjected the division's long defensive perimeter to spoiling attacks designed to prevent the 36th from launching any attacks of its own.

On the evening of 25 August Route Seven, several miles north of Montélimar, was severed by the entire 141st Regimental Combat Team, reinforced by elements of the 143rd. In the process they beat off German infantry and armour. Crucially this attack cut the valley road at a narrow neck of the Rhône south of La Coucourde. Lieutenant Colonel Charles Wilber's mission was to hold the block as long as possible. In the event of the Germans breaking through he and his men were to fall back eastward to Crest and hold the town at all cost, blowing up the bridges as a last resort. Subsequent German counter-attacks did indeed break through the roadblock soon after midnight.

Alarmingly, German armour was soon being reported north and north-west of Crest, in the vicinity of Banlieu and near Grance. The northernmost roadblock, manned by the 36th Cavalry Reconnaissance Troop, was forced back at daybreak by overwhelming German power. Reinforcements in the shape of the 157th Infantry Regiment of the US 45th Division were quickly deployed north of Crest.

Artillerymen turned their guns 180 degrees to pummel the German armour threatening Grance and Crest to the north. The 36th Division salient at Montélimar thrust towards Route Seven several miles north of the city. Running through Condillac, Sauzet and Cleon and anchored, at Crest, the snaking lines of supply and communication ran from the south to Crest. At first the Germans held the initiative and certainly if they had conducted a bold oblique thrust to the east, they might have disrupted the whole of 6th Corps, cutting the only artery up from the beaches.

General Dahlquist decided to hold the little Rubion streambed (in front of a vital supply road) on a flat bowl-shaped plain backed up by a wall of hills. His divisional artillery was deployed onto the hills opening up in a great arc south, west and north. Key terrain held by the infantry allowed gun positions to be disposed in such a manner that the route of German withdrawal along the Rhône was under fire for 16 miles, creating a perfect killing field.

Fleeing German convoys were now blasted off the roads, and the entire zone was literally covered with a mass of burnt-out vehicles, equipment, dead men and animal carcasses. German attacks, initiated simultaneously from three directions, were hammered and repulsed by the same paralysing artillery barrages. On the Rhône side of the line the 36th Division committed to putting a final seal on the main valley highway. American P-47 fighters also swooped in, pounding and destroying all bridges across the river, forcing the enemy to remain on the east bank.

Trapped in the developing pocket were three German divisions hell-bent on holding open their escape route. On two successive days, regiments of the German 198th Division bolted against the centre of the Rubion line at Bonlieu and were thrown back by battalions of the 143rd and 142nd. The 141st, in the hot seat near the Rhône, faced incessant enemy attacks striving to drive them away from Route Seven.

Further American efforts to seize La Coucourde and to recapture and block Route Seven were not completely successful though much damage was inflicted on the enemy. The 3rd Battalion 143rd, held the vital Magranon Ridge near La Coucourde, overlooking Route Seven, during three days of critical fighting. Cut off and isolated in small groups one at one time, the battalion fought on to decisively defeat the exhausted German forces. Toward the end divisional forces were shifted northward to strike again along the Drome River Valley.

For nine days the Germans fought the GIs before retreating on Lyon. In particular, on 25 August 11th Panzer Division and supporting units launched five attacks. Two days later the bulk of 11th Panzer and most of the retreating infantry had crossed the Rhône north of Drome having lost 2,500 PoWs, leaving the Montélimar region in the hands of General Baptist Kniess' fresh 85th Corps.

General Otto Richter's 198th Infantry Division, plus a rearguard engineer detachment to the south, remained at Montélimar. On the night of

27/28 August, he led his remaining two regiments and other survivors in a bid to escape. Richter's group ran straight into the US 36th Division's push on the town, the general and some 700 of his men were captured, but not before the Americans suffered around 100 casualties in a fierce firefight.

The 143rd Regiment shattered German forces around Loriol on 29 August, taking over 1,000 prisoners in the final mop-up. Also that day the 142nd seized Livron but straggling groups of Germans continued to resist strongly until the 30th. Then elements of 3rd Division, pressing the Germans up from the south, contacted the 141st near Clary. Yet, with such terrible destruction wrought on 19th Army, even on the last day of battle, Colonel Paul Adams, commanding the 143rd, reported to headquarters, 'I'm expecting a hell of a fight'. At six o'clock in the morning, the last German counter-attack had formed in the vicinity of La Coucourde, but in an hour the drive had been repulsed and the attackers were destroyed or captured.

It was American artillery at Montélimar, not tanks, that counted most and swayed the tide of battle. During the eight days the 36th Infantry's four field artillery battalions fired well over 37,000 rounds at the confined, retreating German troops. Supporting fire from the attached battalions brought the total number of rounds expended to considerably more than 75,000. It is a wonder that any German soldiers survived to fight another day.

The US 6th Corps' newspaper, *The Beachhead News*, reported triumphantly:

> Under the 36th Division command ... such a great force of artillery was directed on the Germans that more than four thousand vehicles, one 380mm and five other railroad guns were destroyed, and the main escape gap for the fleeing German army was under constant fire and attack. ... the Division moved in and finished off the kill.

By the time the Battle of Montélimar ended 6th Corps had suffered 1,575 casualties, having inflicted five times that number on the Germans. The highway for 11 miles north and south of the town was a smoking double-column of knocked-out vehicles, dead horses and men. There was no stretch of road that did not contain some remnant of destruction.

In total Blaskowitz and Wiese's troops suffered 11,000 casualties and lost 1,500 horses. The Americans took some 5,000 prisoners at Montélimar and destroyed more than 4,000 vehicles, as well as the 189th and 338th Divisions. The Allies secured the region between Nice and Avignon as far north as Briançon via Grenoble to Montélimar mauling General Wiese's 19th Army mainly through artillery and air strikes as it sought to flee. As a result, the Germans were unable to draw up an effective defensive line until after the Americans had crossed the Moselle River.

The retreating Germans conducted delaying actions, notably in the Autun and Dijon regions, but ultimately they were now being driven from the whole of France. The 4th Luftwaffe Field Corps got to Lyon on 30 August, where it found the city's anti-aircraft defences had been fending off French troops to the west. The corps was transferred to the east bank of the Rhône where it joined units of 11th Panzer. However, elements of 4th Corps straggling behind were marshalled on the west bank to cover 85th Corps.

In Lyon the US 36th Infantry found the Maquis and the Milice, the Vichy police who the French hated as much as the Germans, battling it out. The factories on the city's outskirts were burning and all the bridges had been destroyed except one. While the fighting in the industrial area was ongoing, across the river patrols were greeted by great crowds of cheering civilians. The jeeps were surrounded by masses of men and women who just wanted to shake an American hand or stare curiously at the liberators.

The US 7th Army liberated Lyon on 3 September and another 2,000 Germans were captured, they were also driven from Besançon four days later. There were two days of celebrations in Lyon and all sorts of parties in honour of the Americans, drinking bouts in which the French and their guests vied with one another in paying extravagant compliments. Every private home threw open its doors to the liberators.

Meanwhile on the eastern flank the German 148th Reserve Division delayed the Americans once they were over the Var River. Their task was greatly assisted by the Maritime Alps, which run northward to the Cottian and Graian Alps south of Geneva. The Germans had established defensive positions along the Menton–Sospel–Breil road, the Nice–Ventimiglia highway and the Turini Pass. The division was eventually incorporated into the new 75th Corps tasked with defending north-west Italy and preventing the Allies turning the Italian Front. By 8 September the Americans had pushed west of Nice and reached Menton and the Italian border. The advance then came to a halt as there was some concern that the US 5th and British 8th Armies might drive the Germans out of Italy via the Franco–Italian border.

On 12 September 1944 the victorious Allied forces in southern and northern France linked up at Châtillon-sur-Seine, as de Lattre's forces made contact with General Leclerc's French 2nd Armoured Division, part of Patton's US 3rd Army. Luckily for Blaskowitz, the latter was starved of gasoline in favour of General Montgomery. Patton came to a stop at Verdun and for five days his forces were left kicking their heels just 70 miles from the Rhine.

Chapter 13

Patton's Triumph

Once the Germans were in full flight from France, Patton was spoiling for a fight. Following his dramatic breakout from Normandy he was irked that his 4th and 6th Armored Divisions had been sent west to hem in the German garrisons in Brittany. Securing the well-fortified Breton ports was a job for the infantry divisions, but his tanks ended up facing Brest and Lorient. They would not be ordered east until mid-August, which wasted valuable time when trying to catch the Germans heading for the Seine. After he liberated Rennes, Major General John 'Tiger Jack' Wood, commander of the 4th Armored, tried to persuade General Middleton, his corps commander, and Patton that he was heading in the wrong direction. When he attempted to turn about, Patton threatened him with a court martial.

Both the German Army Group G and 19th Army escaped the south of France as coherent formations. Unfortunately, the French 2nd Armoured Division's actions in liberating Paris helped prolong the war, for the delay round the city enabled a greater part of Army Group G's 1st Army to escape intact over the Rhine. After the collapse in Normandy Field Marshal Walter Model's Army Group B, with four armies, was trying to stabilize the situation defending the region all the way from the North Sea down to Nancy.

The remains of Wiese's command streamed north to join Chevallerie's 1st Army, which was evacuating south-western France and heading for the strategic Belfort Gap, the gateway to Germany just north of the Swiss border. The 11th Panzer Division, conducting a fighting retreat, withdrew to Alsace to defend the Belfort Gap in September. The latter forms the pass between the French Jura and Vosges mountains and the Germans knew that if they lost control of it Strasbourg and all Württemberg to the east would be exposed.

The mountains consist of the High and Low Vosges, divided by the Saverne Gap. The Belfort Gap lies at the southern end of the High Vosges, the main route of approach to the Plain of Alsace. The lynchpin of the High

Vosges is Epinal on the Moselle, which has two major routes through the mountains to Strasbourg and the Rhine and the other to Colmar and the Alsace Plain.

By early September Blaskowitz's 1st Army, now under General Otto von Knobelsdorff, was safely behind the Moselle, and Wiese's 19th Army was holding Army Group G's front from Nancy to the Swiss border. Following Blaskowitz's successful withdrawal from southern France Hitler was convinced of his abilities: he would be the man to oversee a much-needed counter blow in Lorraine. Indeed, Hitler was hoping to decisively counter Patton, who was now spearheading the Allies' eastward drive into Lorraine posing a direct threat to the Siegfried Line or Westwall. However, until General Jacob L. Devers' US 6th Army Group pushing up from the south of France could nip off the remaining bulge formed by the German 19th Army, Patton's left flank was precariously exposed.

Despite the failure of Hitler's foolish Mortain armoured counter-attack, he remained convinced that his panzers could successfully envelop the advancing Allies. This view was based on the German Army's performance on the Eastern Front, where time and time again it had managed to snatch victory from the jaws of defeat, not on the reality of the situation in France where Operations Overlord and Dragoon were backed by overwhelming firepower both on the ground and in the air.

Colonel Hans von Luck, from 21st Panzer Division, a veteran of the brutal fighting in Normandy and around the ancient city of Caen, bumped into General Hasso von Manteuffel in the Vosges on 9 September. In their following discussions Manteuffel did not mince his words:

> The US 6th Army Group, including the French 1st Army is approaching from southern France and is supposed to join up with Patton. The remains of our retreating armies from the Mediterranean and Atlantic coast are ... still holding a wedge that extends as far as Dijon, but for how much longer?
>
> The worst of it is, Hitler is juggling with divisions that are divisions no more. And now Hitler wants to launch a panzer attack from the Dijon area to the north, in order, as he likes to put it, 'to seize Patton in the flank, cut his lines of communication, and destroy him.' What a misjudgement of the possibilities open to us.

Hitler hoped a decisive blow against Patton's advancing tanks would stop him getting into Germany and would prevent Devers' army group from linking up with Bradley's 12th Army Group. To this end he gave his forces in Lorraine priority. In contrast the Allies were now at the end of their supply lines and Allied supreme commander General Dwight Eisenhower's attention was focusing on Operation Market-Garden. This was intended to take Montgomery's 21st Army Group through the Netherlands and over the Rhine. Operations in the south were now just an unwanted distraction, though Patton was constantly calling for more fuel and ammunition in order to press on.

Hitler's forces in Lorraine were on the whole under strength and of poor quality. Only the 16th Infantry Division with about 7,000 men was worthy of any note, the rest had been mauled in the fighting during the summer or were newly-raised Volksgrenadier divisions, which were of questionable value. In contrast Patton's divisions were largely up to strength and eager to fight. It was apparent Hitler needed to act quickly or lose the initiative. Gathering a number of newly-raised panzer brigades he planned to surround Patton using the battered 5th Panzer Army, which had only just recently escaped from the chaos of Normandy. Also General Blaskowitz was ordered to commit his only armoured division, the veteran 11th Panzer that was defending the Belfort Gap.

Hitler, as always obsessed with counter-attacking when such action was simply not feasible, felt that the bridgehead west of Dijon would not only provide a haven for 64th Corps but also provide a jump-off point for an attack on Patton's southern front. Looking at his situation reports, Blaskowitz doubted the counter-attack could succeed, while the ability to hold until 64th Corps arrived was of even greater concern. However, he knew that Hitler's orders could not be ignored and on 4 September instructed 47th Panzer Corps into the Neufchâteau region. This though proved impossible in the face of attacks by the US 12th and 20th Corps.

Now under von Manteuffel, 5th Panzer Army was redeployed from Belgium to Alsace-Lorraine. The counter-attack was initially to involve three panzergrenadier divisions, 3rd, 15th (brought up from Italy) and 17th SS (from Normandy) and the newly raised Panzer Brigades 111, 112 and 113. They were to be supported by elements of the Panzer Lehr,

11th and 21st Panzer Divisions and the new Panzer Brigades 106, 107 and 108. On paper this seemed a credible force.

In total Blaskowitz and Manteuffel were able to muster at most about 350 tanks, amounting to barely three weak panzer divisions or a panzer corps, hardly sufficient for Hitler's optimistic plans. Against these Patton could field 1,122 M4 Shermans and M10 and M18 tank destroyers. In addition, 19th Army had just 165 artillery pieces; the rest lay scattered about southern France. Hitler's two generals could see only one outcome.

Manteuffel's army was far from reconstructed following its defeat in Normandy. The panzer forces were in a poor state, for example the 17th SS Panzergrenadier Division had been boosted with reinforcements from units as far away as the Balkans and Denmark. It was able to field just four Panzer IVs and twelve StuG III assault guns. The 21st Panzer Division had also been mauled in Normandy and could only muster a few assault guns.

While the 11th Panzer Division was regarded as the best armoured unit in the region, it had lost a number of its tanks during its withdrawal from the south. For the Lorraine offensive it would be able to field about fifty panzers, over half of which were Panthers. However, it would have to redeploy before it could have any bearing on the fighting. In contrast the 3rd and 15th Panzergrenadier Divisions were in good order and up to strength. The former had a battalion of assault guns and the latter could field thirty-six Panzer IVs, while both also had had a battalion of powerful Panzer IV/70 tank destroyers.

While the Nazi weapons factories alleviated the critical shortage of panzers on the Western Front following Falaise, there was little Hitler could do about his complete lack of experienced tank crews. Furthermore, his senior generals could see little point in raising new panzer brigades when the replacement panzers would have been better issued to the existing depleted panzer divisions.

Instead the bulk of these new panzer brigades were raised from units that had been destroyed when the Red Army crushed Army Group Centre in Operation Bagration in June 1944. For example, Panzer Brigade 106 was created around the tattered remnants of Panzergrenadier Division Feldherrnhalle. Also the first batch of brigades only consisted of single tank battalions. Again it was felt by some that the Eastern Front veterans would be better assimilated into existing units rather than new stand-alone brigades.

With the Allies preoccupied in the south of France, Hitler knew he need not worry about the Italian front. In fact, Field Marshal Kesselring was directed to relinquish his 3rd and 15th Panzergrenadier Divisions to France and the Hermann Göring Panzer Division to Poland. The two panzergrenadier units would form the core of Hitler's opposition to Patton's US 3rd Army push on the Upper Meuse.

Just as the Americans were losing momentum, Hitler planned to stop the US 3rd and 7th armies linking up by cutting off those forces pushing toward the Belfort Gap. This was to be done by a counter-attack from Pontalier toward Plateau de Langres scheduled for 12 September. In the event, with American tanks converging on Dijon these plans were quickly derailed. Also American military activity in the Nancy area soon thwarted Hitler's plans for an armoured counter-attack in Lorraine as Blaskowitz struggle to contain the US Army spilling over the Moselle. Although Hitler's counter-attack was intended to cut off the US 3rd Army, Blaskowitz's was more concerned that it prevent an American wedge between his 1st and 19th Armies.

Nancy was the lynchpin and in the subsequent fighting for the city, Blaskowitz was forced to commit his available armoured forces. Between Metz to the north and Nancy lay the 3rd and 17th SS Panzergrenadier Divisions respectively, while the 553rd Volksgrenadiers defended Nancy itself. Just to the south were deployed the 15th Panzergrenadiers, then Panzer Brigade 112, 21st Panzer and Panzer Brigade 111. Panzer Brigade 113 along with 11th Panzer was near Belfort.

Under mounting pressure, it was not long before Blaskowitz and Manteuffel were falling out. The 5th Panzer Army had to share control of the front with Blaskowitz's 1st and 19th Armies, causing administrative headaches for von Knobelsdorff and Wiese. When Manteuffel visited Blaskowitz on 11 September both knew Hitler's plans were absolute nonsense. General Walter Botsch, 19th Army's Chief of Staff, described their remaining troops as 'badly battered weak units and security forces, very poorly equipped with artillery and anti-tank material and in no position to resist the enemy'. Blaskowitz had no choice but to seek authorization to withdraw toward the Vosges Mountains.

In addition, the US 1st Army was bearing down on the German city of Aachen, causing Field Marshal von Rundstedt to redirect all available forces including Panzer Brigades 107 and 108. This meant that a third of the panzer brigade counteroffensive force was lost already. Rundstedt after being sacked over Normandy had found himself reappointed as CinC West in early September to try and stop the rot.

In the meantime, Panzer Brigade 106 was smashed attempting to prevent the Americans from reaching the Moselle on 8 September. Two days later the US 4th Armored Division and 35th 'Sante Fe' Infantry Division crossed the river south of Nancy in the face of fierce resistance by the 15th Panzergrenadiers. The next day the US 80th 'Blue Ridge' Infantry Division crossed to the north of the city and on 13 September they were counter-attacked by the 3rd Panzergrenadiers with ten assault guns. That day Blaskowitz gave the order to start evacuating Nancy, now that his defences had been ruptured, with the 553rd Volksgrenadier Division covering the withdrawal.

Elements of General Leclerc's French 2nd Armoured then crushed Panzer Brigade 112, south-west of Nancy and north-west of Belfort, at Dompaire on 13 September. His Combat Command Langlade, slipping between Kampfgruppe Ottenbacher and the German 16th Infantry Division, took control of the high ground overlooking Dompaire. Following an American air strike Panzer Brigade 112's Panthers were hemmed in on three sides. German reinforcements in the shape of forty-five Panzer IVs from Panzer Regiment 2112 almost threatened to trap one of the French battle groups.

Luckily a French roadblock formed by armour and anti-tank guns beat off German reinforcements and by the end of the day the panzer brigade had lost thirty-four Panthers and the panzer regiment twenty-eight Panzer IVs. In total Panzer Brigade 112 was reduced from ninety tanks to just twenty-one and suffered 1,350 killed and wounded; the survivors were placed under 21st Panzer. Blaskowitz and Manteuffel had now lost four panzer brigades before their counteroffensive had even started. The 5th Panzer Army was left with just two panzer brigades – the writing was clearly on the wall for Hitler's Lorraine operations.

Blaskowitz was well aware that he could not completely defy Hitler's plan to strike Patton's 3rd Army's southern flank, but the reality was that he no longer controlled the advanced bridgehead assembly area nor had sufficient armoured units to mount such an operation. On 14 September he let Rundstedt know that the proposed offensive by 5th Panzer Army was simply impossible, however he could counter-attack east of the Moselle river. Also

Blaskowitz was of the view that Metz would provide a good rallying point and as a strongpoint would hold Patton up until mid-December.

With the remaining German garrison at Nancy under threat of encirclement by the US 4th Armored, Blaskowitz threw the 3rd and 15th Panzergrenadiers into the counter-attack. They suffered heavy casualties and the US 80th 'Blue Ridge' rolled into the city on 15 September. Task Force Sebree from the US 35th Infantry Division also entered the city and found that the Germans had abandoned it.

When Manteuffel's delayed counteroffensive finally got underway on 18 September, Panzer Brigade 113 ran straight into the Americans at Lunéville south-east of the city and was forced to disengage. The brigade was then redirected to attack towards Arracourt east of Nancy along with Panzer Brigade 111, though the latter became lost. That night Blaskowitz ordered Manteuffel to continue the attack in the morning, 'without regard to the losses already suffered or the crippled condition of the 113 Panzer Brigade'. Manteuffel, thinking of his troops, branded the attack, 'an outright waste of men and material', knowing that Blaskowitz was sticking slavishly to the dictates of Hitler and his high command. In his chance meeting with Manteuffel, veteran Hans von Luck had damned Hitler's plan to attack Patton's flank as, 'senseless, unrealistic' and 'illusory'.

During 19 September Patton's tanks and artillery knocked out forty-three panzers, but Blaskowitz instructed Manteuffel to persist with the futile attack the following day. General von Mellenthin recalled, 'Our Panthers were superior to the American Shermans, but the enemy had very strong artillery and anti-tank support, and when the fog lifted enjoyed all the benefits of overwhelming air power. The German attack cost nearly fifty tanks and achieved nothing.'

Despite Blaskowitz's orders Panzer Brigade 113 did little and 111 committed only a few companies to the fighting. There was now a danger that Patton would indeed drive a wedge between 5th Panzer Army and 1st Army and force its way to the Rhine. Blaskowitz held Manteuffel responsible for this mess, while the latter blamed the poor performance on the inexperienced panzer brigade crews. Hitler was so angry that his new panzer force had been squandered to no affect he sacked the unfortunate commander of Army Group G.

Despite successfully extricating Army Group G from the French Riviera, Hitler held Blaskowitz personally responsible for the failure of his panzer offensive in Lorraine. At Hitler's HQ General von Mellenthin recalled,

> In a voice ringing with indignation Hitler severely criticised the way Blaskowitz had commanded his forces, and reproached him with timidity and lack of offensive spirit. In fact he seems to have thought that Blaskowitz could have taken Patton's Third Army in the flank and flung it back to Reims.

Hitler was deluded if he thought Blaskowitz had the resources to achieve such a feat. The German Army Personnel Office recorded, 'When it became apparent that the retreat actions and measures taken by Army Group G were not in accordance with the way Hitler expected it to be, Hitler ordered Colonel General Blaskowitz … relieved.' Mellenthin was appalled by the ungrateful treatment handed out to Blaskowitz and saw darker forces at work,

> He had just extricated his army group from the south of France under extremely difficult conditions, but his offence was that he had quarrelled with Himmler, first in Poland and recently in Alsace. Like so many others, Blaskowitz was made a scapegoat for the gross blunders of Hitler and his entourage.

Blaskowitz was sent home to Dresden and his wife later wrote to relatives saying, 'Hans is now at home, planting cabbages'.

By 25 September 11th Panzer Division had arrived, but with the new panzer brigades cut to pieces, Manteuffel could only muster fifty tanks. For the attack north of Arracourt that day 11th Panzer only had sixteen panzers and two regiments of panzergrenadiers, but fought on for another four days against the US 4th Armored Division. The 559th Volksgrenadiers were also obliged to renew their attack against the US 35th Infantry Division.

The remains of Panzer Brigade 111 were assigned to 11th Panzer, 112 to 21st Panzer and 113 to the 15th Panzergrenadiers. Patton's US 3rd Army had now gone over to the defensive and American withdrawals enabled Manteuffel to occupy Juvelize and Coincourt east of Arracourt. German attacks on 27 September to take Hills 318 and 293 ultimately ended in failure despite the best efforts of 11th Panzer, with the loss of twenty-three panzers.

By the end of the month the confused fighting in Lorraine between Patton's forces and General Balck's Army Group G had become a general stalemate. Nonetheless, from an overall force of 616 panzers and assault guns committed in Lorraine only 127 remained operational, though another 148 were repairable. Balck visited von Rundstedt at Bad Kreuznach on 29 September and informed him that Army Group G needed a minimum of 140 panzers, as well as artillery, otherwise all its offensive operations would rapidly come to a standstill.

Von Rundstedt made it clear that Hitler was currently preoccupied with Aachen and Arnhem and that there would be no reinforcements. In response Balck instructed Manteuffel to break off his attacks and withdraw the exhausted 11th Panzer in order to husband his dwindling resources. Thus ended Hitler's ill-fated and ill-conceived attempts to cut off Patton's armoured spearhead.

With Hitler's withdrawing armies being pressed from the west and the south, his only remaining escape route from southern France lay in the network of roads and rail lines located in the 15-mile wide Belfort Gap, between the Vosges Mountains to the north and the Jura Mountains to the south-east. Since the days of the Roman Empire this had formed a strategic corridor connecting the Paris basin to the Rhine Valley.

This area also holds the principal tributary of the Rhône, namely the headwaters of the Saone-Doubs River. The latter's river valley formed the natural route that General Patch's US 7th Army would have to follow north. The French Resistance also appreciated the region was ideal for a guerrilla activity as the hilly and heavily forested countryside crisscrossed with numerous streams and rivers, provided ideal locations for ambushes and other acts of sabotage.

Blaskowitz was granted a much-needed breathing space while the Americans and French regrouped. This gave him time to create an effective defensive line. General Wiese recalled, 'It was an enigma to the Army, why the enemy did not execute the decisive assault on Belfort between 8 and 15 September 1944 through a large scale attack.' The tired American and French troops lost their window of opportunity.

After landing in the French Riviera on 15 August 1944 the advance of the seven divisions of General Jean de Lattre de Tassigny's French 1st Army and the fourteen divisions of Patch's US 7th Army was very swift. Bypassing Toulon and Marseilles, the lead elements of 7th Army had reached Grenoble by the 22nd with the objective of linking up with elements of Patton's US 3rd Army near Dijon and pressing eastward down the Belfort Gap. It was now up to General Wiese's 19th Army to bar the way to the encroaching enemy. Blaskowitz had hoped and intended that Wiese should form a loose cordon that would permit the remaining elements of his depleted Army Group G to retreat safely north-eastward into the Belfort Gap.

Apart from 11th Panzer, most of Wiese's combat forces were essentially improvised kampfgruppen or battle groups made up of the remnants of his infantry divisions and fleeing rear-echelon units. To help bolster his army, the German high command ordered the 30th Waffen-SS Division to France for anti-partisan duties. This arrived in Strasbourg on 18 August with instructions to hold the entrance to the Belfort Gap and counter any French units operating in the area.

On 1 September the headquarters of the French 1st Corps was established at Aix to command troops as a subordinate corps of the French 1st Army. It was now under the command of the able Lieutenant General Émile Béthouart, a veteran of the 1940 campaign in Norway and who had aided the Allied landings in French North Africa in November 1942. The corps' main component divisions were colonial formations consisting of the 2nd Moroccan Infantry Division, the 4th Moroccan Mountain Division, the 9th Colonial Infantry Division and the 1st Armored Division. All these units had been forged in the fire of war.

In the south the French Army also had two further divisions available. The French 2nd Armoured Division, formed 1 May 1943, was re-designated 5th Armoured Division on 16 July 1943 (thus allowing 2nd Free French Division to convert to 2nd Armoured) in North Africa. Originally comprising a tank brigade and a support brigade, the 5th Armoured was re-equipped and reorganized to American standards with three combat commands, which were detached to support French infantry divisions. The French 3rd Algerian Infantry Division was created in Algeria on 1 May 1943 from elements of the Constantine Division of the garrison of French North Africa. It moved to Italy in December 1943 and campaigned as far north as Siena as part of the French Expeditionary Corps, then withdrew to prepare for the landing in southern France.

General de Lattre's French 1st Corps was counter-attacked west of Belfort along the Doubs River by German forces in the Montbeliard area on 8 September and the French were driven back. Also that day the German 1st Army returned to Blaskowitz's control and his command became a full Army Group once again. This though was simply a formality as most of the units earmarked for Hitler's planned counter-attack came from 1st Army anyway.

The Allies' logistic situation was improving by early November, coinciding with orders from Eisenhower, now in charge of all Allied forces in northwestern Europe, calling for a broad offensive all along the entire French front. In the meantime, the inactivity of the French 1st Corps misled Hitler into believing they were digging in for the winter and he reduced his forces in the Belfort Gap to a single understrength infantry division.

To the north Patton, with a three-to-one superiority in men, eight to one in tanks and a huge superiority in artillery, struck on 8 November between Nancy and Metz with all the force he could muster. Although the Germans were taken by surprise the bad weather slowed Patton's advancing armour. The 11th Panzer Division counter-attacked two days later claiming thirty American tanks. Rescuing the shaken 559th Volksgrenadier Division, it withdrew on Morhange. The panzers counter-attacked again on the 12 November capturing an entire American battalion. Although the Germans abandoned Morhange, Patton was forced to call a halt. On the night of 17/18 November the German 1st Army withdrew, leaving the ill-equipped 10,000-strong Metz garrison to its fate. The last of the city's forts did not surrender until 13 December.

The French attacked the Belfort Gap on 13 November 1944, killing the commander of the 198th Infantry Division near the front lines while the commander of the 4th Luftwaffe Field Corps narrowly escaped capture. Six days later French armour pushed through the Belfort Gap and reached the Rhine River at Huningue. The defenders were split into isolated pockets, particularly Belfort itself and troops of the 2nd Moroccan, 9th Colonial and 1st Armoured Divisions were able to move through the German lines.

Meanwhile, Leclerc's French armour rolled into Strasbourg on 24 November. At that point the German 308th Grenadier-Regiment was trapped, forcing its men to surrender or intern themselves in Switzerland. The following day

1st Corps liberated both Mulhouse, taken by a surprise armoured drive and Belfort was assaulted by the Moroccans. General de Lattre, appreciating that the Germans were conducting an almost entirely static defence, directed both his corps to advance on Burnhaupt in the southern Vosges Mountains to encircle the German 63rd Corps (formerly 4th Luftwaffe Corps). By 28 November this operation had been completed, capturing over 10,000 German troops and crippling 63rd Corps. French losses were such that plans to clear the Alsatian Plain had to be shelved while both sides reorganized for the next round of bloodletting.

Chapter 14

Hell's Highway and Beyond

In planning Operation Market-Garden Montgomery, normally a cautious general, showed uncharacteristic boldness with his narrow-front thrust through the Netherlands. In particular, he chose to ignore the intelligence about the presence of Lieutenant General 'Willi' Bittirch's battered SS panzer divisions. Monty surmised what threat could these exhausted units pose? Market-Garden was simplicity itself and therein laid its flaw. Market, the airborne element, employing four divisions of the Allied 1st Airborne Army, was to seize the bridges at Einhoven, Son and Vehgel (US 101st), Grave and Nijmegen (US 82nd) and Arnhem and Osterbeek (British 1st plus Polish 1st Parachute Brigade), with the airlifted 52nd (Lowland) Infantry Division securing Deelem on Day Five. This airborne assault was to involve 34,600 airborne troops delivered by a combination of parachute and glider.

On the ground, carrying out the Garden element, Lieutenant General Brian Horrocks' British 30th Corps, with the Guards Armoured Division (comprising an armoured and a mechanized infantry brigade), was to barge its way up Highway 69 (which for reasons that were soon to become apparent was to re-dubbed 'Hell's Highway') followed by the 43rd Wessex and 50th Northumbrian Infantry Divisions. The Guards had come ashore in Normandy in late June and had subsequently experienced a severe hammering along with 11th Armoured during Monty's ill-fated Operation Goodwood. Horrocks' 30th Corps was flanked by 12th and 8th Corps respectively.

In theory Horrocks' tanks were to reach Einhoven on Day One, Nijmegen on Day Two and Arnhem by Day Four. He was not altogether too happy about the timetable. 'The country was wooded and rather marshy which made any flanking operation impossible. The only thing I could do was blast my way down the main road on a comparatively narrow front with as much air and artillery support as I could get.' British 1st Airborne would end up on its own for ten gruelling days thanks to Bittrich's efforts.

There is no disputing that Market-Garden was a potentially decisive plan intended to capitalize on the Germans' apparent disarray. The 1st Airborne Division had been held back on D-Day and was now chaffing at the bit to have a go. Unfortunately, the bulk of 1st Airborne landed around Arnhem by 1400 hours on 17 September 1944 in complete ignorance of the presence of the SS armour. Bittrich and his 2nd SS Panzer Corps learned of the British airborne drop five minutes after it started. He immediately called for the bridges at Nijmegen and Arnhem to be brought down to stop them falling into enemy hands, but Field Marshal Model refused, claiming that they would be needed for the counter-attack. Following some initial confusion Bittrich's two divisions quickly cobbled together various kampfgruppen or battle groups.

The US 101st Airborne achieved the majority of its objectives by 1600 hours on the 17th with 501st Parachute Infantry Regiment securing the road and rail bridges at Heeswijk and Veghel, 502nd PIR the St Oedenrode bridge, though at Son, the road bridge was brought down before the 506th PIR could secure it and at another bridge south of Best they were turned back. The 82nd's 508th and 505th Parachute Infantry established defensive positions either side of Groesbeek village, while the 504th took Grave Bridge. Unfortunately, two of the three bridges over the Maas–Waal Canal were blown. American paratroopers were sent into Nijmegen to reconnoitre the bridge across the River Waal but were halted in their tracks by Kampfgruppe Henke.

At 1400 hours on 17 September, over 400 guns of Horrocks' 30th Corps opened, fire to support the initial advance of the Irish Guards battle group on a front just two tanks wide, with infantry from the 231st Brigade, 50th (Northumbrian) Division. The 12th Corps under Lieutenant General N M Ritchie attacked north with the 15th (Scottish) Division and 53rd (Welsh) Division striking the Germans' Kampfgruppe Chill. Horrocks' initial breakthrough went well, with the dazed Kampfgruppe Walther being unable to withstand the blasting it received.

'To start with everything seemed to be going our way,' recalled Horrocks. 'But suddenly nine of the Irish Guards' tanks were knocked out almost all at once and a furious battle began in the woods in front of me.' The Guards' tanks managed to break out of their Meuse-Escaut canal bridgehead and rolled into the Netherlands an hour later. They then ran into elements of two battalions of the 9th SS and two German parachute battalions.

These were pushed aside but crucially 30th Corps only covered half the anticipated distance. By 1930 hours the Guards Armoured Division was stalled at Valkenswaard.

The 9th SS, although preparing to transit home, quickly sent its reconnaissance battalion south over the Arnhem highway bridge toward Nijmegen. Another battle group sped westward toward Oosterbeek where most of 1st Airborne was located; this would prevent reinforcements reaching those British paratroops already in Arnhem. To avoid losing them, SS-Lieutenant Colonel Walter had removed the tracks and wheels from some of his vehicles and deliberately reported them unserviceable, so it was not until late afternoon that sufficient numbers of tanks were battle ready. The following day the 9th SS reconnaissance battalion, leaving a few self-propelled guns to guard the southern approaches of Nijmegen bridge, headed north to Elst. A column of twenty-two vehicles then attempted to force a crossing of Arnhem bridge, the northern end of which was by now firmly in British hands, half were destroyed and the SS were driven off amidst a blaze of gunfire.

The 10th SS was despatched to Nijmegen to hold the main bridges against the Guards' advancing armour, this was key to isolating and destroying the paratroops at Oosterbeek west of Arnhem. However, with Arnhem bridge in British hands the bulk of the 10th SS was obliged to use the ferry at Pannerden eight miles south-east of Arnhem. Twelve Panthers reached the Nijmegen area and Arnhem bridge was finally secured on 20 September.

'It was 1100 hours on the morning of Thursday 21 September,' according to Geoffrey Powell, a company commander with 4 Para Brigade, 'before the Irish Guards received orders to break through to Arnhem Bridge ... Waiting for them were German infantry, by now well dug-in and supported by tanks and SP guns.' Unfortunately, they did not move off until 1230 hours (19 hours after the capture of Nijmegen road bridge) and within twenty minutes had lost three tanks blocking the highway.

'For three days now,' recalled Powell, 'the dogged resistance of Brigadeführer Harmel's SS troops, fighting in the Betuwe between Nijmegen and Arnhem, had slowed the pace of the British advance.' To the south the Panthers of Kampfgruppe Walther attacked toward Veghel between Eindhoven and Nijmegen on the 22nd. The 9th SS reinforced by Heavy Panzer Battalion 506 consisting of some sixty powerful King Tigers set about eliminating the defenders at Oosterbeek. Luckily for the paras these attacks were not very well coordinated.

The 10th SS were eventually forced back, so Bittrich sent forty-five Tigers and a company of Panthers to reinforce them, following the landing of the Polish 1st Parachute Brigade at Driel south of Oosterbeek. Geoffrey Powell noted, 'defeated at Nijmegen, the 10th SS Panzer Division had retired towards Arnhem and was now waiting for 30th Corps' next move'. The continually delayed British tanks struggling north along the single exposed road, under constant counter-attack, could simply not get through and on 26th the decision was taken to evacuate the exhausted paratroops trapped at Oosterbeek. The SS had lost 3,300 casualties, including 1,100 dead in the fighting. The British 1st Airborne Division at the start of the operation numbered just over 10,000, only 2,163 escaped back across the Rhine, leaving behind 1,485 dead and 6,414 captured.

While the Allies managed to seize eight of the crossings, the failure to secure the ninth at Arnhem, thanks to the presence of Bittrich's panzers, meant the failure of Montgomery's laudable plan. His fundamental objective had been to force the Maas and Rhine in one bound, but the presence of the SS ensured that he failed. Total Allied losses for the operation were in excess of 17,000 while the Germans lost up to 10,000 troops. Horrocks, not Monty, got the blame for not acting with enough urgency.

Although the British 11th Armoured Division liberated Antwerp on 4 September 1944, the Germans remained firmly dug in along the vital Scheldt Estuary to the west. Once the British were in the city the German 15th Army fell back to a fortified bridgehead at the mouth of the Scheldt estuary, thereby blocking the approach to the port. It would take the Allies almost two months of heavy fighting to secure it and the Scheldt, in the meantime much-needed supplies had to rumble across Europe from the French ports by truck. While the armour of the British 2nd Army was preparing itself for Operation Market-Garden the Canadian 1st Army was given the task of driving the Germans from the estuary.

The Canadian 4th Armoured Division was instructed to clear the south shore around the Breskens Pocket and drive along the Ghent-Terneuzen Canal on 21 September. The Polish 1st Armoured Division struck north of Antwerp and along the Dutch-Belgian border. The Canadian tanks had to fight their way over the Ghent, Leopold and Schipdonk Canals suffering heavy casualties. The Poles succeeded in taking Terneuzen and clearing the south bank of the Scheldt east toward Antwerp.

Following the failure of Market-Garden, opening the Scheldt to Allied shipping became a priority. The Canadians focused on the neck of the South Beveland peninsula. Their 4th Armoured Division attacked north of the Leopold Canal and captured Bergen-op-Zoom; this was followed by fighting to reduce the Breskens Pocket, advance down the South Beveland peninsula and secure the island of Walcheren. Amphibious landings were carried out in two parts on 1 November and five days later the island's capital Middleburg was taken. German resistance ended on 8 November.

The defensive obstacles presented by northern Europe's rivers meant that by late 1944 the British Army was integrating increasing numbers of new amphibious vehicles. Up to that point the American Landing Vehicle Tracked (LVT) or Water Buffalo had mainly been employed in the island hopping campaigns in the Pacific against the Japanese, but coming into service in North-West Europe it saw action during the bitter fighting to clear the Scheldt estuary.

During the Scheldt battles 100 Buffaloes striking from Terneuzen helped ensure the south bank was cleared of Germans after an attack turned their eastern flank on 8 October 1944. Working west from Antwerp the Canadian 2nd Corps started to clear the north bank, but ran into difficulty on South Beveland. In response 174 Buffaloes carrying an assault force from the 52nd Lowland Division supported by a squadron of DD tanks crossed the Scheldt on 24 October. Buffaloes were then involved in the capture of Walcheren Island that dominated the mouth of the estuary. In particular, 102 Buffaloes were used to attack Westkapelle on the western end of the island. The town of Middleburg was seized by a Buffalo force from the 11th Royal Tank Regiment.

In the DD tank regiments, the 3-ton trucks were replaced with eighteen wheeled DUKWs and eleven tracked M29C Weasels. The amphibious 6x6 DUKW was a veteran of the campaigns in the Mediterranean and D-Day. The prototype was built around the cab over engine six-wheel-drive GMC military truck with the addition of a watertight hull and a propeller. It was not an armoured vehicle and at 7.5 tons managed just 6.4mph in water or a respectable 50–55mph on land. The DUKW rode the waves well and its bilge pumps meant it could be kept free of water and for ship to shore stores ferrying it was ideal. More than 21,000 DUKWs were manufactured with large numbers supplied to the British Army.

In contrast the British-built Terrapin, intended as a possible DUKW stand-in, was poorly designed in terms of storage and visibility. Also its lack of rear loading ramp restricted its operational usefulness. One member of the 199th General Transport Company, Royal Army Service Corps (RASC) recalled it as slow and cumbersome on both the water and land, with the steering lever making it very difficult to handle. In addition, if one of the two V8 Ford engines broke down the Terrapin was left going round in circles with no way of getting back to the shore without help.

Although 500 Terrapins were ordered in 1943 and it equipped the 1st Assault Brigade of the Royal Engineers, its only notable operational use was during the Scheldt operations. The Terrapin first went into action following the attack from Terneuzen when forty were used to carry stores after most of the Buffaloes had broken down. During the South Beveland attack the follow up force consisted of Buffaloes and twenty-seven Terrapins. Perhaps not surprisingly the improved Terrapin Mk II and the British LVT equivalents, the Argosy and Neptune, never went into production.

Likewise, the American M29C Weasel's main claim to fame in North-west Europe was during the operations in the Scheldt. At the end of April 1944 the US Army Engineer Board summarized:

> From the results of the investigation and test of the M29C Cargo Carrier to determine its suitability for Engineer use, it is concluded that this special purpose amphibious vehicle has high cross coun-try mobility and is particularly suited for operation over swampy, muddy, and extremely rough terrain for crossing small bodies of calm water; it is suitable for the same general applications in swamp, jungle, or rough terrain for which the ¼-ton 4x4 truck or the ¾-ton weapons carrier is used under average conditions . . .

Issued to the British Army under Lend-Lease in late 1944 the Weasel formed part of the establishment of those regiments equipped with Buffaloes. For the attack on Walcheren a whole platoon of the 259th General Transport Company, RASC, operated Weasels supporting the 52nd Lowland Division. Nearly seventy M29Cs were used in the assault on Walcheren on 1 November 1944.

Hitler's surprise winter offensive in the Ardennes commenced on 16 December 1944 under the cover of heavy cloud and snow that kept the enemy fighter-bombers at bay. The 1st SS and 12th SS Panzer Divisions launched the 6th SS Panzer Army's main thrusts. Their spearhead formed by Kampfgruppe Peiper drawn from 1st SS consisted of 100 Panzer IVs and Panthers, about forty formidable Tiger IIs and twenty-five assault guns. In addition, Otto Skorzeny's Panzer Brigade 150's three kampfgruppen were also assigned to the 1st SS and 12th SS Panzer and the 12th Volksgrenadier Division.

Directly in the line of 12th SS Panzer's northern attack was the Elsenborn ridge. It was here that the Germans were halted dead in their tracks by the US Army and the panzers singularly failed to contribute to the huge bulge cut into the Allied lines further south. The defending US 99th Infantry Division were well dug in and their artillery and anti-tank guns played havoc with the German advance. It also forced Kampfgruppe Pieper further south and south-east of Elsenborn the 1st SS Panzer Division was held up. Key amongst the American anti-tank units were elements of the 612th Tank Destroyer Battalion equipped with towed 3in guns around Höfen.

Alarm was caused when a reconnaissance tank company from Kampfgruppe Peiper's spearhead threatened Wirtzfeld on 17 December. Occupation of Wirtzfeld and the twin villages of Krinkelt-Rocherath would roll up the 2nd and 99th Infantry Divisions from the flank. If Peiper reached Bütgenbach and moved north to Elsenborn the two divisions would be caught in the rear completely unhinging the American defences and trapping up to 30,000 men. With the panzers making for Bullingen, the Americans set up an improvised defence south of Wirtzfeld with clerks, cooks, drivers and military police. They were reinforced by divisional artillery under Brigadier General John H Hinds who deployed a battery of 105mm field guns and another of heavy 155mm howitzers to cover the approaches to Wirtzfeld and Bullingen. The defenders also had some 57mm anti-tank guns and four half-tracks with quad .50-calibre machine guns.

Panzers and armoured half-tracks roared out of the mist on the Bullingen road at about 0800 hours on 17 December and crossed a ridge outside Wirtzfeld to be met by a hail of fire. At this point the Americans received welcome reinforcements in the shape of five self-propelled tank destroyers from the 644th Tank Destroyer Battalion. They destroyed four enemy vehicles in quick succession and the others withdrew to Bullingen.

Near Krinkelt-Rocherath the 12th Volksgrenadiers, supported by 12th SS tanks, set about the 99th Infantry. Even in the face of five Tigers the Americans fell back grudgingly on the twin villages. In front of Rocherath the ground was littered with German dead and seventeen tanks. The streets of Krinkelt-Rocherath became a killing ground for the panzers where they were caught by bazooka teams and hidden tanks and tank destroyers. American artillery and mines also took a toll, often leaving panzers disabled and at the mercy of bazookas. Remarkably, two Shermans claimed five Tigers in Rocherath after the Germans became trapped in the narrow streets.

Nonetheless, tanks of the US 741st Tank Battalion covering the American withdrawal were destroyed by the advancing Panthers. Desperate to drive the Americans from Elsenborn, the Germans threw themselves at Höfen and Monschau only to be stopped by US artillery fire. They renewed their attacks on the twin villages on 18 December supported by Jagdpanthers of the 560th Heavy Anti-tank Battalion. Armed with the 88mm gun they seemed unstoppable. However, Shermans from the 741st Tank Battalion as well as artillery and bazooka fire ensured the panzers did not break through to the open ridgeline. In the meantime, two US infantry divisions moved to reinforce the defenders who withdrew to the ridge.

Switching their emphasis, the 12th SS supported by the 12th Volksgrenadier Division attacked Domäne Butgenbach on the southern end of the ridge on 19 December. Two days later the 12th SS were halted by M36 tank destroyers of the 613th Tank Destroyer Battalion. The last German attack on the right took place on 22 December and was greeted by a devastating 10,000 rounds fired by US artillery. Cole Barnard, a rifleman with the US 11th Armored Division deployed south-west of Bastogne, recalled:

> There are some interesting aspects to the attack and one of them was that Hitler had created a special brigade which would go along with the lead elements of the attack, get behind our lines, and capture the Meuse River bridges so they could hold those until the rest of the troops got up there. This brigade was outfitted with all captured American and British tanks. They had all captured American weapons and were all dressed in American uniforms.

Under Operation Grief, Otto Skorzeny had been personally appointed by Hitler to command Panzer Brigade 150 tasked with capturing the vital Meuse bridges at Amay, Andenne or Huy before they could be demolished. Skorzeny was summoned to Hitler's Rastenburg HQ on 22 October 1994, where he was congratulated on the success of his mission to Hungary and promoted from major to lieutenant-colonel. The Hungarian operation had used several hundred commandos from the 500th SS Parachute Battalion and the Jagdverbande. Skorzeny's coup in Budapest though had hardly been very subtle, as a company of massive Tiger II tanks had backed his seizure of Hungarian dictator Admiral Horthy.

'Stay awhile,' said Hitler. 'I am now going to give you the most important job of your life. In December Germany will start a great offensive that may decide her fate.' He outlined Operation Herbstnebel (Autumn Mist) or Wacht am Rhein (Watch on the Rhine), the forthcoming Ardennes counter-offensive. 'He told me about the tremendous quantity of material which had been accumulated,' noted Skorzeny 'and I recall that he stated we would have 6,000 artillery pieces in the Ardennes, and, in addition, the Luftwaffe would have about 2,000 planes, including many of the new jet planes. He then told me that I would lead a panzer brigade which would be trained to reach the Meuse bridges and capture them intact.'

Despite Skorzeny's repeated complaints, he found himself being supplied with German equipment rather than American. Skorzeny grumbled that 'he had to make up the difference with German vehicles. The only common feature of these vehicles was that they were all painted green, like American military vehicles.' Initially his unit was equipped with five Panther tanks, five assault guns, six German armoured cars and six armoured personnel carriers.

Skorzeny's brigade was supposed to include two companies of panzers and by late November had been supplied with twenty-two Panther tanks and fourteen assault guns with the tank crews provided by the 6th Panzer Division. Panzerjäger crews for the assault guns came from Heavy Panzerjäger Battalion 655 and the armoured car crews came from the reconnaissance battalions of the 2nd Panzer Division and 90th Panzergrenadier Division. When they finally went into battle they only seem to have deployed ten Panthers and five assault guns.

There was simply no way to make a Panther look like a Sherman, so Skorzeny's men ingeniously opted to make then look like the Sherman's tank destroyer cousin, the M10 Wolverine, based on a Sherman chassis but with a much more angular hull and turret. To do this the Panthers were disguised with sheet metal, painted olive green and given prominent white five-pointed American recognition stars. These Skorzeny cynically noted were only sufficient to, 'deceive very young American troops seeing them at night from very far away'.

Once Hohes Venn was reached, Skorzeny's three kampfgruppen were to pass round their assigned units, but things did not run smoothly and they got horribly tangled up at Losheim. Skorzeny realized by the evening of the second day of the offensive that Panzer Brigade 150 would simply not reach the Meuse bridges, so he suggested that his unit serve as a regular combat force. Under the direction of Colonel Wilhelm Mohnke he was ordered to help take Malmédy to open up the roads to reach Kampfgruppe Peiper.

Although the Germans destroyed 300 American tanks, Eisenhower countered Hitler's offensive by moving the US 7th Armored Division to St Vith and elements of the 10th Armored and US 101st Airborne Divisions to Bastogne. The Panzer Lehr Division was not quick enough and the GIs beat them to the town. Although the 116th Panzer Division slipped between Bastogne and St Vith, Bastogne's defenders held up 2nd Panzer. St Vith fell on 21 December but heavy American artillery fire forced the two Panzer armies to become ever more entangled.

All three of Skorzeny's battle group joined 1st SS Panzer and were thrown into the attack on Malmédy on the 21st. However, any chance of his kampfgruppen achieving surprise was lost after one of his men was captured the day before and spilled the beans. To make matters worse Skorzeny's planned attack lacked artillery support to soften up the defenders or conduct counter-battery fire when the American artillery inevitably retaliated. Luftwaffe fighter cover was also completely out of the question.

Predictably, Hauptmann Scherff and Kampfgruppe Y were met by such heavy shelling that he quickly broke off his assault. This was not the covert operation he had planned and trained for. On the left Willi Hardieck's Kampfgruppe X attacked with two companies of infantry supported by five fake M10 tank destroyers. They pushed from Ligneuville, through Bellevaux and along the Route de Falize striking west of Malmédy. The main force headed toward the Warche River bridge and Rollbahn C. Trip-wire flares illuminating the early morning gloom quickly alerted the American defenders and the fake M10s ran into a minefield and the 823rd Tank Destroyer Battalion command post, which was quickly surrounded and attacked.

Skorzeny watched from the hill on the Route de Falise as one of his fake M10s supported by German infantry attack toward Malmédy, but it was driven off by an American anti-tank gun. The other nine tanks attempted to capture a bridge over the Warch in order to reach Stavelot, but the first tank was lost to a mine and began to burn. American infantry manning a road-block were forced back, but when the Germans attempted to cross the bridge GIs armed with bazookas knocked out two more tanks. Two American tank destroyers then accounted for two further German tanks.

Seeing how things were progressing, Skorzeny ordered his men to fall back, but none of his remaining armour made it. One fake M10 coded B5 was disabled at Malmédy, another, B10, crashed into the café at La Falize. B7 got as far at the Ambléve Bridge at Malmédy but was brought to a halt by US bazooka fire. Several sturmgeschütz in American markings were knocked out at Géromont. A knocked-out snow-covered Sherman, belonging to the 5th Parachute Division, photographed outside the Hotel des Ardennes epitomised the failure of Hitler's Operation Grief. Skorzeny's fake Shermans had got him nowhere, 2nd Panzer got closer to the Meuse than special Panzer Brigade 150 ever did.

Chapter 15

Monty to the Rescue

The Battle of the Bulge, as the Ardennes offensive became known, was exactly the type of rough-and-ready scrap that Patton excelled at. Just three days after the German offensive opened, Eisenhower had ordered Patton and his US 3rd Army, comprising the 3rd, 8th and 12th Corps, north to attack the left flank of the German assault. But Patton was already ahead of the game; his 3rd Corps had been ordered to move from Metz to north of Luxembourg. Its 4th Armored Division under Major General Hugh Gaffey moved to Longwy, while 12th Corps' 80th Infantry Division was sent to Luxembourg. Both these tough divisions had most recently seen combat during Patton's push to the Saar River and they were also veterans of Normandy. Gaffey's 4th Armored had seen heavy fighting in Lorraine and Major General McBride's 80th Infantry had fought hard to get over the Moselle River.

Patton's 12th Corps, under Major General Manton Eddy, also included the 4th and 5th Infantry Divisions and the 10th Armored Division (minus Combat Command B in Bastogne), Combat Command A of 9th Armored, plus the 109th Infantry from the 28th Division. The plan was that Major General John Millikin's 3rd Corps would relieve Bastogne. Millikin was told by Patton to, 'Attack in column of regiments and drive like hell.' The only snag was that some of the routes north and the bridges had been destroyed by the Americans to stop the Germans turning south.

General Barton's 4th Infantry were highly experienced. They were D-Day veterans, having landed on Utah Beach. After fighting in Normandy they helped liberate Paris, then penetrated the Siegfried Line on the Schnee Eifel and fought in the Hürtgen Forest. General Irwin's 5th Infantry had arrived in Normandy in July and had suffered heavy losses during the fighting for Metz. In contrast General Morris' 10th Armored were largely greenhorns. His division had not entered the line until late September 1944 in Lorraine in time to take part in the encirclement of Metz and the drive to the Saar.

Patton's H-Hour was 0600 hours on 22 December. The 80th Division moved on Merzig and came into contact with the German 352nd Volksgrenadier Division, which they cut through to reach Heiderscheid and Ettelbruck. This helped take pressure off 4th Armored's thrust to Bastogne by holding up both the 352nd and 79th Volksgrenadier Divisions. On the left the US 26th Infantry Division took Grosbous from the Germans, but was checked at Arsdorf and Rambrouch by the Führer Grenadier Brigade, which consisted of a battalion of Panzer IVs and Panthers, a battalion of panzergrenadiers and a battalion of infantry. The 26th Infantry, commanded by General Willard Paul, had only just been pulled from the line to take in replacements after fighting near Verdun so was nowhere near combat ready.

On the western flank 3rd Corps was led by Combat Command A, 4th Armored, which pushed up the Arlon–Bastogne road, with Combat Command B to the west using the secondary roads. At Martelange Combat Command A were held up by a German parachute company until 23 December, when the village was secured and the bridge over the Sûre repaired.

In contrast Combat Command B had reached Burnon by midday on 22 December, just seven miles south of Bastogne. Here though, they were delayed by more demolition damage and elements of the German 5th Parachute Division. The village was not secured until midnight and heavy resistance was encountered at Chaumont, which was also defended by Luftwaffe fighter aircraft. Some twenty-two Shermans of the US 8th Tank Battalion and supporting infantry moved round the village and, despite a slight thaw that bogged down some of the tanks, captured Chaumont.

General Kokott was not complacent about this threat developing on his left flank and launched a counter-attack, with units from the 11th Assault Gun Brigade and the 39th Grenadier Regiment. This force emerged from the woods to the north of Chaumont and drove down the hill into the village before the Americans could react. Very swiftly sixty-five Americans were killed and eleven Shermans lost. By the end of the day Chaumont was once more in German hands.

That same day, 23 December, the US 35th Tank Battalion, 4th Armored attacked the Germans holding Warnach to the north of Martelange. The village was held by a parachute battalion and a battery of assault guns, which successfully drove off the first assaults. The following day the Americans struck from three sides and once in Warnach fought house to house.

The defenders did not give up easily and counter-attacked, claiming four Shermans and sixty-eight American lives. Once the village was secured the Americans found 135 German dead and a similar number of prisoners. When Bigonville was taken the village yielded 328 German paratroop prisoners.

General Millikin's armoured thrust had been weakened by the efforts of the German 5th Parachute Division, so he then decided to recuperate ready for another go on Christmas Day. In Bastogne McAuliffe was understandably disappointed, but was optimistic 4th Armored would punch its way through. Tintange was taken after a costly struggle, along with Hollange and Chaumont. On the left Remoiville was pounded by four US artillery battalions. When the German defenders who had been keeping their heads down attempted to reach their firing positions they were mown down by American tanks using their machine guns. When the fighting stopped the Americans had captured 327 prisoners.

By 26 December the German 5th Parachute Division was in a precarious position. Its men were slowly being driven from their positions, killed or captured and its artillery was running out of ammunition. At nightfall the Americans reached Homprè just 4,000 yards from Bastogne's defensive perimeter. Early on the 27th Lieutenant Walter Carr led a patrol in but they were not the first.

On Boxing Day Combat Command Reserve fought its way through Remichampagne to the north-west of Chaumont and toward Clochimont. The plan was to hook to the left and through Sibret and on to Bastogne. However, Sibret was defended by the German 26th Reconnaissance Battalion so it was decided to carry straight on up the road through Assenios. This village was held by elements of both the exhausted 5th Parachute and 26th Volksgrenadier Divisions. Fierce fighting followed, but the lead Shermans, under Lieutenant Charles Boggess, reached the US 326th Airborne Engineers at 1650 hours and 20 minutes later Lieutenant Colonel Abrams reported to General McAuliffe. The German siege had been lifted.

On Christmas Day, General Harmon's US 2nd Armored Division, striking south-west from Ciney, had split 2nd Panzer in two in the Celles area. At Foy Notre Dame, just four miles from Dinant, elements of 2nd Armored and the British 3rd Royal Tank Regiment, 29th Armoured Brigade attacked 2nd Panzer's reconnaissance battalion and some of its artillery units. They resisted until they were overrun, losing seven Panthers and 148 prisoners.

In the closing days of December 1944 the fighting around snow covered Bastogne reached its a climax. The 1st SS Panzer and the 167th Volksgrenadiers desperately attempted to sever the American lifeline into the town. To do so they had to cut their way through the US 26th and 35th Infantry Divisions. The latter had gained combat experience in Normandy and had fought to help stop Hitler's Mortain counter-attack, so they knew what to do. The German attacks were driven back by ground fire and air attacks that claimed fifty-five panzers.

Meanwhile the US 11th Armored and 87th Infantry Divisions to the south-west fought to widen the relief corridor. They ran head long into Panzer Lehr and the 26th Volksgrenadiers who had launched a counter-attack. A fierce battle followed with heavy losses on both sides, but eventually the depleted German divisions were forced back to their start line. General Patton drove into Bastogne on 30 December to congratulate McAuliffe and his garrison.

The Battle of the Bulge was to have potentially serious repercussions for the British and the Americans. It was at this point that Montgomery completely overstepped the mark with Eisenhower. He had not been impressed by the Americans' handling of the battle and renewed his call that he should be given operational control not only over his own 21st Army Group, but also the whole of Bradley's 12th Army Group.

Monty's logic was that this chain of command would make it easier to liquidate the German bulge. As always he was thinking of the military implications and not the political ramifications of what he was insisting on. He did not appreciate that to take over at the very point a major Allied counter-attack was launched would be a slur on American military prowess. If Eisenhower agreed, it would be a vote of no confidence in General Bradley's handling of 12th Army Group. Behind the scenes it was common knowledge that while his subordinates had shone, Bradley's leadership had been rather lacklustre.

Monty and the British press had already formed the opinion that he had saved the day. In light of American bravery, tenacity and losses this was an insult that could not be tolerated. Eisenhower, who had always shown the upmost patience and diplomacy with his British allies through some extremely trying times, decided that this was the final straw. He drafted a signal to the Combined Chiefs of Staff saying either Monty went or he would.

Fortunately for Monty, Major General Francis de Guingand, his very able 21st Army Group Chief of Staff, was aware of the mounting tensions and did all he could to defuse the dangerous situation. De Guingand went to see Eisenhower and informed him Monty had no idea of the trouble he was causing and asked for a 24-hour stay of execution. He then flew back to Monty's headquarters and warned his boss that he faced the sack. At this stage of the war the last thing Monty wanted to do was lose his command. In addition, the situation would put Churchill in an impossible position because if he had to sack Monty it would cause an almighty political row in London.

There was no question of Eisenhower being replaced, which meant the war could be delayed while there was a tense stand-off between London and Washington. Fortunately, Monty agreed to sign a message drafted by de Guingand promising full cooperation with Eisenhower and asking for his signal that had caused offence to be destroyed. Eisenhower, ever the diplomat, content that Monty had been contrite, let the whole incident pass. It was lucky that Eisenhower was not a vindictive man.

In the meantime, the Allies completed their plans for a counter-attack in the Ardennes. The intention was to cut the German salient in half at Houffalize, with Hodge's US 1st Army striking south and Patton's US 3rd Army attacking north. They would also swing eastward toward Germany and the Siegfried Line. In order to free up the US 2nd Armored and 84th Infantry Divisions for the attack, General Horrocks' British 30th Corps moved to take up their positions west of the Ourthe. Supported by the British 6th Airborne Division they were to deploy in the Marche area. The paras took over the foxholes of the frozen US 84th Infantry overlooking the German positions.

Horrocks was to move forward toward Houffalize, to the right of the US 7th Corps, with the 6th Airborne on his right and the 53rd Welsh Division to the left. Due to the transfer of the US 1st Army to Monty's command and the criticism of the US conduct of the battle in the British press, there was some grumbling in American circles that Horrocks should be assigned a greater role. Monty though was right to hold him back. 21st Army Group was short of reserves and to extend Horrocks' corps further east would have been foolish.

Hitler though was not done yet and had one final grand but ultimately futile gesture as part of his Ardennes campaign. As the New Year commenced the Luftwaffe belatedly sprang into action. Over 1,000 German planes attacked British and American airfields, successfully destroying

150 aircraft and damaging another 111. Whilst this impressive massed attack came as a surprise, it was too little too late as it had little impact on the fighting on the ground. The Luftwaffe had to call on its air defence units employing experienced and inexperience pilots. In pressing home their raids, the Luftwaffe lost 280 aircraft and several hundred irreplaceable aircrew.

Undeterred, the Allied counter-attacks commenced on 3 January 1945 amidst the snow, mud and fog. The weather once again greatly hindered Allied air support. In the following days frost and heavy snow made for firmer going, but hid German fixed positions and their minefields. In the face of very stiff resistance on the first day 7th Corps managed to advance just two miles. The US 2nd Armored and 84th Infantry secured Beffe and 3rd Armored got to Floret and Malempré. The British 53rd Division drove the enemy toward La Roche, but came up against determined counter-attacks by the 116th Panzer Division.

That day the British 6th Airborne fought all afternoon against Panzer Lehr to take Bures, suffering heavy losses. The following day Panzer Lehr repeatedly counter-attacked but were unable to hold onto Bures. By 7 January 1945 Horrocks' 53rd Division had captured Grimbiemont, just four miles from Marche. The following day his 51st Highland Division took over the attack and by 11 January were in La Roche. A few days later they made contact with Patton's men. By mid-month Horrocks' corps was redeploying north back to 21st Army Group, ready for the battles to clear the west bank of the Rhine from the Ruhr to the Netherlands.

Also by the end of the first week of January the US 84th Infantry had reached Marcouray and 2nd Armored had retaken Dochamps and Baraque de Fraiture. It was now that Hitler had to face up to the reality of the situation, as there was little he could do to cling onto his hard-fought battlefield gains. Reluctantly on 9 January he agreed to the withdrawal of 5th Panzer Army east of the Liege-Bastogne road. It was now that Patton commenced his main attack, employing the US 4th and 6th Armored, 26th, 35th, 87th and 90th Infantry as well as the 17th and 101st Airborne Divisions. The going proved to be a tough struggle against increasingly desperate German units.

The 6th SS Panzer Army was ordered into reserve north of St Vith, though it would take it four days to comply due to Allied air attacks, blocked roads and the weather. German soldiers were not happy with what they saw as favouritism towards the SS units, but it seems to have occurred to few that they were actually destined for the Eastern Front, so were hardly being done any favours by Hitler. Shortly afterwards the US 1st and 3rd Armies linked up in the Ardennes. By 27 January 1945 American lines were back where they started when the Battle of the Bulge first commenced on 16 December 1944.

Hitler's grand plan had all been for nothing. Nevertheless, his Ardennes offensive proved to be a remarkable battle. He had thrown three armies at five US divisions over a 50-mile front, achieving complete surprise. This resulted in an embarrassing breakthrough that left the British and Americans at loggerheads. But Manteuffel and Model never came close to getting to Brussels or Antwerp. Despite some American units being thrown into a state of confusion, ad hoc battle group fought with bravery and distinction on the northern shoulder, at St Vith and Bastogne. This significantly derailed the German timetable.

Hitler severely underestimated the speed of the Allied response and the power of their air forces. Within the space of just four days the Allies reacted by redeploying half a million men to the Ardennes. Once the weather had cleared his forces were at the mercy of Allied fighter-bombers. His own airborne operations were ill-fated. The parachute drop during the attack ended in failure and the Luftwaffe's grand-slam was too late to influence the battle. Hitler also underestimated the terrain over which his armies had to fight. This slowed his advance and crucially delayed his second wave of attack forces.

The US armed forces paid a heavy price for their victory, suffering 8,497 killed, 46,170 wounded and 20,905 missing or captured. German losses were hard to gauge, but it is believed they lost 13,000 dead and 50,000 captured. Other estimates have put German losses in excess of 90,000. The key point was that Hitler's panzer armies, so carefully reconstituted and re-equipped after defeat in Normandy, had been thrown away. Some senior generals argued that they would have been much better used to defend the Rhine and Oder.

Chapter 16

Reichswald to the Rhine

In early 1945 Operation Veritable was an armoured thrust designed to drive the Germans back and occupy the ground between the Maas and Rhine Rivers. This heavily forested region greatly favoured the defenders, as did the soft ground and local floodwaters. Once again this terrain was highly unfavourable for the conduct of massed armoured warfare. Delays in launching the American southern pincer against the Siegfried Line gave the enemy precious time to prepare for the Anglo-Canadian attack. The Germans, whose three lines of defences were anchored on Schottheide, Cleve and Goch, were determined not to give up the west bank of the Rhine, which behind the Reichswald running from Nijmegen to Calcar, was completely flooded.

The Canadian 1st Army was directed to attack along the northern flank, while the British 2nd Army, supported by the Guards and 11th Armoured Divisions, were to punch their way through the Reichswald to the Rhine. The US 9th Army was to conduct Operation Grenade, the southern element of the assault. German formations defending the area were a mixture of infantry and paratroops, the only armoured units in reserve being the battered 116th Panzer and 15th Panzergrenadier Divisions with just ninety tanks between them.

Following the Ardennes offensive in late 1944, the Colmar Pocket, way to the south, unnecessarily distracted Eisenhower's attention. During late January and early February 1945 French and American forces attacked General Siegfried Rasp's 19th Army trapped around Colmar. Although the pocket was sealed by 9 February and the Germans lost 22,000 PoWs, the bulk of 19th Army escaped over the Upper Rhine.

In preparation for the advance of Montgomery's 21st Army Group (Canadian 1st, British 2nd and US 9th Armies), the Allies' air forces sought to sever communications within the German industrial region of the Ruhr and between the Ruhr and the rest of Germany. Significantly these air attacks helped ensure that much of Field Marshal Model's Army Group B, consisting of General Hasso von Manteuffel's 5th Panzerarmee and General Gustav von Zangen's 15th Army, remained trapped in the Ruhr.

On 8 February 1945 Montgomery launched Veritable, one of his usual plodding set-piece battles, thrusting the Canadian 1st Army, under Lieutenant General Sir Henry Crerar, in the Netherlands supported by the British 2nd Army, under Lieutenant General Sir Miles Dempsey, into the Rhineland. The attack by 30th Corps involved three British and two Canadian infantry divisions supported by the Guards Armoured Division. Success relied on surprise and the weather. Massing tanks, other vehicles and guns in the Nijmegen area was no easy feat. General Horrocks recalled, 'Thirty-five thousand vehicles were used to bring up the men and their supplies. One million, three hundred thousand gallons of petrol were required. Five special bridges had to be constructed over the Maas. One hundred miles of road must be made or improved.'

Over 1,000 tanks were gathered for the Reichswald offensive. General Horrocks recalled, 'When the attack was launched, 50,000 troops were on the start line, supported by 500 tanks and some 500 specially adapted tracked vehicles. In addition, there were another 10,000 waiting to advance northeast, in order to secure the left bank, and another 15,000 frontline troops in reserve with over 500 tanks.' In the face of such strength it seemed that the Germans would be simply overwhelmed.

Attacking through the Reichswald Horrocks' 30th Corps came up against General Alfred Schlemm's 1st Parachute Army. The German 84th Division was successfully forced out the way, but fierce resistance was encountered from the 7th Parachute Division. While Horrocks was faced solely by German infantry and tough paratroops he noted, 'It was estimated that the enemy also had three infantry and two panzer divisions in reserve available to intervene rapidly in the battle.'

The forest was not suitable for Horrocks' wheeled vehicles, let alone tracked ones, and there were no east-west roads of any note and there were only two north-south routes. This meant that the tanks were held back leaving the infantry to conduct a major frontal assault following a huge aerial and artillery bombardment. On 9 February, the very day after Veritable commenced, the Germans blew the Roer dam and flooded the valley. It was a desperate act, but the Germans knew it would impede the Allies' armour. The bitter fighting lasted until 21 February culminating in the capture of Goch. This was followed by Operation Blockbuster, which took the Canadians to the Rhine itself. 'From now on the battle developed into a slogging match as we inched our way forward through mud and rain,' recalled Horrocks after the Germans breached the banks of the Rhine upstream. 'Slowly and bitterly we advanced through the mud supported by our superb artillery.'

The Americans hoped to launch Operation Grenade across the Roer to the south, but were delayed for two weeks by the flooding. Eleven days after Veritable commenced, Lieutenant General William H. Simpson pushed his US 9th Army forward from Geilenkirchen to the Rhine around Dusseldorf. At the same time Lieutenant General Alexander M. Patch's US 7th Army advanced to the Upper Rhine. After bitter resistance in the Reichswald had been overcome, the Allies regrouped before pushing on the Hochwald forested ridge and Xanten to the east. Once the Roer floodwaters had gone down the US 9th Army was able to cross the Roer on 23 February. Of those German forces on the west bank of the Rhine 290,000 were captured. Such haemorrhaging of manpower could not go on indefinitely.

By 1945 the Germans, expecting a big Allied push over the Rhine, did everything they could to stiffen the defences of this vast natural barrier. Minefields were strengthened, as were the bunker and trench complexes as well as the gun pits. They assessed the Allies would strike down stream of Emmerich, so General Blaskowitz, commander of Army Group H, deployed the stronger of his two armies the 25th, under General Gunther Blumentritt, there. General Schlemm's battered 1st Parachute Army was left to cover the 45 miles between Emmerich and Duisburg.

'We felt quite a professional affection for these paratroops,' recalled Corporal Wingfield of the 7th Armoured Division. 'They were infantry-trained, liked to use their own initiative. They had the same system of "trenchmates." They fought cleanly and treated prisoners, wounded and dead with the same respect they expected from us. If our uniforms had been the same we would have welcomed them as kindred spirits.' After capturing Xanten on the west bank of the Rhine the brigadier commanding the 43rd Infantry Division ordered his men to salute the defeated fallschirmjäger as they filed past. By mid-February Montgomery was facing the remains of four parachute, three infantry and two panzer or panzergrenadier divisions.

It seemed to the Germans that the Allies' resources and firepower were limitless. They also knew in the back of their minds that continued resistance was increasingly pointless. With the Red Army just 35 miles from Berlin the fighting in the west seemed futile to many senior German officers. Following the German counter-attacks into the Ardennes and Alsace reserves were now exhausted. The remaining mobile reserve consisted of the 47th Panzer Corps with the 116th Panzer Division and the 15th Panzergrenadier Division. These sounded formidable but they could scrape together just thirty-five panzers.

The prognosis for the Germans did not look good. On 23 March Montgomery assessed:

> The enemy has lost the Rhineland, and with it the flower of at least four armies – the Parachute Army, 5th Panzer Army, 15th Army, and 7th Army; 1st Army, farther to the south, is now being added to the list. In the Rhineland battles, the enemy has lost about 150,000 prisoners, and there are many more to come; his total casualties amount to about 250,000 since 8 February.

While Operation Plunder was the key armoured assault across the Rhine, during the Malta Conference Eisenhower announced additional crossings south of the Ruhr. It was as if the Americans were intent on stealing Montgomery's thunder. They launched Operation Lumberjack using Hodge's US 1st Army and Patton's US 3rd Army attacking between Koblenz and Cologne on 1 March 1945. The plan was to barge Model's Army Group B back through the Eifel region to the Rhine. Six days later Hodges met his 7th Corps commander, General Collins, on the Rhine at Cologne. The US 3rd Armored Division drove the remnants of the 9th Panzer Division from the city, but the Hohenzollern Bridge was destroyed before it could be secured or crossed.

More importantly, just an hour to the south armoured Combat Command B of the US 9th Armored Division, supported by elements of the US 78th Infantry Division, reached Remagen at the same time. Dramatically, they seized the Ludendorff Railway Bridge, one of the only remaining spans over the Rhine, before the Germans could blow it up. The Americans had secured a bridgehead two weeks before Montgomery was ready to go. Ironically this bridge had originally been constructed during the First World War to move men and material to the Western Front. The bridge had two railway lines and a footpath, but one line had been boarded over to allow road traffic. The Americans wanted Lieutenant General William H. Simpson's US 9th Army to cross at Urdingen, but Montgomery refused, perhaps smarting that he had lost the opportunity to breach the Rhine defences first.

Ten days after its capture the battered Ludendorff Bridge fell into the Rhine, killing twenty-eight American soldiers. Its loss mattered little as by 21 March the Americans had five pontoon bridges over the Rhine at Remagen. Its capture cost Field Marshal von Rundstedt his job as commander in the West. Albert Kesselring replaced him, but although he was a very able general who had fought with skill in Italy, there was little he could do to restore the deteriorating situation.

On 13 March Patton's 3rd Army crossed the Moselle, then on the night of the 22nd he further stole Montgomery's thunder by throwing the US 5th Infantry Division across the Rhine at Nierstien and Oppenheim southwest of Frankfurt. As part of the preparations the US 249th Engineer Battalion was given special training on the floating Bailey bridge in Trier. 'On 19 March, our headquarters was at Adenau, Germany,' recalled Captain John K. Addison of the 249th, 'where we were alerted to join the engineer task force for the Rhine crossing at Oppenheim. We would man the assault boats for the crossing of the second wave of the 5th Infantry Division, to be followed with the construction of the heavy pontoon bridge.'

German resistance to the crossing was negligible. 'Our engineer work went off like clockwork,' adds Captain Addison, 'although one raft was sunk, two of our men were lost, and as many as 200 Germans drowned. The sinking was caused by the sudden shifting of passenger weight brought on by panic.' Hitler immediately declared this a greater threat than the Remagen bridgehead, as this section of the Rhine was virtually unguarded. Hitler wanted to send a panzer brigade but all that were available were five disabled Jagdtigers at the tank depot at Sennelager. By the evening of 24 March Patton had captured 19,000 prisoners.

South of Koblenz at 0200 hours on 26 March Patton's US 8th Corps pushed the US 89th and 87th Divisions across the Rhine at Boppard and

St Goar. The powerful 89th was supported by the US 748th Tank and the 811th Tank Destroyer Battalions. Altogether the division plus supporting and attached forces numbered well over 23,000 men. To oppose them were Luftwaffe anti-aircraft battalions fighting as infantry and Volkssturm home guard.

The US 354th and 353rd Infantry Regiments spearheaded the crossing. The 1st Battalion, 354th attacked towards Wellmich and the 2nd towards St Goarshausen from St Goar. Over a company and a half of 1st Battalion reached the east bank on the first wave with little resistance, but once ashore they came under heavy fire from the hillside behind Wellmich. German machine-gun and 20mm AA fire along with the swift current prevented the assault boats from returning to the west bank. The 2nd Battalion on the way over were greeted with point-blank grazing fire just above the water-line. Nonetheless, a pontoon bridge was completed between St Goar and St Goarshausen the following day allowing the tanks to cross and over 2,700 prisoners were eventually taken. Further south Lieutenant General Patch's US 7th Army crossed the Rhine at Worms on 26 March, allowing a break-out towards Darmstadt.

The British Buffalo Landing Vehicles Tracked were noisy. There was no way of masking them and no element of surprise, though Montgomery had a good try. The banks of the Rhine were shrouded in a thick man-made fog; this may have concealed things visually but from the racket it was clear to the Germans that an awful lot of mechanized vehicles were being brought up to various jump off points. On the night of 23 March 1945 the Allies crossed Germany's last major defensive barrier and after Operation Overlord this was the second largest operation undertaken by the British Army during the entire war.

The logistics were staggering. As well as the amphibious Buffalo there were also landing craft, powered rafts, DUKWs, Terrapins, Weasels and DD Sherman swimming tanks gathered for the Rhine crossing. Forty-five medium landing craft and a similar number of landing craft vehicle/person-nel were shipped to Ostend from Britain. Under their own power they then made their way to Antwerp and were picked up by Army transporters for the onward journey. To many it must have looked like D-Day all over again.

The lead assault formation was Major General Sir Percy Hobart's British 79th Armoured Division, affectionately known as the 'Funnies' because of its unique armour. This division had served the Allies well on D–Day and ever since. It consisted of five brigades operating almost 2,000 specialized vehicles and gun tanks including approximately 500 Buffaloes, which were allocated to the various assault infantry divisions. Additionally, about 100 DD Sherman tanks were to support the initial waves, while eight Class 50/60 rafts were to ferry over almost 800 tanks. Some 200 DUKWs were refurbished by the British ready for the Rhine operation. In stark contrast, the weak 47th Panzer Corps was the Germans' only mobile reserve. In the face of Allied air supremacy it was hardly capable of going anywhere without being met by a deluge of rockets and bombs.

Despite their massed power the Rhine crossing presented particular problems for the Allied planners, not least the steep and very muddy river banks. To counter this, hard-won lessons from the Scheldt were called upon. The Buffalo Carpet-Layer was developed after fourteen Sherman DD tanks had become stuck fast in the mud during the assault on South Beveland. The net result was that they and their crews had become sitting ducks and they had been unable to support the assaulting infantry. For the assault over the Rhine Special Buffalo Troops were to lay chespale wooden carpeting to assist the supporting tanks up and over the banks.

In total Montgomery's 21st Army Group could call on 1.2 million men of General Crerar's Canadian 1st Army, General Dempsey's British 2nd Army and General Simpson's US 9th Army. For 10 days before the crossing Montgomery's gathering forces at Wesel were shrouded in a dense, choking smokescreen making it obvious that something was about to take place. First into battle were the men of the 51st Highland Division, which had been strengthened by the addition of the 9th Canadian Infantry Brigade. Major General Tom Rennie was supported by 150 Buffaloes, which carried his four assault battalions. The Buffaloes ploughed resolutely through the Rhine's strong current, but the DUKWs struggled in many places and often ended up on the wrong stretch of bank. All the DD tanks of the Staffordshire Yeomanry were across by 0700 hours and in action engaging enemy strongpoints.

The Black Watch took just four minutes to cross and were the first British troops over. The defenders, stunned by the preceding bombing and artillery attacks, offered sporadic mortar and machine-gun fire in response to the forces ploughing toward them. Remarkably the 7th Black Watch lost just one Buffalo in the opening attack to a German Teller mine. The commanding officer of the 4th Battalion, Royal Tank Regiment was in the first Buffalo to reach the opposite bank on 23 March at 2104 hours. At Xanten the assault battalions encountered a stone-lined bank, which their Buffaloes could not climb and the units became widely scattered. Fortunately, this obstacle proved to be the only serious difficulty as the German defenders put up little resistance. The ground north-east of Rees was quickly secured, but German paratroops resolutely held onto the town until the next day.

The 43rd Division then moved up on the 51st's left to attack Esserden, while the 9th Canadian Infantry Brigade pushed on Androp and Bienen, reaching Emmerich by the 27th. The 3rd Canadian, 15th (Scottish), 43rd, 51st (Highland) Divisions and the equipment of the 6th Airborne Division were ferried across by 425 Buffaloes. They made almost 4,000 crossings, with 55 damaged and nine written off; not a bad casualty rate for such an enormous operation.

By the afternoon of the 26th the four Class 50/60 rafts on 12th Corps' front had ferried over about 250 tanks, while on 30th Corps' front another four rafts had shifted 437 tanks by the 27th. Montgomery then prepared to commit his other four corps and by the 26th seven 40-ton bridges had been put over the Rhine. The logistics of bridging the Rhine were mind-boggling. To get the Allies' armoured fighting vehicles and motor transport over the river required 22,000 tons of assault bridging including 25,000 wooden pontoons, 2,000 assault boats, 650 storm boats and 120 river tugs.

This allowed the British 12th Corps' 7th Armoured Division, under Major General L.O. Lyne, and the US 16th Corps' 8th Armored Division, under Brigadier General John M. Devine, to move into the bridgehead. There was no stopping these formations and by midnight on 28 March the bridgehead had expanded considerably. The 7th Armoured thrust forward as far as Borken some 20 miles and the 8th Armored got to Haltern about 25 miles. Within a week of the crossing Montgomery had amassed 20 divisions with 1,500 tanks. There was simply nothing the Germans could do to withstand this steamroller and 30,000 PoWs went into the 'bag' after they threw down their weapons. Other elements of the British 2nd Army and Canadian 1st Armies were pushing into northern Germany and southern Holland. The US 9th Army struck south into the northern end of the Ruhr between Duisburg and Essen.

'Cover Girl' of the US 775th Tank Battalion engaging Japanese troops on Luzon in the Philippines in early 1945.

The most common Allied tanks in Normandy were the Sherman M4 and M4A1 – they equipped the bulk of the American, British, Canadian, French and Polish armoured forces.

At the time of D-Day upgunned Shermans were in short supply. Only 800 M4s armed with a 105mm howitzer were produced during 1943. The follow-on M4A3 105mm only went into production in April 1944.

The M4A1 and M4A3 equipped with a 76mm gun only became available in early 1944.

To compensate for the Sherman's lack of punch, in June 1942 the Americans began to produce the M10, armed with a 3in gun, using the Sherman chassis.

The British Sherman IIC, IVC and VC Firefly were the only Allied tanks capable of taking on the Panther or Tiger on equal terms (using the M4A1, M4A3 and M4A4 respectively).

Specialized armour supporting D-Day included the Sherman Crab. Designed to clear minefields and barbed wire, it consisted of the M4A4 fitted with a rotating flail.

This mobile Normandy hedgerow is concealing an American M10. To the right is a burnt-out Sherman.

Sherman with the Canadian 2nd Armoured Brigade, which consisted of the 6th, 10th and 27th Armoured Regiments.

Cromwell tanks of the 4th County of London Yeomanry (Sharpshooters), 7th Armoured Division, who were mauled at Villers-Bocage.

US Military Policeman directs an M5 light tank bearing the name 'Concrete' in Normandy.

M5 light tank engages enemy targets as a GI dashes for cover.

Another US Army M5. Note the prong on the front of the hull designed to dig up the Normandy hedgerows.

French half-tracks and a M8 Howitzer Motor Carriage, Free French 2nd Armored Division, on parade through the Arc de Triomphe, Paris.

Churchill Mk VI, armed with a 75mm gun, in the Netherlands.

Sherman with the call sign 'Bramble 5', serving with the 79th Armoured Division in the Netherlands.

US Sherman and supporting infantry crossing the Siegfried Line in September 1944.

M10 tank destroyer with the Régiment Blindé de Fusiliers Marins, Free French 2nd Armored Division, outside Halloville, France on 13 November 1944.

Camouflaged Sherman tank, belonging to the French 5th Armored Division, engaging enemy targets during the liberation of Belfort on 20 November 1944.

M36 tank destroyers of the US 703rd Tank Destroyer Battalion, attached to the US 82nd Airborne Division, near Werbomont, Belgium, 20 December 1944.

M18 Hellcat tank destroyer knocked out during the Battle of the Bulge.

Snow-covered M10, US 654th Tank Destroyer Battalion, supporting the US 35th Infantry Division during the winter of 1944.

American Sherman tanks rumbling through the snow.

Churchill tanks in December 1944, north of the German town of Geilenkirchen, just east of the Dutch border.

British Sherman tank in early 1945. The crew have enhanced the front armour with spare road wheels and track – a common practice.

Shermans of the US 781st Tank Battalion just before the Rhine crossing.

M24 Chaffee light tank ferried over the Rhine by landing craft.

Sherman crossing the Rhine. The Allied armoured build-up once over the river was quite remarkable.

British Sherman Firefly, M3 half-track, at least four Carriers and a Humber armoured car in Germany in early 1945.

This tank is a M4A1 (76mm) Sherman with a cast hull. Behind it is a M7 Howitzer Motor Carriage.

The M24 Chaffee was a late entrant to the war. American tank battalions first received it in late 1944 when it began to replace the M5.

M18 Hellcat Gun Motor Carriages on the streets of Leipzig. This proved to be one of the best tank destroyers of the war.

Major Peter Carrington of the Guards Armoured Division was full of praise for his opponents, recalling:

> The Germans were very, very good soldiers. After the Rhine crossing, we had 15th Panzergrenadier Division in front of us fighting a rearguard action all the way to the very end of the war; in circumstances in Germany when they must have known they were going to lose the war and didn't have much hope. They fought absolutely magnificently with great courage and skill.

Further south the US 1st Army broke out of the Remagen bridgehead, while the spearhead of the US 9th and 1st Armies – the 8th Armored Division and Major General Maurice Rose's US 3rd Armored Division – linked up on 2 April 1945 at Lippstadt east of the Ruhr. Everywhere you looked Allied tanks drove the scattered enemy back. The Allies meantime pushed on to meet up with the Red Army on the Elbe. The Buffaloes swan song was ferrying Allied troops over the Elbe in late April/early May just before the German surrender.

Chapter 17

Industrial Muscle

There can be no denying that ultimately the outcome of the Second World War largely boiled down to industrial muscle. Between 1940 and 1945 Britain churned out 24,800 tanks, a figure comparable to Germany's 24,360, but nowhere near the enormous numbers achieved by America and the Soviet Union. The Commonwealth also did its bit for the tank effort. Between 1939 and 1945 Canada built 1,420 Valentine tanks, plus 1,144 Ram tanks and 188 Grizzlys. Most of the former were converted to armoured personnel carriers for use in Europe. The Canadians also built 2,150 Sexton self-propelled guns, which used variations of the Ram chassis, for the British and Canadian armies. All this work was conducted by Canadian Pacific's Montreal Locomotive Works – its parent company was American Locomotive, which under guidance from Washington, initially thought it necessary to set up a tank arsenal in Canada.

Even the Australians, from a cold start, produced a cruiser tank known as the Sentinel. Very few were ever built as America's enormous tank manufacturing capacity was able to meet Australia's needs. The number of tanks produced by Britain's factories would never have been sufficient to fill the requirements of the British and Commonwealth armies. There is no hiding from the fact that British-designed tanks were not up to the job and the British Army would not have overcome the Wehrmacht but for the supply of American tanks. These were principally the M3 and M5 Stuart light, M3 Lee/Grant medium and M4 Sherman medium tanks. In particular, a staggering 15,153 Shermans had been shipped to Britain by the end of 1944 to arm the Allied armies. America also sent almost 2,000 to the Russians, over 900 to the Chinese Nationalists and 656 to the Free French.

American factories turned out 88,410 tanks, as well as 18,620 armoured fighting vehicles based on tank chassis. Remarkably all this was achieved from a standing start. America's tank building went from just 330 in 1940 to 29,500 at its peak in 1943. The Detroit Tank Arsenal, which was constructed from scratch, between 1940 to 1945 accounted for 25 per cent of all America's tanks – producing over 25,000 vehicles. In total the Sherman made up almost two-thirds of all American tank construction. This means that more Shermans were produced than the combined output of Britain and Germany. Like the Russian T-34, it was easy to manufacture and easy to operate. Although light tanks were built in considerable numbers in the opening stages of the war, the Americans, like the British and Russians, largely dropped them in favour of massed medium armour.

The Chrysler Car company initially constructed the massive Tank Arsenal factory in Detroit to build the M3 medium tank. American Locomotive and Baldwin Locomotive were also contracted to help with full-scale production, which was underway by August 1941. By the end of the following year some 6,258 of the M3 series had rolled out these factories. Pressed Steel and Pullman also each received orders for 500 M3s from Britain. Production of the Sherman commenced in March 1941 at Lima Locomotive Works, Pacific Car and Pressed Steel. By the autumn of the following year it was being built by almost a dozen plants, including a second giant purpose built tank facility run by Fisher at Grand Blanc, Michigan. Production of the Sherman and all its variants amounted to 48,000 compared to just over 55,000 T-34s.

Just three months after Hitler's invasion of the Soviet Union, Churchill began to supply Stalin with much-needed replacement tanks. He held a 'Tanks for Russia' week in September 1941 when the entire British tank production run was donated to the Soviet Union's war effort. The first tank to be officially handed over was a Valentine, suitably dubbed 'Stalin', which was publicly accepted on 22 September by the Russian Ambassador M. Maisky. By the end of the year 481 tanks had been supplied.

Britain and the Commonwealth shipped almost 3,300 tanks to the Red Army during 1941 and 1942. America then stepped in providing Stalin with a further 7,000 from 1942 to 1945. On the whole Russian tank crews did not like the British Matilda and Churchill tanks, as they were poorly armed and slow in comparison to their own tanks – particularly the T-34. Likewise, the American-supplied M3 Lee and M4 Sherman gained a poor reputation. The only foreign tank the Red Army seems to have taken to its heart was the British Valentine.

By way of comparison Allied wheeled vehicle production was even bigger than that of tanks and other fighting vehicles. Whilst tanks and artillery provided the cutting teeth of the armies on the ground, without adequate motor transport (MT) they would have gone nowhere. In 1939 the British Army found itself with a fleet of some 85,000 motor vehicles (26,000 were pressed into service). In fact, procurement had been so slow that two private firms supplied MT for manoeuvres. The Army was predominantly equipped with the 15-cwt 4x2, 30-cwt 4x2 and 6x4 and 3-ton 4x2 and 6x4. The term truck, covering vehicles up to 15-cwt, lorry encompassing 3-tonners and over, and light-lorry covering everything in between defined British MT. The Americans used the term truck for all load carriers.

In Britain there were three vehicle categories: 1) Army 'A', 'B', 'C' plus Royal Army Service Corps (RASC); 2) RAF and 3) RN. 'A' vehicles consisted of all wheeled and tracked Armoured Fighting Vehicles (AFVs); 'B' encompassed trucks of all types, cars, motorcycles and artillery tractors; 'C' vehicles were special purpose ones used by the likes of the Royal Engineers. The RASC category covered all second-line MT operated by the Corps, but in 1942 was included in the 'B' classification.

After the Fall of France and the British Expeditionary Force's escape from Dunkirk, the British Army found itself bereft of transport. The Army left behind almost 21,000 vehicles and about 600 tanks. It managed to extricate 3,000 vehicles; more could have been saved, but many were often abandoned prematurely. For example, the Army had over 10,000 30-cwt light lorries, but over half were left behind.

Afterwards the British motor industry went to work with gusto and vehicles were also ordered from the US and Canada. Britain's vehicle producers included AEC, Alvis, Austin, Bedford, Daimler, Foden, Leyland, Scammell, Thornycroft and Vauxhall. Incredibly four months of increased production made good the losses of wheeled vehicles in France. By the end of the war, excluding AFVs, British forces had about 1.25 million vehicles (including 35,000 civilian vehicles pressed into service). The basic 6x4 chassis became standard across the British Empire, with the 3-ton (medium) version remaining in production throughout. Prior to the war the 30-cwt six wheeler was numerous, but quantity production ceased by the end of 1940. Various 4x4 load carriers went into bulk production in 1941, with Bedford producing 52,245 QLs, Austin 12,280 K5s and Thoryncroft 5,000 Nubians.

Having defeated the Italians in 1941, in North Africa Britain was able to outproduce the Germans. In August 1942 British and Commonwealth forces received 7,000 vehicles, Rommel needed 1,500 trucks, not to mention more panzers, but got none. Many British vehicles were shipped to Egypt in kit form, where four assembly plants turned out 180 a day, totalling 45,000 by October 1942. Some 37,000 vehicles were assembled in Britain in 1944 and shipped across the Channel after D-Day. Between June 1944 and May 1945 176,000 'B' vehicles passed through the workshops of Montgomery's 21st Army Group in Europe. Following D-Day the introduction of 80 Octane fuel rendered over 1,400 British lorries unserviceable at a crucial time when the Channel ports were still closed to the Allies.

The biggest supplier of military vehicles to the British Commonwealth was Canada. In July 1940, Britain asked Canada to supply 7,000 desperately needed replacement motor vehicles. The Canadians successfully combined British War Office designs with American mass production. Within a year Canada was the main supplier to the whole British Empire, producing 189,178 military MT vehicles during 1941 alone. Between 1939 and 1945 the Canadians manufactured a total of 815,729 transport vehicles, of these 345,831 were 4x4 types predominantly in the 3-ton payload class. Canada also produced 10,054 wheeled AFVs.

The Canadian motor industry consisted of subsidiaries of American Ford, Chrysler and General Motors, which helped standardization. Indeed, in 1936 Ford and GM merged military production to produce Canadian Military Pattern (CMP) vehicles. The first CMP transport arrived in Britain with Canadian troops in the spring of 1940. While Canada concentrated on building 8-cwt to 3-ton trucks, lighter and heavier vehicles were obtained from the US.

Transport vehicles produced in Australia, India, South Africa and New Zealand were usually of Canadian origin, although bodywork and some components were of local manufacture. Until the outbreak of the war Australia depended mainly on Canadian chassis, which were then fitted with locally produced cabs and bodywork. The end result was dubbed initially Local Pattern and then Australian Pattern vehicles to distinguish them from complete British, Canadian, Indian and American imports.

America of course beat everyone hands down in the mass production stakes churning out 3.2 million transport vehicles, 41,170 half-tracks and well over 82,000 tractors. The bulk of the trucks fell into the light (up to ¾ ton) class of which 988,167 were built followed by 812,262 light-heavy (2½ ton) class. Medium and heavy accounted for almost another 582,000 vehicles. Peak procurement occurred in June 1942 when the US Army received 62,258 trucks of all types. Under the Lend-Lease programme America's allies were provided with thousands of military vehicles, prior to that thousands had been supplied on a commercial basis. Many destined for France ended up diverted to Britain or in German hands.

The American Quartermaster Corps was responsible for transport procurement for the US Army and Army Air Force until August 1942, at which point the Ordnance Department took over. This made sense as the latter was already overseeing tracked and wheeled combat vehicle acquisition. In addition, the US Marine Corps and Navy procured their own vehicles. America's automotive industry was vast and included such names as Buick, Cadillac, Chevrolet, Dodge, Ford, GMC, Harley-Davidson, Oshkosh, Studebaker and Willys, all were rallied to the war effort. Where America excelled was in the standardization of vehicle types and the production of spare parts.

After the German invasion of the Soviet Union, America supplied the Red Army with over 400,000 military vehicles. About 25 per cent of the trucks were 2½-ton 6x4 and 6x6 Studebakers, the rest comprising of Jeeps, Dodge Weapons Carriers, and Chevrolet and Dodge 4x4 1½-tonners. Many Lend-Lease trucks were assembled in Iran and then driven northward. Canada also supplied GM trucks and Britain sent Albion, Austin, Bedford and Fords.

Gun production proved to be one of Britain's greatest weaknesses, which caused a fatal flaw in its tanks. Early British tanks were hamstrung by their deficient tank guns based on the anti-tank guns of the day. The British Army went to war with wholly inadequate anti-tank guns, principally the 2-pounder (40mm) developed in the mid-1930s and the slightly better 6-pounder (57mm) developed in the late 1930s. The latter did not enter production until 1941 because the War Office insisted on first replacing those 2-pounders lost in France. This was a significant error. These weapons were easily outgunned by the German 50mm, 75mm and 88mm guns. Yet all the early British tanks were armed with the 2-pounder and could not fire high explosive.

By the beginning of 1942 prototypes of a 3in (76mm) weapon firing a 17lb shot were in hand and by May 1942 the powerful 17-pounder gun was introduced. The latter was the best anti-tank gun possessed by the British

Army toward the end of the Second World War and was a real tank killer, capable of penetrating up to 230mm armour at 1,000m. As a result, it was to be employed in a wide variety of guises, as a towed gun, tank gun and self-propelled gun. At first hurriedly fitted to 25-pounder field gun carriages, as the spilt-trail carriage was not ready, about 100 were rushed to North Africa to help counter the appearance of the German Tiger tank in 1943.

By mid-1944 the 17-pounder had become the mainstay of the anti-tank regiments of the British and Canadian armies. The same cannot be said for their tank regiments. Unfortunately, it was never available in really decisive numbers. Also by this stage existing British tank designs were incapable of taking a larger gun, because the hull was not wide enough to take a bigger turret. This led to the Archer and Challenger, which were little more than unsatisfactory stopgaps. Only the American Sherman provided a sufficient platform.

The question remains which of the Allied tanks was ultimately the best. In terms of British and American armour certainly none of them were perfect. It is fair to say American designs largely proved to be better than their British counterparts. Despite all its faults, it has to be the Sherman, especially the British modification in the shape of the Sherman Firefly. For the Russians the T-34 was certainly a war winner, while for the Germans the Panzer IV did all the hard work – despite the reputations of the Panther and the Tiger. War correspondent Alan Moorehead observed in Tunisia, 'Most of the American stuff was first-class, and even as good or better than the German ... The diesel Sherman was certainly the best tank of its class.'

The Germans, who were on the receiving end of the Sherman after El Alamein, initially thought it was a good tank, especially its rugged reliability. A Sherman captured near Sbeitla in Tunisia on 22 February 1943 was driven the 217 miles to Tunis in four and a half days. It was then shipped to the German Army Weapons Office test centre at Kummersdorf, where the engineers and technicians were impressed. However, at this stage the Germans had already deployed their new Tiger heavy tank and the Panther medium tank was on its way – both were vastly superior to the Sherman. The captured tank simply confirmed to the Germans how easy it was for their tank guns to penetrate the Sherman's armour.

American and British tank crews found they could not win a head-to-head fight and had to develop lifesaving panzer-stalking tactics. They were helped in this by the Sherman's gyrostabilizer and power traverse, which gave a greater rate of fire than the panzers. Just a week after D-Day the perils of such tactics were graphically illustrated on the streets of Villers-Bocage, when British Shermans and Cromwells tangled with the Tiger tank at very close quarters. The Americans had similar experiences amongst the Normandy hedgerows.

Fortunately for the Allies, although the Germans had gained the techno-logical lead, panzer crew training became progressively worse. Poorly-trained young panzertruppen often found themselves thrown into battle piecemeal and lacking adequate support. In contrast Sherman crew training was vastly superior. They found that the use of white phosphorus smoke or high explo-sive rounds sometimes led to inexperienced panzer crews abandoning their tanks in panic. If this did not happen the smoke gave Sherman crews time to manoeuvre onto the flanks or rear of their prey, where their 75mm gun could penetrate the armour. This did not always work, but the Allies had plenty more Shermans to spare. Allied tankers in North-west Europe also had the advantage of regular close air support and artillery fire support.

The Sherman was well past its prime by 1944 and ought to have been replaced by a new tank. This never happened despite British and American efforts to come up with a successor before the end of the war. The result was that the Sherman had to rely on weight of numbers made possible by American industrial might. Nevertheless, the skill and bravery of Allied tank crews should not be maligned. For example, American tank ace Staff Sergeant Lafayette Pool and the crew of a Sherman called 'In the Mood', accounted for 12 panzers, 258 armoured vehicles and self-propelled guns, 1,000 Germans killed and 250 captured. Their tank kills included a Panther outside Liège, which they knocked out at a range of 1,500 yards. In the Mood's' luck finally ran out when it was hit by a Panther at Munsterbusch, south of Aachen. The crew only just managed to escape their stricken tank.

The British Comet and the American Pershing might had compensated for the Sherman's deficiencies, but they both appeared too late to have any impact on the battlefield. In some quarters, with the benefit of hindsight, it has been argued that the continued use of the Sherman was nothing short of scandalous, but it was all the Allies had and as a weapon of war it served them faithfully to the best of its abilities. It has also been said that the Sherman was the tank that won the war – this might be a little generous – but it certainly came a close second after the T-34.

Appendices

Allied Armoured Divisions 1940–1945

The Allied armies created thirty-eight armoured divisions, but some of these were destroyed in the very early stages of the war, or were not deployed overseas and subsequently disbanded. This figure does not include the numerous independent armoured and tank brigades, nor the tank battalions, supporting the infantry divisions. Nor does it include the four French heavy cavalry divisions that were destroyed in 1940, as they were not equipped with British or American armour.

American tank divisions expanded very rapidly from just two in early 1941 to fourteen by the end of the following year. By 1945 the US Army had sixteen active armoured divisions and one depot division, which contained fifty-four tank battalions. This was not a true reflection of its enormous tank strength. If it had grouped all its independent armoured units into divisions this would have given the US Army almost thirty-six full armoured divisions. For example, by the end of 1944 there were an additional sixty-five tank battalions with a further twenty-nine being formed. The US Marine Corps also formed six tank battalions, which fought in the Pacific.

By far the greatest concentration of American tanks was in North-west Europe, where they deployed fifteen armoured divisions and thirty-seven separate tank battalions. There were also seventeen American amphibian tractor battalions that could be classified as tanks. On top of this there were the tank destroyer units equipping the anti-tank regiments. By early 1943 there were 106 tank destroyer battalions. Thanks to changing priorities and heavy casualties, there were only sixty-eight remaining at the end of March 1945. The US tank destroyer force was then disbanded, with some units subsumed by the tank force.

The Australian Army formed three armoured divisions, but these were retained for home defence against possible invasion by Japan. Britain formed eleven armoured divisions, four of which were disbanded before the end of the war and of these half did not serve overseas. The French formed three armoured divisions, which were equipped with American tanks, that fought during the 1944–5 campaigns. The Canadians provided two divisions and the Poles and South Africans one apiece. The Nationalist Chinese deployed a so-called armoured division in Burma. This started life designated a mechanized division, but in reality was little more than a weak motorized infantry division with a supporting tank unit.

Nationality	Areas of Operation
American	
1st Armored Division 'Old Ironsides'	North Africa, Italy
2nd Armored Division 'Hell on Wheels'	North Africa, Sicily, Normandy, North-west Europe
3rd Armored Division 'Spearhead'	Normandy, North-west Europe
4th Armored Division 'Breakthrough'	Brittany, North-west Europe
5th Armored Division 'Victory'	Brittany, North-west Europe
6th Armored Division 'Super Sixth'	Brittany, North-west Europe
7th Armored Division 'Lucky Seventh'	North-west Europe
8th Armored Division 'Tornado'	North-west Europe
9th Armored Division 'Phantom'	North-west Europe
10th Armored Division 'Tiger'	Southern Europe, North-west Europe
11th Armored Division 'Thunderbolt'	North-west Europe
12th Armored Division 'Hellcat'	Southern France
13th Armored Division 'The Black Cats'	North-west Europe
14th Armored Division 'Liberator'	Southern France
16th Armored Division 'Armadillo'	North-west Europe
20th Armored Division	North-west Europe
50th Armored Division 'Jersey Blues'	This unit did not serve overseas

Nationality	Areas of Operation
Australian	
1st Armoured Division	This unit did not serve overseas (disbanded 1943)
2nd Armoured Division	This unit did not serve overseas (disbanded 1943)
3rd Armoured Division	This unit did not serve overseas (disbanded 1943)
British	
1st Armoured Division	France, North Africa, Italy
2nd Armoured Division	North Africa (disbanded 1941)
6th Armoured Division	North Africa, Italy
7th Armoured Division 'Desert Rats'	North Africa, Italy, Normandy, North-west Europe
8th Armoured Division	North Africa (except for HQ disbanded in 1942 before El Alamein)
9th Armoured Division	This unit did not serve overseas (disbanded 1944)
10th Armoured Division	North Africa
11th Armoured Division 'The Black Bull'	Normandy, North-west Europe
42nd Armoured Division	This unit did not serve overseas (disbanded 1943)
79th Armoured Division 'The Funnies'	Normandy, North-west Europe
Guards Armoured Division	Normandy, North west Europe
Canadian	
4th Armoured Division	Normandy, North-west Europe
5th Armoured Division	Italy
French	
1st Armoured Division	Southern France, South-western Germany
2nd Armoured Division	Normandy, North-west Europe
5th Armoured Division	Southern France, South-western Germany
Polish	
1st Armoured Division	Normandy, North-west Europe
South African	
6th Armoured Division	Italy

Note: The North-west European campaign was divided officially into five separate campaigns: Normandy, Northern France, Rhineland, Ardennes-Alsace and Central Europe. In the case of the US 11th–20th Armoured Divisions they only saw combat from the Rhineland onwards.

Appendix B

British and Commonwealth Tanks and Armoured Fighting Vehicles 1939–1945

Archer Self-Propelled Gun

In 1942 it had been hoped to use the British Bishop self-propelled gun, based on the Valentine tank chassis, as a mounting for the new 17-pounder, but this was not possible and instead the British Army ended up with the Archer variant. The drawback with this was that the weapon, installed in an open fighting compartment, faced to the rear. While far from perfect 665 were constructed from 1944 to 1945 and it proved a popular and useful weapon.

Bishop Self-Propelled Gun

The Bishop was the first British designed self-propelled gun of the war, consisting of a Valentine chassis with a 25-pounder gun in a large, high-sided fixed turret. The later only permitted limited elevation for the gun. It was intended to provide self-propelled anti-tank gun support for British armoured divisions, but by the time it entered service the 25-pounder was no longer being used in a dual anti-tank role. Although it was dubbed 'a for-midable combination', only about 150 were ever built. Limited numbers were supplied to the 8th Army, but it was rapidly eclipsed by the M7 Priest using the M3 medium tank chassis. The Bishop was crude and unsophisticated in comparison and was rapidly phased out of service after 1943.

Centaur Mk IV Close Support Tank

The Centaur Cruiser Tank Mk VIII (A27L) was essentially the same as the Cromwell, but with a different engine (Liberty rather than the Meteor). About 950 Centaurs were built, of which only 80 were Mk IV close support models, with a 95mm howitzer replacing the standard 6-pounder gun. The Mk IVs were assigned to the Royal Marines Armoured Support Group and saw action on D-Day, providing covering fire from LCTs and then on the beaches. The Centaur Mk III was armed with a 75mm gun and most were converted into Cromwells. Some Centaur IIIs were also used in a dozer role, with the removal of the turret and the addition of a dozer blade.

Challenger Cruiser Tank (A30)

The Challenger used a modified A27 chassis and, like the Valentine-based Archer self-propelled gun, was armed with the powerful 17-pounder. The Cromwell was too narrow to allow for a larger turret ring that was needed to house the gun. As a result, the Cromwell chassis had to be widened and extended, meaning that the Challenger had six rather than five road wheels. The large turret gave the tank a very prominent silhouette and it had limited ammunition stowage. Weight greatly hampered the Challenger's performance. Although development commenced in 1943 it was not ready for production until March 1944. It was then realized no provision had been made for waterproofing and it could not be used on D-Day.

Only small numbers of the Challenger were used in North-west Europe during 1944–5, as the Sherman Firefly proved more successful. These were deployed with the reconnaissance regiments of the armoured divisions, in order to bolster the firepower of the Cromwell. A self-propelled gun variant using the A30 chassis, known as the Avenger, was also developed. It was not ready until 1944 and was made superfluous by the American M10 tank destroyer. Consequently, it did not appear until 1946.

Churchill Infantry Tank (A22)

The British Churchill infantry support tank was first bloodied during the disastrous Dieppe raid in 1942, then in Tunisia and France on D-Day. After Dunkirk, British Prime Minister Winston Churchill was left with fewer than 100 tanks for the defence of the mainland, so losses had to be swiftly replaced to repel Hitler's anticipated invasion. The British company Vauxhall were asked to work on the A20 Infantry Tank, which was still in development, and to get it into production within a year. The A20 was a throwback to the First World War intended to cope with heavily-shelled areas and obstacles such as wide trenches.

Originally the Belfast shipbuilders Harland and Wolff had been tasked to provide four mild steel prototype A20s, the first of these though showed that the design needed to be revised. A pilot model of the subsequent A22, Infantry Tank Mk IV, appeared in November 1940 and 500 were ordered, with the first 14 being delivered in mid-1941. Weighing in at 38 tons it was by far the heaviest British tank in service. Dubbed the Churchill tank in honour of the Prime Minister, the A22 was built by a production group of eleven manufacturers under the direction of Vauxhall. The hull was of composite construction with the outer armour bolted or riveted on. Notably it was the first British tank to have controlled differential steering, provided by the then new Merritt-Brown four-speed gearbox. With a crew of five it had a top speed of 17mph and a range of 100 miles.

In the best traditions of the British military, due to the dire situation, this tank was understandably a rushed job. The engine was inaccessible, the petrol pump shaft tended to snap and the hydraulic tappets often broke requiring an engine replacement. The list went on. Therefore, the early A22s required constant fine-tuning until all the bugs were ironed out, this gained the tank a reputation that stuck even after it had proved itself. During 1942–3 Vauxhall engineers on secondment became familiar faces with those units issued with the temperamental tank.

Britain sent some Churchill Mk I, II and IIIs to Russia and three Mk IIIs fought at El Alamein with the 8th Army. However, the Germans next properly came up against the Churchill tank in Tunisia where it served with the British 1st Army, most notably with the 142nd Royal Tank Regiment at the Battle of Medjez el-Bab in March 1943. Production was to have stopped but its success in Tunisia meant it continued to be built and was employed in the Italian campaign.

Churchill I

Like so many British tanks the initial model Churchill was woefully under-gunned. The Churchill Mk I's armament consisted of a 2-pounder gun (with 150 rounds) and 7.92mm Besa machine gun mounted in a cast turret plus a close support 3in howitzer (with 58 rounds) in the front hull. The later was required because the 2-pounder could not fire high-explosive shells. The post-Dunkirk emergency requirements meant the ineffective 2-pounder had been kept in production way past its sell-by date.

Churchill II

This inability to fire HE was a major shortcoming especially in the Mk II, which was the same but with a 7.92mm Besa machine gun replacing the howitzer. These were issued to the newly-raised British tank brigades and the exiled Polish Army tank brigade. A few Mk IICs were produced which featured the 2-pounder in the nose and the 3in howitzer in the turret. Both the Churchill I and II had exposed tracks and engine intake louvres on the hull sides. Track covers and armoured front horns were fitted from May 1942. Likewise, the air intake was redesigned so that the opening was at the top to prevent engine flooding when wading.

Churchill II Oke Flamethrower

In 1942 the Petroleum Warfare Department developed the Churchill Oke flamethrower tank. This comprised the Mk II with the Ronson flamethrowing system (with a range of 40–50 yards), which had been designed for the tracked Universal Carrier. Once more this was a rushed job in order that the concept of a flamethrower tank could be tested under combat conditions at Dieppe in the summer of 1942.

Churchill III

In 1942 the Churchill Mk III appeared with a larger turret and upgunned to a 6-pounder.

Churchill IV

As above but with a new cast turret. Apart from the turrets the III and IV were identical.

Churchill IV (NA 75)

Usually armed with a 6-pounder gun, some of 1st Army's tanks in Tunisia were upgunned with the M3's 75mm gun to produce the Churchill IV (NA 75).

Churchill VI and VII

The Mk VI and VII were both armed with 75mm guns. The former was converted from the Mk IV. In contrast the Churchill VII was a new mark with thicker integral armour (rather than the earlier composite construction), a new cast/welded turret with cupola and circular instead of square hull side escape doors. Both were used in the North-west Europe campaign of 1944–5.

Churchill V and VIII

The Mk V and VIII were armed with a 95mm howitzer. These were essentially rearmed Churchill IVs and VIIIs respectively.

Churchill Armoured Vehicle Royal Engineers (AVRE)

The Churchill tank in various guises played a highly specialized engineering role in the D-Day landings. From its creation in 1942 the 79th Armoured Division was conceived as a regular armoured unit, but the following year, with the impending invasion of German-occupied France, it was earmarked for a key role. British military authorities, having learned a sharp lesson after the disastrous Dieppe raid, realized it was vital to have specialized armoured fighting vehicles that could punch through the hard crust of the Germans' Atlantic Wall defences. The 79th was allocated this tough task.

Dubbed 'The Funnies', the division was equipped with specialized AFVs. Amongst these the AVRE (Armoured Vehicle Royal Engineers) consisted of various developments mounted on the Churchill tank chassis. Churchill Mk III and IVs were equipped with a 290mm Petard spigot mortar for bunker-busting. Some nicknamed the 'Bobbin' were fitted with a carpet layer for crossing soft clay. Other variants included the ARK (Armoured Ramp Carrier), the mine-clearing Bullshorn Plough and the SBG (Small Box Girder) Assault Bridge. These vehicles were operated by the 5th and 6th Assault Regiments Royal Engineers.

Churchill Crocodile Flamethrower

Another key specialized Churchill was the Crocodile. This flamethrower variant used the Mk VIII. The flame projector was fitted in place of the hull machine gun. The flame fuel and nitrogen gas cylinders were carried in a two-wheeled armoured trailer, with the fuel being pumped under the belly of the tank via a shielded pipe. The flamethrower had a range of up to 120 yards, firing eighty one-second bursts. The Crocodile equipment came in kit form so Churchills could be converted in the field. About 800 kits were produced, but not all these were used, with about 250 set aside for potential use against Japan.

This was the only tank-mounted flamethrower used operationally by the British Army during the war. The Crocodile arrived in Normandy with the 141st Regiment, Royal Armoured Corps (The Buffs) just after D-Day. Although not originally part of the 79th Armoured it came under the division's command in France. The regiment helped with the American assault on Brest and as a result many members were awarded American decorations. A second unit equipped with the Crocodile, the 1st Fife and Forfar

Yeomanry, joined the 79th Armoured in early October 1944, in time to help clear S'Hertogenbosch in the southern Netherlands. A third, the 7RTR, joined in February 1945.

Super Churchill

A 'Super Churchill' variant, the Black Prince, armed with the 17-pounder gun, was developed, though it never went into production. By the end of the war 5,640 Churchills of all types had been built.

Comet Cruiser Tank (A34)

One of the few new Allied tank designs introduced in the closing days of the war was the Comet. This drew on the design work for the A27 Cromwell and the A30 Challenger, with a view to creating a more powerful gun tank. Although the Comet was essentially supposed to be an improved Cromwell, in reality over 60 per cent of its components were new. Notably the turret was larger and the suspension featured four return rollers, which were not used on the Challenger or Cromwell.

Armed with a 77mm gun, which was shorter and lighter than the 17-pounder, it proved to be reliable and fast and was the first British production tank capable of matching the Panther. However, its late arrival meant it did not play a prominent role in British tank actions. Although called the Ordnance Quick Firing (OQF) 77mm Mk 2, the gun was actually of 76.2mm calibre but was dubbed a 77mm to avoid confusion with the 17-pounder. It was first issued to the 11th Armoured Division after the Rhine crossing in March 1945.

Cromwell Cruiser Tank (A27M)

Two-thirds of the tanks used by British, Canadian and Polish armoured units in Normandy were Shermans, the rest being mainly British-built Cromwell and Churchill tanks. The Cromwell cruiser tank was numerically and qualitatively the most significant British-built tank and along with the Sherman formed the main strength of the British armoured divisions. However, even armed with a 75mm gun it was inferior to the late model Panzer IVs and the Panther. Although fast, the narrowness of the hull made upgunning it very difficult.

Cruiser Tank Mk I–V (A9–A13)

The early British cruiser tanks the Mk I (A9), Mk II (A10) and Mk III and Mk IV (A13 and A13 Mk II) built during the 1930s were too slow and thinly armoured. All were armed with the inadequate 2-pounder gun and armour ranged from just 14mm to 30mm. It had been planned to arm them with a 3-pounder (47mm gun), but they ended up with the new 2-pounder as it had a higher muzzle velocity. The A9 had the distinction of being the first British tank to have a power-operated turret and an auxiliary engine. A few were armed with 3.7in howitzers for a close support role.

The British 1st Armoured Division was equipped with the Mk I (A9), Mk II (A10), Mk III (A13) and Mk IV (A13 Mk II) cruiser tanks, all of which saw service in France in 1940. They were also deployed with the 7th Armoured Division in North Africa. While adequate for fighting the Italian Army, they were clearly outclassed by the time the Afrika Korps arrived in Libya. The A13 Mk II was the last of the series to see combat with the 7th Armoured Division. The Cruiser Tank Mk V (A 13 Mk III) Covenanter was relegated to training duties in the UK.

Cruiser Tank Mk VI, Crusader (A15)

Introduced in 1941, the Mk VI (A15) Crusader suffered from many of the same problems as its predecessors and proved extremely mechanically unreliable. Like so many British tanks the Crusader was a rushed job, resulting in many mechanical issues. The Crusader I and II were armed with the 2-pounder gun, though some were converted to close support roles by replacing this with a 3in howitzer. Although the Crusader III had increased armour and was armed with the 6-pounder gun, only 144 were built between May and July 1942. Although total output for the Crusader tank was an impressive 5,300 vehicles, German anti-tank guns never had any trouble picking them off in the desert fighting, especially if they had broken down.

Despite being completely obsolete by the end of 1943, some Crusaders were kept in service in a support role until the end of the war. The Gun Tractor Mk I used the Crusader II chassis to tow the 17-pounder anti-tank gun. The turret was removed and replaced by an open-topped superstructure and ammunition lockers. This vehicle was employed by the anti-tank regiments with the British armoured divisions in 1944. Some were fitted with side extensions on the superstructure for deep wading during Operation Overlord. Others were converted into observation posts and anti-aircraft gun platforms.

Loyd Carrier

During 1943–4 Vivian Loyd & Co, in cooperation with other manufacturers, produced 4,213 tracked Loyd Carriers. This design drew on Ford, and like the American T16 and Canadian Windsor had four paired road wheels and two return rollers either side. This type was used in a variety of carrier and gun towing roles.

Mk VIB Light Tank

The Mk VI light tank series were numerically the most important armoured fighting vehicles of the British Army in 1939–40. The Mk VI like its predecessors was designed by Vickers-Armstrong Ltd and was chosen in 1935, along with other armoured fighting vehicles, to be built by manufacturers outside the armaments industry to give companies experience in tank building. The Mk VIB was an improved version of the initial model and was built in far greater numbers.

In the same style as its predecessors the Mk VI's engine was installed on the right-hand side of the hull, with the transmission led forward to the front drive sprockets. The driver was seated to the left and the turret housing the commander and gunner was also off set to the left. The tank used the Horstmann suspension which, while simple and dependable, did have a habit of shedding the tracks. Fortunately, they could be replaced fairly easily. The suspension was formed by two, two-wheel bogie units on each side, that were sprung on twin coil springs, with the rear road wheel acting as the trailing idler. The Mk VIB was armed with a Vickers 0.303in water-cooled machine gun and a Vickers 0.5in heavy machine gun.

Mk VIC Light Tank

The subsequent Mk VIC was very similar, but lacked the large turret cupola and was armed with Besa 7.92mm and 15mm machine guns. On both models the armour was just 14mm thick, meaning the Mk VI was only suitable for fast reconnaissance work. Even so, Mk VIBs were utilized by all the divisional cavalry regiments with the infantry divisions of the British Expeditionary Force. They were also employed as headquarters tanks with the 1st Tank Brigade.

In the British 1st Armoured Division Mk VICs formed a large proportion of its tank strength due to a delay in supplying the newer cruiser tanks.

They were to prove no match for the panzers encountered in 1940. Although designed as a reconnaissance tank the Mk VI was often used in a cruiser role, its inadequate armour and armament invariably lead to heavy losses when facing anything heavier than a Panzer I. This tank type likewise served in the 1st Tank Brigades' Headquarters.

Matilda I Infantry Tank (A11)
The much heavier Matilda I (A11) Infantry Tank was first delivered to the British Army in 1936. It was a fine example of poor funding and inadequate design. Utilizing an underpowered lorry engine, initially the suspension kept shedding the tracks. The first batch of 60 were ordered in April 1937, later increasing to 140, all of which had been delivered by the summer of 1940. While the more numerous Matilda I's armour was almost impervious to the Germans' standard 37mm anti-tank guns, its Vickers machine gun lacked hitting power. Without an anti-tank gun, it simply could not take on the panzers.

Matilda II Infantry Tank (A12)
Designed in the mid-1930s, the Matilda II benefited from work conducted on the A7 medium tank, which never came to fruition. In late 1937 an order for 165 Matilda IIs was placed. Disastrously, due to the shape and size of the armour castings the tank was not easy to mass produce. This was to prove a major problem and two years later there were just two in service. Although heavily armoured, its frontal plating was more than twice that of the Panzer II and III, cross country it was slow and its 2-pounder main armament lacked penetrating power.

The early production Matilda II, deployed to France, is recognizable by the Vickers machine gun on the right-hand side of the turret, rather than the smaller 7.92mm Besa fitted in the Mk IIA. The Matilda II Infantry Tank proved a nasty shock for the Germans at Arras in May 1940. Despite being unavailable in sufficient numbers, lacking adequate infantry and artillery support and no air cover, the tank's measure of success was largely due to its 78mm-thick frontal armour. This proved invulnerable to the German 37mm anti-tank gun.

Priest Kangaroo Armoured Personnel Carrier
After the Sexton self-propelled gun replaced the Priest, the latter was first used as an APC by the Canadian 2nd Corps in August 1944 during the Allied

breakout from Normandy. The Canadians simply removed the 105mm gun and plated over the aperture. This was the first time that fully-tracked APCs were deployed by Montgomery's 21st Army Group in North-west Europe. From October 1944 to April 1945 around 100 Priests were converted into Kangaroo APCs by the 8th Army in Italy. This involved removal of the gun mount and ammunition stowage bins, then platting in the gun opening. This conversion required two crew and could carry twenty infantry.

Ram Kangaroo Armoured Personnel Carrier

During the early 1940s Canada developed the Ram cruiser tank drawing on the American M3 medium tank. The first fifty Ram Is were armed with the 2-pounder and the subsequent RAM II with the 6-pounder. In total 1,094 of the latter were built, but they did not see action, being retained for crew training in Canada and Britain. However, many were converted to Ram APCs and used to equip the armoured troop carrier battalions of the 79th Armoured Division. Removal of the turret and fighting compartment equipment permitted ten infantry to be carried plus two crew.

The Canadian Army replaced the Priest Kangaroo with the Ram Kangaroo in September 1944. These were used to equip the newly formed Canadian 1st Armoured Carrier Regiment. Likewise, the British issued it to the 49th Armoured Personnel Carrier Regiment (previously 49th Royal Tanks, 1st Tank Brigade). In December 1944 both regiments were assigned to the 79th Armoured Division.

Sentinel Cruiser Tank

In 1940, with the prospect of war looming in the Pacific, the Australians decided to build an indigenously-designed cruiser tank armed with the 2-pounder known as the AC I Sentinel. The British colonel sent out to help oversee the project was influenced by the US M3 medium tank, which was clearly reflected in the prototype. In general appearance and layout, it bore a passing resemblance to the Canadian Ram. The turret featured an overhang on either side, which would have created a shot trap. Steps were taken to remedy this on the AC III and IV prototypes that would have had larger guns. The Chullona Tank Assembly Shops, managed by the New South Wales State Railways, produced the first Sentinel in August 1942. Only sixty-six were ever completed by the summer of the following year as the programme was cancelled in favour of American-supplied tanks. The Sentinel never saw combat and was retained for training purposes only.

Sexton Self-Propelled Gun
The British answer to the American M7 Howitzer Motor Carriage was the Sexton built in Canada using the M3 and M4 bogies. This mounted the standard British 25-pounder field gun in place of the 105mm. The Sexton was used to replace the M7, which had entered British service in 1942 with the field regiments of the armoured divisions; a process largely completed by mid-1944 ready for D-Day.

Stuart Kangaroo Armoured Personnel Carrier
This was a late-war British conversion during 1943–5 using redundant Stuarts by removing the turret. These were used by the infantry units of the armoured brigades.

Universal Carrier
The British Army had a liking for tracked carriers and 50,000 were built by 1945. The first, bearing the Vickers machine gun, appeared in 1935. The subsequent Bren Carrier was then superseded by the Universal Carrier from 1940, though the generic name Bren Carrier stuck. Directed by a steering wheel, this made driver training much easier. Maximum hull armour went up to 12mm and the crew and passenger compartments remained open.

Other variants included the Cavalry Carrier and Scout Carrier; only 50 of the former were built, whereas the latter amounted to 667. Initially built as a replacement for the Mk VI light tank the Carrier was developed from Vickers-Armstrong's Light Dragon artillery tractor. The latter was built from 1933 to 1935. Notably its Horstmann suspension, with inclined double compression springs, provided the basis for all subsequent British carriers and was also used on the Mk VI light tank. During the war Canada built almost 29,000 Mk I Universal Carriers with a number of different weapon variants.

Valentine Infantry Tank
The British Valentine tank drew on the A9 and A10 and used the same gun, suspension and many other components. Its small turret, which prevented

installing a larger gun, as well as its poor speed meant that it was really obsolete by late 1942. However, the following year it accounted for almost a quarter of British tank production. It proved to be one of the most widely built British tanks with 8,275 completed by the time production ended in early 1944. Although it first went into production in 1940, it only joined 8th Army's tank brigades in June 1941 and had a key role in Operation Crusader. Due to Britain's tank shortage at that time the Valentine tended to be used as a cruiser tank.

It subsequently played an important part in the desert fighting, but again like the Crusader it was armed with the inadequate 2-pounder gun. In contrast the Valentine gained a reputation for reliability, although it was slow cross country. It is reported that after El Alamein some drove over 3,000 miles on their own tracks. Eventually the main armament was replaced by a 6-pounder in the Valentine VIII, IX and X and eventually a 75mm gun in the Valentine XI. The Canadians also built the Valentine, but most of these were shipped to Russia.

Windsor Carrier

Along with the British Universal Carrier, Canada also built a larger indigenous design known of the Windsor Carrier of which 5,000 were manufactured. This was employed as a weapons carrier or gun tractor for 4.2in mortar platoons and 6-pounder anti-tank gun crews respectively. Like the American T16, the lengthened Windsor suspension included an additional road wheel and an addition return roller.

Appendix C
United States' Tanks and Armoured Fighting Vehicles 1939–1945

Landing Vehicle Tracked Bushmaster

Designed and built by Berg Warner, the tracked LVT3 Bushmaster, with a stern ramp, was similar to the LVT4 Water Buffalo. It used two Cadillac engines which were more efficient than the Continental powering the latter. Almost 3,000 were produced in 1943–5 for the US Marine Corps. The Bushmaster first saw action at Okinawa. It suffered from many of the same limitations as the Water Buffalo.

Landing Vehicle Tracked (Armored) Water Buffalo

The American LVT concept evolved from the Alligator, designed by Donald Roebling, for emergency relief work in the Florida Everglades in response to the regular hurricanes in the mid-1930s. A militarized version was produced by Roebling in 1940 for the US Marine Corps known as the LVT1, which was followed two years later by the LVT2. The third variant, the LVT4, was designed with a rear loading ramp enabling the vehicle to come into its own as a ship-to-shore military cargo carrier. It could take thirty troops or a Jeep, Universal Carrier or field gun. Armoured cargo and support variants were produced in the shape of the LVT(A)1 and LVT(A)2. The LVT(A)4 included the M8 Motor Carriage turret armed with a 75mm howitzer, making it an amphibious tank or Amtank.

The Water Buffalo was propelled through the water by its tracks at a speed of just 7½mph. Due to the large track grousers, which were in a W shape to provide propulsion, the vehicle could not drive on hard surfaces for any length of time before causing damage, therefore the LVT was unable to stray far from the water. This meant the Buffalo was usually moved on roads on a trailer towed by the Diamond T tractor. LVTs saw action in Europe and the Pacific with the US Army and US Marine Corps respectively. During the war over 18,600 were built by the USA.

British Designation

Those supplied to the British Army were classified as Amphibian Tracked and were used in northern Italy, on the Scheldt and along with American ones on the Rhine. They were issued to the Royal Engineers and the Royal Tank Regiment. Most were the LVT2 and LVT(A)2, designated the Buffalo II, and the LVT4, designated the Buffalo IV. The standard armament of the Buffalo was two .30in machine guns at the sides, with a .50in machine gun over the driving compartment. On the Mk II the side machine guns were carried on a rail around the hold, while on the Mk IV they were pintle mounted. On most British Mk IIs the rails were removed and the guns fitted to sockets mid-way on the hold, likewise the 0.5in guns were usually replaced with a 20mm Polsten cannon. Some British Mk II Buffaloes were converted to carry the 17-pounder anti-tank gun. In the water many British crews found the Buffalo a dreadful beast: not only was it slow, but rather than ride the waves it simply ploughed through them. In choppy seas it alarmingly took on a lot of water. Likewise, vehicle drivers had to be very careful when driving from the ramp as the Buffalo could flounder and sink. A number of crewmen were lost in this way during training.

M3 Stuart Light Tank

An early welcome addition to the British tank inventory was the American-supplied M3 Stuart light tank. The first 84 arrived in Egypt in July 1941 and by November this number had risen to 163. Simply known as the Stuart, its British crews also affectionately dubbed it the 'Honey'. While it was under-gunned, with a 37mm gun, and poorly armoured, it was reliable and very mobile in a reconnaissance role. It too was blooded during Operation Crusader. The M3 was followed by the M3A1 and M3A3 (the M3A2 designation was not used). Along with the M5 light tank, it continued to see service on all fronts throughout the war with the British, American and French armies. Turretless M3s were employed as Kangaroo armoured personnel carriers, command tanks and reconnaissance tanks. Many were also used as artillery tractors. In total 5,811 M3s were built.

British Designations

Stuart I – M3 with Continental engine.
Stuart II or Stuart Hybrid – M3 with Guiberson diesel engine.

Stuart III – M3A1 with Continental engine.
Stuart IV or Stuart Hybrid – M3A1 with Guiberson engine.
Stuart V – M3A3.

M3 Lee and Grant Medium Tank

The British-specification M3 General Grant is identifiable from the standard M3 Lee by the lack of the commander's machine-gun cupola on the turret. It was a welcome replacement for the inadequate British Crusader tank and could not have arrived at a better time. Its main armament was a 75mm gun, but the sponson mount in the right-hand side of the hull only offered a 30-degree traverse. Nonetheless, its firepower and numbers alone gave the 8th Army much-needed punch. By October 1942 nearly 600 M3 Grant/Lee tanks had been delivered to the British in North Africa.

The Grants were issued to the units of the 7th and 10th Armoured Divisions ready for the Battle of El Alamein. Afterwards they were sent to Burma, where they proved to be the workhorse of the British and Indian armoured units. Notably the US 2nd Tank Battalion, 13th Armored Regiment, US 1st Armored Division, equipped with the M3 Lee was the only medium tank battalion to take part in the initial landings in French North Africa in November 1942.

British Designations
Grant I – Version manufactured to British specifications.
Grant II – American M3A5.
Lee I – Basic M3.
Lee II – M3A1.
Lee III – M3A2, none were delivered.
Lee IV – M3A3.
Lee V – M3A3 with diesel engine.
Lee VI – M3A4.

M4 Sherman Medium Tank

The famous American M4 Sherman first came into service in 1942. As the most numerous of Allied tank types it was involved in all the major battles from El Alamein, D-Day, Arnhem, Ardennes and on to the Elbe. The M4 medium tank was easily the most common tank of the war, with over 40,000 produced. It was a straightforward design that was easy to manufacture and was adaptable to numerous other roles, such as self-propelled gun and tank destroyer platforms. The General Sherman, or Sherman for short, was actually a British name that became popular with all other users including the Americans. The British 8th Army received about 270 Shermans by October 1942. Churchill claimed that he had 'gone on his knees' to persuade President Roosevelt to send these tanks and then complained bitterly when he was informed they could not go into battle immediately.

M4/M4A1–A4 Sherman

Design of the M4 as a medium tank armed with a 75mm gun started in early 1941 and was intended to replace the stopgap M3. The latter was flawed by its main armament being mounted in the hull, but many of the other elements of the M3 such as the power pack, transmission and suspension design had proved utilitarian and were incorporated. On the Sherman the 75mm gun was designed to be mounted in a fully rotating turret. The prototype was completed by September 1941 and after some tinkering the M4 went into production the following year. The Sherman was employed by the American and British armies on almost every front from 1942 onwards.

Ensuring adequate engine supplies meant different versions of the Sherman employed different engines. Most notably the Wright engine was used in the M4 with the welded hull, M4A1 was the M4 but with a cast hull, the General Motors 6046 12-cylinder diesel engine was used in the M4A2, the Ford GAA V-8 petrol engine in the M4A3 and the Chrysler A57 30-cylinder petrol engine in the M4A4 (longer hull). These were dubbed the Sherman I to V respectively by the British Army. Space does not permit a fully comprehensive survey of all the different Sherman production models and the array of special purpose variants.

The basic shape of the hull included a well-sloped glacis plate, though construction varied with the A1 cast rounded hull being the closest to the original design. The M4, although the first in designation was the third type to enter service, featured an all-welded hull as did the A2, A3 and A4. The combinations though did vary enormously. The Sherman started life armed with a 75mm M3 gun with a coaxial 0.30in Browning machine gun.

A second machine gun was fitted in a ball mounting in the front of the hull. Changes to the armament during production included replacing the 75mm gun with a 76mm or 105mm gun.

By 1944 the main Allied tank in service with the Red Army was the American M4A2 Sherman, which had a diesel engine and all-steel tracks and usually included extra fuel drums and ditching beams. The Soviet tankers nicknamed it *Emcha*, after the first letter and number – M4 being *M-Chetyrye* in Russian. For Stalin's Operation Bagration offensive the 3rd Guards Tank Corps was one of the Soviet units equipped with the ubiquitous Sherman.

M4A1 (76mm) Sherman

The American upgunned M4A1 armed with a 76mm gun went into production in early 1944. The gun was also fitted to the M4A2 and M4A3 as well as the new M4A3 horizontal volute spring suspension or HVSS Sherman. Both types of M4A3 were also built armed with the 105mm howitzer to provide close support tanks. The 76mm gun was not much of an improvement, because it could not penetrate the frontal armour of either the Tiger or Panther.

M4A3E2 Sherman Assault Tank

In lieu of a heavily armoured infantry support tank, this was a late-war addition to the Sherman family. The M4A3E2 was an up-armoured assault tank variant of the Sherman M4A3 and because of its bulky appearance was known unofficially as 'Jumbo.' While sporting armour ranging from 100mm–150mm thick it still was armed with the standard 75mm gun. A few of these infantry support tanks were refitted with 76mm guns. Only 254 were ever ordered.

Sherman Calliope

Towards the close of the war the Sherman was used as a rocket launcher mount. The Rocket Launcher T34 Calliope, installed on the M4, consisted of 60 x 4.6in rocket tubes in a frame above the turret. The two bottom sets of tubes could be jettisoned on all variants except the M4A1. This was first used by the US 2nd Armored Division in France in August 1944. It saw limited combat until the end of the war.

Sherman Crab

The British Sherman Crab designed to clear minefields and barbed wire was produced to support the British and Canadian D-Day landings at Gold, Juno and Sword beaches. It consisted of a Sherman V (M4A4) gun tank fitted with a rotating flail, driven by the main drive shaft, with an effective depth of about five inches. Three regiments of the 79th Armoured Division were equipped with Crabs, the 22nd Dragoons, 1st Lothian and Border Yeomanry and the Westminster Dragoons.

Sherman Dozer

The M4 Dozer first appeared during the Italian campaign in 1943 as a field modification utilizing parts from Caterpillar D-8 dozers. As a result, the M1 and M1A1 dozer blades were specially designed for the Sherman the following year. The US Engineer Corps variant had their turrets removed.

Sherman Duplex Drive

The British amphibious Sherman Duplex Drive (DD) was also developed to support the D-Day landings. The DD tank consisted of steel decking around the hull, upon which a screen could be raised by thirty-six air tubes and secured by hinged struts. The front screen could be lowered to facilitate firing. Propelled by twin screws, hence duplex drive, the tank could swim at 4–5 knots. Three regiments of the 79th Armoured Division were equipped with DD tanks, the 4th/7th Royal Dragoon Guards, the 13th/18th Hussars and the 1st East Riding Yeomanry. Three US tank battalions were also equipped with the DD tank, which were deployed in support of the Omaha and Utah Beaches.

Sherman Firefly

Some Shermans supplied to Britain were modified to take the British 17-pounder gun. These were dubbed the Firefly and issued in 1944 for the Normandy campaign. Unfortunately, a shortage of 17-pounders due to the delayed Challenger tank programme meant Fireflies were only issued one per Sherman troop. Production was not made a priority until February 1944 and larger numbers were unavailable until early 1945. The British Sherman IIC, IVC and VC Firefly, using the M4A1, M4A3 and M4A4 respectively, were the only Allied tanks capable of taking on the Panther or Tiger on equal terms.

The Germans soon realized that the larger gun in the Sherman Firefly constituted the biggest threat, and as a resulted they tended to be targeted first. The artist Rex Whistler, who was serving with the Guards Armoured Division, came up with a disruptive camouflage pattern that was designed to disguise the length of the barrel. By painting the last half with a lighter colour it was intended to make it look like the regular 75mm gun from a distance.

Sherman Grizzly

The Canadian Montreal Locomotive Works started building the M4A1 under the designation Grizzly I. Between September-December 1943 only 188 were produced because the Americans decided to concentrate all M4 production in the US. The Grizzly was largely identical to its American cousin, though featured British radio equipment, Canadian tracks, a 2in smoke mortar in the roof and a stowage box on the rear of the turret. Some Grizzlys, alongside US-built M4s, served with Canadian armoured units in North-west Europe.

Sherman Kangaroo Armoured Personnel Carrier

The successful deployment of the Canadian Ram Kangaroo in North-west Europe in the autumn of 1944, convinced the commander of the 8th Army in Italy that he wanted a regiment of tracked APCs. During October 1044 and April 1945 some 75 Sherman IIIs (along with redundant M7 Priests) were converted by field workshops. Removal of the turret allowed for ten infantry plus two crew.

British Designations

Sherman I – Basic M4 with Continental engine and welded hull.
Sherman Hybrid I – Late production M4.
Sherman IB – M4 with 105mm gun.
Sherman IBY – Late M4 with 105mm gun.
Sherman II – M4A1 with cast hull.
Sherman IIA – M4A1 with 76mm gun.
Sherman IIC (Firefly) – M4A1 with 17-pounder gun.
Sherman III – M4A2 with twin General Motors engines.
Sherman IIIAY – Late production M4A2.
Sherman IV – M4A3 with Ford engine (not many supplied).

Sherman IVA – Late production M4A3.

Sherman IVB – M4A3 with 105mm gun.

Sherman IVC (Firefly) – M4A3 with 17-pounder gun.

Sherman V – M4A4 with Chrysler Multibank engine.

Sherman VC (Firefly) – M4A4, main version with 17-pounder gun.

M5 Light Tank

The American M5 light tank is easily distinguished from the M3 light tank by the stepped rear deck. This was done to accommodate the large coupled engines. Otherwise the M5 was very similar to the M3A1 and featured a welded hull and 37mm gun. Originally it was designated the M4, but this was changed to avoid confusion with the Sherman. From early 1943 the M5A1 replaced the M5 on the production line, which mirrored the improvements made on the M3A3. The M5 series proved even more popular than the M3.

British Designation

Stuart VI – M5 (only a small number were delivered during 1943–4).

M7 Howitzer Motor Carriage

The M7 and M7B1 self-propelled howitzer, which used the M3 and M4 medium tank chassis, were standard equipment of the artillery battalions in all US armoured divisions. By 1944 each division had sixty-three M7s. It was first used by the British Army in North Africa. A major drawback was that the 105mm ammunition was not standard issue for the British, which meant it had to be supplied by the Americans. The M7 also equipped some of the artillery battalions with British armoured divisions during D-Day, but the Canadian-built Sexton armed with the 25-pounder howitzer replaced these shortly after the landings.

British Designation

105mm SP, Priest – M7 HMC, the name was in part due to the pulpit-shaped machine-gun turret

M8 Howitzer Motor Carriage

The M8 Howitzer Motor Carriage utilized the M5's chassis armed with a 75mm howitzer in an open-top turret. This was used to equip the headquarter companies of the US Army's medium tank battalions from the summer of

1942. It saw action in Italy and North-west Europe, but was slowly replaced by the Sherman armed with the 105mm howitzer.

M10 Gun Motor Carriage

To compensate for not producing a successor tank soon enough, the Americans developed tank destroyers based on the Sherman, that could penetrate at least 80mm of armour at 1,000 yards. Notably the M10 was armed with a 3in gun and the M36 was armed with a 90mm gun, though these were never available in sufficient quantities. They were introduced into service in 1943 and 1944 respectively.

The M10 was one of the few Allied armoured fighting vehicles capable of taking on the panzers with any parity. The 3in gun was intended to tackle the Tiger, but being only able to penetrate the frontal armour at 50 yards rendered it all but ineffective against this panzer. The M10 used the M4A2 chassis and the M10A1 utilized the M4A3.

British Designation

3in SP, Wolverine – M10 and M10A1.

17pdr SP, Achilles – Wolverine upgunned in late 1944 with the 17-pounder gun.

M18 Gun Motor Carriage

The M18 Hellcat GMC, the M36's smaller cousin armed with a 76mm, specialized in 'hit and run' tactics. The Hellcat's low silhouette made it less of a target for German anti-tank gunners. It proved to be one of the best tank destroyers of the war; with a top speed of 50mph it was also the fastest AFV during 1944–5. Hellcats equipped US tank destroyer battalions in northern Europe where their speed and firepower made them very effective. Between July–October 1944 2,507 M18s were produced, all of them going to the US Army.

M24 Chaffee Light Tank

Late-war American armour included the M24 Chaffee light tank, armed with a 75mm, that came into service in 1944. Three types of Motor Gun Carriage, the M19, M37 and M41, were built using the same chassis, but very few saw action before the end of the conflict. The Chaffee was first delivered to US tank battalions in Europe in late 1944 to replace the M5. It saw combat in North-west Europe and Italy and proved to be a fast and efficient reconnaissance vehicle. Between April 1944 and June 1945 over 4,000 Chaffees were built and they went on to give notable post-war service.

M26 General Pershing Heavy Tank

British and American tank designers were not convinced of the heavy tank concept and various projects never came to fruition. There was only one exception to this and it had started life as the American T20 Medium Tank, which was originally intended as a successor to the Sherman. This culminated in mid-1944 with the T-26 which was re-designated a heavy tank. The production M26 General Pershing heavy tank, armed with a 90mm gun, appeared largely too late to see action in Europe and only a few saw combat in Germany.

Twenty Pershings arrived at Antwerp in January 1945 and were issued to the US 3rd and 9th Armored Divisions. Following crew training, they did not get off to a good start when a Tiger knocked out one on 26 February 1945. This was quickly avenged and 3rd Armored went on to claim a Tiger and two Panzer IVs at Elsdorf. Those Pershings operated by 9th Armored made their debut at Remagen, where they provided fire support against German defences around the Ludendorff Railway Bridge.

M29 Weasel Cargo Carrier

Looking slightly similar to the British Universal Carrier, the American tracked Studebaker Weasel was designed early in the war for use in snowy conditions and special operations. It could be deployed as a supply, personal or weapons carrier. The M28, the first version (originally T15), was superseded by the M29 (T24) in 1943, which had the engine at the front right instead of the rear. The later was deployed with the US Army in Normandy. The M29C Water Weasel, the amphibious variant, was used by the British and Americans in the Scheldt and Rhine crossings. M29s also saw service in Italy, the Far East and the Pacific. Studebaker built around 15,000 M29 and M29C.

M36 Gun Motor Carriage

The M36B1 and M36B2 Gun Motor Carriage utilized an M4A3 Sherman and M10 chassis respectively, fitted with an open-top M36 type turret armed with a 90mm gun. This was capable of tackling both the Tiger and Panther at long range. It entered service in late 1944.

T16 Universal Carrier

American Ford built 13,893 of the US-designed Universal T-16 Carrier, its equivalent of the British Universal Carrier using the Horstmann-type suspension. Although similar to the Universal the lengthened chassis included an additional road wheel and an additional return roller either side. The Universal had a pair of road wheels with a single return roller then a single road wheel.

Bibliography

This work draws on a number of previous Pen & Sword books all of which are listed below.

Ambrose, Hugh, *The Pacific* (Edinburgh: Canongate, 2011)

Barnett, Correlli, *The Desert Generals* (London: Pan, 1983)

Baverstock, Kevin, *Breaking the Panzers* (Stroud: Sutton, 2002)

Bayly, Christopher & Harper, Tim, *Forgotten Armies: Britain's Asian Empire and the war with Japan* (London: Penguin, 2005)

Beevor, Antony, *Ardennes 1944: Hitler's Last Gamble* (London: Viking, 2015)

Breuer, William B., *Operation Dragoon: The Allied Invasion of the South of France* (Shrewsbury: Airlife, 1988)

Burton, Reginald, *Railway of Hell* (Barnsley: Pen & Sword, 2014)

Butcher, Captain Harry C., *Three Years with Eisenhower* (London: William Heinemann, 1946)

Calvert, Mike, *Slim* (London: Pan/Ballatine, 1973)

Cavanagh, William C.C., *The Battle East of Elsenborn and the Twin Villages* (Barnsley: Pen & Sword, 2012)

Chamberlain, Peter & Ellis, Chris, *British and American Tanks of World War Two* (London: Silverdale, 2004)

Church, John, *Military Vehicles of World War Two* (Poole: Blandford Press, 1982)

Crookenden, Napier, *The Battle of the Bulge 1944* (Hersham: Ian Allan, 1980)

Cross, Robin, *The Battle of the Bulge 1944: Hitler's Last Hope* (Staplehurst: Spellmount, 2002)

Daglish, Ian, *Operation Goodwood: The Great Tank Charge July 1944* (Barnsley: Pen & Sword, 2004)

Delaforce, Patrick, *Churchill's Desert Rats: From Normandy to Berlin with the 7th Armoured Division* (London: Chancellor Press, 2001)

Delaforce, Patrick, *Monty's Iron Sides: From the Normandy Beaches to Bremen with 3rd Division* (London: Chancellor Press, 1999)

D'Este, Carlo, *Bitter Victory: The Battle for Sicily July–August 1943* (London: Collins, 1988)

D'Este, Carlo, *Patton: A Genius for War* (New York: HarperPerennial, 1996)

Duncan, Nigel, *79th Armoured Division: Hobo's Funnies* (Windsor: Profile 1972)

Eisenhower, Dwight D., *Crusade in Europe* (London: William Heinemann, 1948)

Ellis, Chris, *Tanks of World War II* (London: Chancellor Press, 1997)

Ellis, Chris & Chamberlain, Peter, *The Great Tanks* (London: Hamlyn, 1975)

Ellis, John, *Cassino: The Hollow Victory, The Battle for Rome January 1944–June 1944* (London: Andre Deutsch, 1984)

Farrel, Brian P., *The Defence and Fall of Singapore 1940–1942* (Stroud: Tempus, 2005)

Feifer, George, *Okinawa 1945: The Stalingrad of the Pacific* (Stroud: Tempus, 2005)

Finnerty, Major John 'Tim', *All Hell on the Irrawaddy* (Bognor Regis: Anchor, 1985)

Fletcher, David, *Universal Carrier 1936–48: The 'Bren Gun' Carrier Story* (Oxford: Osprey, 2005)

Forty, George, *7th Armoured Division: The 'Desert Rats'* (Hersham: Ian Allan, 2003)

Forty, George, *Fifth Army at War* (Shepperton: Ian Allan, 1980)

Forty, George, *Tank Action: From the Great War to the Gulf* (Stroud: Alan Sutton, 1995)

Forty, George, *United States Tanks of World War II* (Poole: Blandford Press, 1983)

Forty, George & Livesey, Jack, *The Complete Guide to Tanks & Armoured Fighting Vehicles* (London: Hermes House, 2006)

Futter, Geoffrey W., *The Funnies: The 79th Armoured Division and its specialized equipment* (Hemel Hempstead: Bellona, 1974)

Gander, Terry & Chamberlain, Peter, *American Tanks of World War 2* (Cambridge: Patrick Stephens, 1977)

Gander, Terry & Chamberlain, Peter, *British Tanks of World War 2* (Cambridge: Patrick Stephens, 1976)

Grant, Roderick, *The 51st Highland Division at War* (Shepperton: Ian Allan, 1977)

Hills, Stuart, *By Tank into Normandy* (London: Cassell, 2003)

Hogg, Ian, *Twentieth-Century Artillery* (Kingsnorth: Grange, 2000)

Holland, James, *Burma '44: The Battle that Turned Britain's War in the East* (London: Corgi, 2016)

Horton, D.C., *New Georgia: Pattern for Victory* (London: Pan/Ballatine, 1972)

Johnson, Curt, *Artillery* (London: Octopus, 1975)

Katcher, Philip, *The US Army 1941–45* (London: Osprey, 1977)

Keegan, John, *Six Armies in Normandy* (Harmondsworth: Penguin, 1983)

Latawski, Paul, *Falaise Pocket* (Stroud: Sutton, 2004)

Latimer, John, *Burma: The Forgotten War* (London: John Murray, 2004)

Leckie, Robert, *Helmet for my Pillow* (London: Ebury Press, 2011)

Linklater, Eric, *The Campaign in Italy* (London: HMSO, 1977)

Lomax, Eric, *The Railway Man* (London: Vintage, 1996)

Lucas, James, *War in the Desert: The Eighth Army at El Alamein* (London: Arms and Armour Press, 1982)

Lucas, James & Barker, James, *The Killing Ground: The Battle of the Falaise Gap August 1944* (London: B.T. Batsford, 1978)

MacDonald, Charles B., *The Battle of the Bulge* (London: Weidenfeld and Nicolson, 1984)

Macksey, Kenneth, *Beda Fomm* (London: Pan/Ballatine, 1972)

Markham, George, *Japanese Infantry Weapons of World War Two* (London: Arms & Armour Press, 1976)

Masters, John, *The Road Past Mandalay* (London: Cassell, 2012)

Maule, Henry, *Caen: The Brutal Battle and Break-out from Normandy* (Newton Abbot: David & Charles, 1976)

McKee, Alexander, *Caen: Anvil of Victory* (London: Souvenir, 1964)

Miller, David, *The Illustrated Directory of Tanks of the World: From World War I to the Present Day* (London: Greenwich, 2004)

Mollo, Andrew, *The Armed Forces of World War II* (London: Black Cat, 1987)

Morris, Eric, *Tanks* (London: Octopus, 1975)

Neillands, Robin, *The Desert Rats: 7th Armoured Division 1940–45* (London: Aurum Press, 2005)

Pack, S.W.C., *Operation 'Husky': The Allied Invasion of Sicily* (New York, Hippocrene, 1977)

Perrett, Bryan, *Armour in Battle: Wavell's Offensive* (Shepperton: Ian Allan, 1979)

Pitt, Barrie, *The Crucible of War: Western Desert 1941* (London: Futura, 1981)

Province, Charles M., *Patton's Third Army* (New York: Hippocrene, 1992)

Reynolds, Michael, *Monty and Patton: Two Paths to Victory* (Stroud: Spellmount, 2007)

Rohmer, Major General Richard, *Patton's Gap: An Account of the Battle of Normandy 1944* (London: Arms and Armour Press, 1981)

Rooney, David, *Burma Victory: Imphal, Kohima and the Chindt issue, March 1944 to May 1945* (London: Arms and Armour Press, 1995)

Rutherford, Ward, *Fall of the Philippines* (London: Pan/Ballatine, 1972)

Sandars, John, *8th Army in the Desert* (Cambridge: Patrick Stephens, 1976)

Saunders, Tim, *Hell's Highway: US 101st Airborne & Guards Armoured Division* (Barnsley: Pen & Sword, 2018)

Sledge, E.B., *With the Old Breed* (London: Ebury Press, 2011)

Slim, Field Marshal Sir William, *Defeat into Victory* (London: Cassell, 1956)

Smith, Steven, *2nd Armoured Division: 'Hell on Wheels'* (Hersham: Ian Allan, 2003)

Strawson, John, *The Battle for North Africa* (London: B.T. Batsford, 1969)

Sumner, Ian & Vauvillier, François, *The French Army 1939–45: Free French, Fighting French & the Army of Liberation* (London: Osprey, 1998)

Thompson, Julian, *The Imperial War Museum Book of Victory in Europe* (London: Sidgwick & Jackson, 1994)

Toland, John, *The Battle of the Bulge* (Ware: Wordsworth, 1998)

Tout, Ken, *A Fine Night for Tanks: The Road to Falaise* (Stroud: Sutton, 1998)

Tout, Ken, *Roads to Falaise: 'Cobra' & 'Goodwood' Reassessed* (Stroud: Sutton, 2002)

Trevelyan, Raleigh, *Rome '44: The Battle for the Eternal City* (London: Secker & Warburg, 1981)

Tucker-Jones, Anthony, *Armoured Warfare in the Battle of the Bulge 1944–1945* (Barnsley: Pen & Sword, 2018)

Tucker-Jones, Anthony, *Armoured Warfare in the Battle for Normandy* (Barnsley: Pen & Sword, 2012)

Tucker-Jones, Anthony, *Armoured Warfare and the Fall of France 1940* (Barnsley: Pen & Sword, 2013)

Tucker-Jones, Anthony, *Armoured Warfare in the Far East 1937–1945* (Barnsley, 2015)

Tucker-Jones, Anthony, *Armoured Warfare in the Italian Campaign 1943–45* (Barnsley: Pen & Sword, 2013)

Tucker-Jones, Anthony, *Armoured Warfare in the North African Campaign* (Barnsley: Pen & Sword, 2011)

Tucker-Jones, Anthony, *Armoured Warfare in North-west Europe 1944–1945* (Barnsley: Pen & Sword, 2013)

Tucker-Jones, Anthony, *Armoured Warfare from the Riviera to the Rhine 1944–1945* (Barnsley: Pen & Sword, 2016)

Tucker-Jones, Anthony, *D-Day 1944: The Making of Victory* (Stroud: The History Press, 2019)

Tucker-Jones, Anthony, *The Battle for Arnhem 1944–1945* (Barnsley: Pen & Sword, 2019)

Tucker-Jones, Anthony, *Tank Wrecks of the Western Front 1940–1945* (Barnsley: Pen & Sword, 2019)

Turner, John Frayn, & Jackson, Robert, *Destination Berchtesgaden: The Story of the United States Seventh Army in World War II* (Shepperton: Ian Allan, 1975)

Tute, Warren, *The North Africa War* (London: Sidgwick and Jackson, 1976)

Urquhart, Alistair, *The Forgotten Highlander* (London: Little Brown, 2010)

Vader, John, *New Guinea: The Tide is Stemmed* (London: Pan/Ballatine, 1972)

Vanderveen, Bart, *Historic Military Vehicles Directory* (London: Battle of Britain Prints, 1989)

Vanderveen, Bart, *The Observer's Fighting Vehicles Directory World War II* (London: Frederick Warne, 1969)

White, B.T., *Tanks and other Armoured Fighting Vehicles of the Blitzkrieg Era 1939–41* (London: Blandford Press, 1972)

White, B.T., *Tanks and other Armoured Fighting Vehicles 1942–45* (Poole: Blandford Press, 1975)

Whiting, Charles, *Ardennes: The Secret War* (London: Century, 1984)

Whiting, Charles, *Bounce the Rhine* (London: Leo Cooper, 1985)

Whiting, Charles, *First Blood: The Battle of the Kasserine Pass* (London: Leo Cooper, 1984)

Whiting, Charles, *Last Assault: 1944 – The Battle of the Bulge Reassessed* (Barnsley: Pen & Sword, 2004)

Whiting, Charles, *Patton's Last Battle* (Staplehurst: Spellmount, 2002)

Wilmot, Chester, *The Struggle for Europe* (London: Collins, 1952)

Wise, Terence, *D-Day to Berlin: Armour Camouflage and Markings of the United States, British and German Armies, June 1944 to May 1945* (London: Arms & Armour Press, 1979)

Wright, Derrick, *Pacific Victory: Tarawa to Okinawa 1943–1945* (Stroud: Sutton, 2005)

Zaloga, Steven J., *US Marine Corps Tanks of World War II* (Oxford: Osprey, 2012)

Index